DON'T
TEACH
CODING

DON'T
TEACH
CODING

Until You Read This Book

STEPHEN R. FOSTER
LINDSEY D. HANDLEY

JB JOSSEY-BASS™
A Wiley Brand

This edition first published 2020

Registered Office(s)
John Wiley & Sons, Inc., 111 River Street, Hoboken, NJ 07030, USA

Editorial Office
John Wiley & Sons, Inc., River Street, Hoboken, NJ 07030, USA

For details of our global editorial offices, customer services, and more information about Wiley products visit us at www.wiley.com.

Wiley also publishes its books in a variety of electronic formats and by print-on-demand. Some content that appears in standard print versions of this book may not be available in other formats.

Library of Congress Cataloging-in-Publication Data

Names: Handley, Lindsey, author. | Foster, Stephen, 1985- author.
Title: Don't teach coding : until you read this book / Lindsey D. Handley,
    Stephen R. Foster.
Description: First edition. | Hoboken, NJ : Jossey-Bass/John Wiley & Sons,
    2020. | Includes bibliographical references and index.
Identifiers: LCCN 2019055396 (print) | LCCN 2019055397 (ebook) | ISBN
    9781119602620 (paperback) | ISBN 9781119602644 (adobe pdf) | ISBN
    9781119602637 (epub)
Subjects: LCSH: Computer programming—Study and teaching.
Classification: LCC QA76.27 .H364 2020 (print) | LCC QA76.27 (ebook) |
    DDC 005.13—dc23
LC record available at https://lccn.loc.gov/2019055396
LC ebook record available at https://lccn.loc.gov/2019055397

Cover Design: Wiley

Set in 9/13pt, Ubuntu by SPi Global, Chennai, India.

V10018100_031720

To our students,
you taught us to teach.
To our teachers,
you taught us to learn.

Contents

About the Authors

Dr. Stephen R. Foster is a researcher, author, and co-founder of multiple social enterprises with a mission to teach teachers how to teach coding. A fierce advocate for the power of coding to bring about worldwide change, he has himself coded to generate peer-reviewed scientific results, coded to build educational technology solutions for teachers and students, and coded to bootstrap educational startups and non-profit organizations out of thin air. All in all, these countless lines of code have all been in service of a single vision: to establish coding education as a basic human right across the globe. In short, he codes to teach coding.

Dr. Lindsey D. Handley is a researcher, entrepreneur, teacher, and author. For the last 10 years, the National Science Foundation has funded the research, design work, and the social enterprises that she operates. As a skilled coder, data scientist, and biochemist, she envisions a world in which we no longer suffer from a worldwide shortage of scientific fluency. To this end, she fights for the unification of science and education on two fronts: the use of science to improve education; and the improved teaching of science worldwide. In short, she applies science to design better ways of teaching science.

Together, they are the co-founders and leaders of ThoughtSTEM and MetaCoders.org – two social enterprises that have touched the lives of hundreds of thousands of beginning coders worldwide.

Acknowledgments

Thank you to the following people for taking time to read and provide feedback on earlier drafts: Dr. Jody Kelly, Dr. Shriram Krishnamurthi, Dr. Janet Siegmund, Kelly Foster, Matthew Butterick, and Allan Schougaard. Your contributions helped make this book what it is.

Thank you to the creators of Racket for their trailblazing work in language-oriented programming, without which we wouldn't have been able to design the programming languages for this book about programming languages.

Introduction

If there's one thing this book seeks to address, it is: What are programming languages?

It sounds simple, but answering this question deeply will require us to ask other questions: Why do we call them "languages"? Why are there so many? Why do people fluent in them get paid so much? How are they related to those other things we call "languages" (like English, Spanish, or American Sign Language)? Where do they come from? Where are they going? How do we learn them? What happens in your brain when you do?

And, above all:

How do we teach them?

Japan, Italy, England, and Finland are just a few of the countries that have begun to mandate coding education throughout K-12 public education. Computer science educational standards now exist in 22 U.S. states – two of which have passed legislation that requires coding education statewide from elementary to high school.

As the world embarks on a global change to its collective education systems, it is worth asking some basic questions.

Technically, this book is about what you should know *before* you start teaching (or learning) a programming language. But the book will also teach you a few simple languages in order to make headway on some of the deeper questions.

There is a structure that frames the four chapters in this book, each of which have five parts – five arcs that recur from chapter to chapter.

The **Wizard's Tale** is the only fictional arc of the book. At the beginning of each chapter, this narrative introduces the main ideas in a lighthearted way. Sometimes the truest things can only be said in fiction.

The pair of arcs called **A Language Without** and **A Language Within** are where you'll learn about coding – one language at a time. In **A Language Without**, we'll examine how the design of a language gives its users certain cognitive powers, and cognitive pitfalls. In **A Language Within**, you'll be given exercises to help you actually learn those languages (if you wish) – meditating on the gaining of those powers for yourself, while learning to avoid the pitfalls. The languages will increase in power and complexity as the book progresses – ending with the

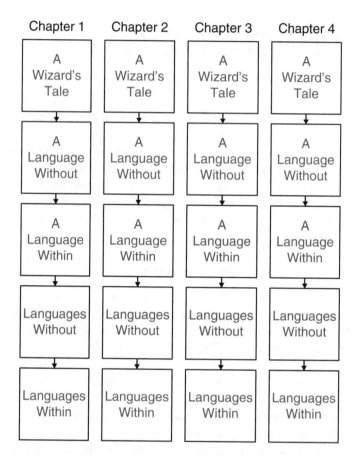

Chapter 1	Chapter 2	Chapter 3	Chapter 4
A Wizard's Tale	A Wizard's Tale	A Wizard's Tale	A Wizard's Tale
A Language Without	A Language Without	A Language Without	A Language Without
A Language Within	A Language Within	A Language Within	A Language Within
Languages Without	Languages Without	Languages Without	Languages Without
Languages Within	Languages Within	Languages Within	Languages Within

most powerful kind of programming languages: what computer scientists call "the Turing-complete languages."

The arcs called **Languages Without** and **Languages Within** will "zoom out" – beyond you, beyond us, beyond this book, beyond the present day. In **Languages Without**, we'll piece together the epic story of language – literally, the story of stories themselves. It began before this book, indeed before the invention of writing and is still unfolding today. In **Languages Within**, we'll examine recent neuroscience about how the human brain processes language, how it acquires fluencies – and ultimately, how it earns the right to participate in that epic story of language that is unfolding all around us.

Human beings are linguistic creatures; and programming languages are one of the weirdest linguistic things we've done in the last few thousand years. The bigger our historical lens, the easier it is to see just how weirdly magical they are.

WHO IS THIS BOOK FOR?

Mainly, this book is for K-12 teachers of coding, or any educated adult with an interest in the teaching and learning of programming languages. We assume no prior coding knowledge on the part of the reader, however.

This is because, increasingly often in the coming years, teachers who once taught a different subject will find themselves suddenly teaching coding. So we wanted this book to be of use to teachers in those situations. As a rhetorical strategy, we'll often seem to be speaking to the reader as if they were a coding student. If you are a teacher who *is* also a student, feel free to assume we are speaking to you.

If you are a teacher who is not also a student – ask yourself, why *aren't* you a student? In this field, the learning never stops. There's always another language, another library, another framework, another tool-chain, another repository, another engine, another platform, another service, another environment, another paradigm, another sub-field, another beautiful idea.

The teaching and learning don't stop. The job titles just change.

Finally, because our goal is to teach coding teachers what all too many do not know before they begin teaching – even expert coders may find insights here that they were never taught (because their teachers did not know). Thus, your expertise in coding will not prevent you from enjoying this book. We expect the book to be readable by: industry veterans while their unit tests run, computer science grad students in between meetings with their advisors, and battle-tested hackers amidst contributions to open-source projects.

Many of us appreciate the power of K-12 education. The students of today will be our colleagues tomorrow.

LET'S DO IT!

We hope this book will empower teachers and students to write the future of education – one line of code at a time.

At any time, for any reason, join us.

dont-teach.com/coding

Chapter 1
Prologues

*"The programmers of tomorrow are the **wizards** of the future. You're going to look like you have magic powers compared to everyone else."*

Gabe Newell, founder, Valve

*"Any sufficiently advanced technology is indistinguishable from **magic**."*

Arthur C. Clarke

*"The programs we use to conjure processes are like a **sorcerer's spells**. They are carefully composed from symbolic expressions in arcane and esoteric programming languages."*

Harold Abelson and Gerald Jay Sussman,
Structure and Interpretation of Computer Programs

A WIZARD'S TALE

The Sorting of Wizards

"A sorting shall now commence!" an ancient wizard announced. "We must assign all of you into your various Houses. Each House at this prestigious school champions a slightly different way of learning how to become a coding wizard. I will now explain precisely how that works..."

Henry, who could not pay attention to lectures for very long, leaned over and asked his new friends, "How does it work? How many Houses are there?"

His better-informed friend Harmony replied, "There are over a thousand, with more being added every day."

"Over a thousand!" hissed Henry. There was no *way* he was going to end up in the same House as his new friends.

"But," his goofy yet loyal friend Rob said, "I've heard that the sorting algorithm takes your preferences into account. So you can basically choose which House you start in."

Henry sighed with relief. "Good, which one are you both picking?"

"Definitely Python," said his friend Harmony, as if there were no doubt in the matter.

"Really?" says his friend Rob, doubtfully. "My dad said I should pick Scratch."

This sparked a debate between Harmony, whose position was that none of the great wizards actually use Scratch in their day-to-day work, and Rob, whose position was that Scratch was a better House for beginners to start in, and that they could always switch Houses later.

"You can switch?" asked Henry.

But Rob and Harmony didn't hear him. They were busy debating.

Henry's heart was starting to pound. The ancient wizard had already begun directing the students standing at the front of the Great Hall to start queuing up for the sorting process. One by one, they went onto the stage and sat on a stool. One by one, the ancient wizard placed upon them a weird cap with blinking lights. Each time, after a few moments of making beeps and boops, the cap's lights flashed green. Each time, it announced with a mechanical voice the House into which the candidate had been sorted:

"Java," it said for one. "C plus plus," it said for another. "Javascript," it said for another.

"Is Java part of the JavaScript House?" Henry tried to ask his friends. But they were too deep in conversation.

Henry noticed that he was being watched by a nearby group of "cool kids." One boy said to his friends, "This kid doesn't even know what JavaScript is."

Henry tried to ignore them, but their snickering hurt.

Meanwhile the hat continued to drone out the names of Houses. "C sharp," it said for one. "Ruby," it said for another. "C," it said for another. After receiving the hat's proclamation, each student grinned and exited the Great Hall through a door in the rear of the stage, presumably to meet the other students in their Houses. The number of students left in the Great Hall was beginning to thin.

Henry began to make his way through the crowd of students, toward the back of the Great Hall. Other kids gave him strange looks as he squeezed between them.

Finally, at the rear of the hall, just as he was about to curl into a fetal position between a suit of armor and a damp stone corner, he discovered that Harmony and Rob had followed him.

"What's wrong?" said Rob. "Where are you going?"

"It's just . . ." said Henry.

"You don't know which House to pick, do you?" said Harmony. "Not to worry. I'll help. The top 10 Houses right now are JavaScript, Python, Java, C++, PHP, Swift, C#, Ruby, Objective-C, and SQL. But you obviously wouldn't want to go into the SQL House – because they don't do general purpose magic, just database magic. And you might want to be careful if you go into the Swift or Objective-C Houses – because their magic is proprietary. With C#, some people think that's proprietary magic too, but there's an open source –"

Henry covered his ears to stop the flood of words he didn't understand. "I wasn't born into a coding family. Maybe I'm just not cut out for –"

"Neither was Harmony," his friend Rob interrupted. "She just spends a lot of time on Google. My parents, on the other hand, were both wizards." He said this proudly. "My father sorted into Java, and my mother sorted into Ruby. But both of them always say that it doesn't really matter where you start." He gave Harmony a pointed look. "It's where you end up that matters."

"But," said Henry, frantic, "they can't ALL be equally good places to start. If they were all equally good, why are there so many different ones?"

"Each House does magic," said Harmony. "They just use a different language to express their magic. At the end of the day, though, magic is magic."

Meanwhile, over half of the students had already been sorted. Still the cap droned on. "Objective-C," it announced. "FORTRAN," it said. "HTML," it said.

Harmony and Rob both winced at the "HTML" announcement.

"See?" exclaimed Henry. "They aren't all equal. What is HTML? What was that face you both made?"

"Okay," said Harmony, "maybe they aren't ALL created equally. HTML is a kind of magic, don't get me wrong. But it's a less powerful kind of magic. You wouldn't want to spend your whole time here just studying HTML. If you did, you might not be able to get a job as a wizard afterward."

Henry sank to the ground and rested his head against the cold metal of the suit of armor.

"My mom and dad say you shouldn't worry about getting a job," said Rob. "You should just learn to love magic."

Henry said, "I just want to be in a House with you two. But even you two can't agree."

Rob and Harmony exchanged a look. "Give us a moment," said Rob, pulling Harmony aside. They conferred in hushed tones.

Henry couldn't hear them over the constant drone of the sorting hat: "Prolog. Scratch. Algol. Perl. XML. Scratch. Haskell. CSS. Racket. Bash. Ruby. Python. TypeScript. Scratch." And so on.

When they came back, Rob said:

"Okay, we've decided. You'll go first, and whatever you get sorted into, we'll pick that too."

Harmony didn't seem happy about it, but she nodded. "Wizards work in teams," she said. "At the end of the day, what matters is that we stay together."

Henry was dumbfounded. He didn't deserve friends like these. They helped him to his feet, where he did his best to hide that his knees were shaky and weak. Arm in arm, they joined the end of the queue – the last of the young wizards to be sorted.

By the time Henry stepped up on the stage, the Great Hall was empty, save his two friends behind him, and the ancient wizard in front of him. Henry sat upon the stool and closed his eyes as the hat settled upon his head.

He could hear it talking through a speaker near his ear. "Well, well, well . . . what have we here?" it said. "Henry doesn't know what House he wants to be in . . . Hmmm . . . I suppose we could put you in HTML, and –" Henry stiffened. "No? What about Scratch?" Henry didn't know what to say. "Why am I asking you, any- way? I could put you anywhere, and you wouldn't know the difference." Henry shifted uncomfortably. "Still, I sense a great power within you – greater even than any of the cool kids who came onto the stage before you . . ." Henry wasn't sure whether he should feel complimented about his mysterious "great power" or worried that he was uncool. "Yes, the more information I gather, the more I'm certain of it. You're a very special young wizard. Much too special for the lesser Houses. Perhaps I could sort you into a venerable old House, such as C. Or perhaps an ancient House, such as Lisp. Or perhaps you'd excel in a hip, newer House, like Rust, or an obscure but powerful House like Prolog or Haskell. Or perhaps a solid, popular House, like Python or Java. Interesting . . . I've never had so much trouble sorting someone before," Henry's heart was beating so hard that he could barely hear the hat anymore. Was he really destined for greatness? The suspense was so painful that he wanted to just shout the name of a House at random in hopes that the hat would put an end to it all. Somehow, he didn't. "Hmmm, well, if I can't tempt you by dropping the names of these Houses, I suppose I have no choice," said the hat, "but to place you into a House that I've only assigned a handful of young wizards before . . ." Henry tensed.

To his surprise, the ancient wizard took the hat off of him. The look on his face was grave.

"Henry," said the ancient wizard, "do you know what this means?"

Henry tensed. "I didn't hear it say anything."

"You're right," said the ancient wizard. "It has been many, many years since I've heard the hat say nothing at all. In fact, the last time this happened, I was the one sitting on that very stool." He scratched his beard. "Perhaps the three of you," he said, "have been chosen by fate."

Voice trembling, Henry asked, "What House did you get sorted into?"

The ancient wizard said, "This House has no name."

"The House of No Name!" gasped Rob. "My parents said it was just a myth."

The ancient wizard turned his attention to Rob and Harmony, still standing in the queue line, waiting to be sorted.

"No," said the ancient wizard. "If we called it the House of No Name, that would be a name, and therefore contradictory. When we refer to it, we must resort to 'This House has no name.' It's a sacrifice we must make to avoid the contradiction."

"I've never heard of a House with no name," said Harmony, skeptically. "There's no wizard language without a name."

"This House," said the ancient wizard, "is the only House that isn't named after a wizard language. That's because we don't subscribe to any particular wizard language."

Harmony scoffed. "One can't do magic unless one has a wizard language," she said, as if she were the authority on the matter.

"You're right," said the ancient wizard. "Focusing on a single language is not our main approach to learning magic. Rather, we study language itself."

As if to underscore that the ancient wizard had made his main point, the phrase "language itself" echoed throughout the now empty Great Hall.

"It definitely sounds way cooler . . . " said Rob. He and Henry both looked at Harmony.

"No way," she said. "I'm joining Python. I want to actually get a job."

The ancient wizard shrugged. "The sorting hat will ultimately respect your wishes. However, if I may impart just a small moment of wisdom . . . " The ancient wizard cleared his throat. "If a job is what you seek, many roads will take you there. At the end of the day, though, when you're looking back on your life, don't you want to take comfort in the fact that you took the road that was way cooler?"

The words "way cooler" seemed to echo throughout the Great Hall.

Harmony waivered.

"Come on, Harmony," said Henry. "Wasn't it you who said that wizards always work in teams?"

With a sigh, she said, "Fine. I'll do it. I'll join the House of No Name – or this House which has no name, or whatever it is. But for the record, I think it sounds weird, and I don't like it."

The Call to Action

The ancient wizard motioned for them to follow him. "Come," he said, "I will personally teach you three the ways of this House which has no name."

He reached into his robe and pulled out three copies of a book, giving one to each of them. The title: *Don't Teach Coding*.

Henry glanced nervously at Harmony. She did not look pleased.

To be continued…

A LANGUAGE WITHOUT

Our Strange Protagonists

This book is about those languages that make computers do things.

Most people today call them "programming languages" – though they weren't always. These languages, oddly enough, are the protagonists of this book – and a mysterious set of heroes they are indeed. On the one hand, they are the tools with which programmers weave the software of the world. On the other hand, the act of learning these languages is what makes us into programmers. They are both tools and rites of passage.

As if that wasn't strange enough, once becoming programmers, we use programming languages to make other software – including, oddly enough, more programming languages. If this sounds like a loop, it is – one that affects everyone who has ever learned programming, and anyone who ever will.

Many of us can outline our personal histories as programmers by listing the languages we learned in different chapters of our lives. One of the authors first learned to program in a language called Applesoft BASIC, which came with his parents' first PC. Back then, people were still calling Apple computers PCs, up until IBM-compatible PCs re-wrote that definition. These new "real" PCs also shipped with a version of BASIC called QuickBASIC – itself an evolution over earlier versions of BASIC. He learned Java, Logo, Visual BASIC, Perl, and Pascal in high school. In college, it was more Java and Haskell, with an additional helping of C, C++, Ruby, Python, and Lisp. When he went into industry, it was Ruby, PHP, SQL, Bash, XML, HTML, CSS, and JavaScript. For his master's degree, it was C#, more Java, more Haskell, and Racket. For his Ph.D. and beyond, it was more Racket, and–

You get the point.

And that's just *his* story. Ask any programmer what languages they've mastered in their lifetime, and you'll get a different story. Sometimes it will be a long story, sometimes short. The details will change depending on when and where they were born, which languages were in vogue when they were going through grade school, which ones were taught in college, which ones were used by the companies that offered them jobs, which ones they selected for personal projects.

As working programmers, we have many cognitive tools, yet our languages are truly special. They are what we use to magically convert the vague linguistic utterances of non-coders – that is, "Solve problem X for client Y" or "Make an app that makes money" or "Get us more users" or "Make this data comprehensible" – into precise programs that, when run, actually *do* those things that non-coders could only talk about. Our languages are what make us look like wizards to others.

The story of how a programmer's mind develops feels like a personal experience – yet every programmer's origin story is woven into that larger story of programming languages. There are common threads. There are patterns. The larger story knits us together as a community. Linguistic history is our history; linguistic future is our future. Languages are the tools that shape us; we are shaped by the programmers who shaped those languages.

Ironically, few of us know the larger stories before beginning to wield a language. It is a rare student indeed who picks up one of these sacred tools for the first time with full knowledge of its true history, or its true power. Rather, most of us made our first steps as programmers by pulling one of the many magic swords from its stone and proceeding to chop vegetables with it – unable to see the tool for what it truly was. Languages, after all, are strange things: tools of the mind. As such, they cannot be correctly seen until *after* they have been learned.

These cognitive tools also deeply affect the teaching arts. Their sheer number poses an Eternal Conundrum: Teachers and students must reckon with their multitude year after year. The twin questions of the conundrum are: "Which one should I learn?" and "Which one should I teach?"

The Eternal Conundrum serves as the backdrop while our society embarks on a historic first: to install the first large-scale public infrastructures for teaching coding in a world that has finally seen that the light of the software dawn is only growing brighter. It took time, but the direction has become quite clear. K-12 computer science educational standards have been drawn up in 22 states (Lambert 2018). Iowa and Wyoming have passed legislation mandating coding in all elementary, middle, and high schools statewide (Iowa 2019) (Goldstein 2019). Non-profit advocacy groups like Code.org and CS For All continue to success-fully drive the teaching of computing classes from Pre-K to 12th grade (Code.org 2019) (CSforALL 2019). The National Science Foundation has invested several million in the CS 10K initiative (Brown and Briggs 2015) – its mission: to pro-duce 10,000 new high school computer science teachers across America. Even big tech companies like Google and Microsoft are spending money and labor on the effort – developing free or low-cost out-of-the-box curriculum and software to facilitate coding education.

England has already mandated computer science classes for all children between 5 and 16 years of age (United Kingdom 2013). Italy has launched an endeavor to introduce computing logic to over 40% of its primary schools (Passey 2017). Japan will mandate computing education starting in primary school by the year 2020 (Japan 2016). Finland introduces coding and computa-tional thinking starting in 1st grade (Kwon and Schroderus 2017). One by one, the countries of the world join in this unified initiative.

When a society changes its public school systems, it is changing its very defini-tion of "basic literacy" and therefore of "educated person." Let's take the current trend to its extreme and imagine, for a moment, a world in which coding flu-ency is acquired by all students throughout all grade levels and beyond. In other words, the average person walking down the street will have had 12 years of computer science education. It's safe to say, that if school systems do an even moderately good job, the average citizen will be fluent in one or more program-ming languages. For many, this fluency will start so early in life that they will have no recollection of *not* knowing how to code.

Because of the growing importance of these enigmatic things called program-ming languages, which we are eagerly welcoming into the minds of our children, this book examines a loop of linguistic ideas – each so interconnected with the others that they are best pondered together, in a single book.

Programmers design new programming languages. Teachers teach program-ming languages to non-programmers. Learning programming languages makes non-programmers into programmers. This means, some of the programmers we teach today will design languages that the teachers of tomorrow will use. These languages will help shape the minds of students the day after tomorrow. So the wheel turns.

This means that some of the programmers of today will directly affect the teaching and learning of programming tomorrow. And by corollary: All of the teaching and learning of programming today has already been affected by programmers who created the languages of yesterday. As schools across the world engage in their individual experiments to teach coding, let us not lose sight of what connects us all.

Our programming languages can be learned, wielded, taught, and created. They are many-faced and multifaceted. In this book, we will sometimes speak of them all as a unified thing – a single entity named "the programming languages of the world." Sometimes we will speak of them as individual things: like "Java," "BASIC," or "Racket."

We said these languages are "the protagonists." And that is true: Sometimes we will study them as protagonists. But languages are tricky things.

Sometimes they may seem to shrink down and become objects of interest in some other protagonist's story. That is how we as students first encounter a language: They pop into the story of our lives, perhaps helping us, perhaps frustrating us, perhaps intriguing us, perhaps boring us. There is no shame in any of these.

Even for a single student, the metaphors may shift over time: A language is the road beneath your feet, the magic sword you are wielding, the mentor you meet along the way, the mountain you are climbing, or even (at times) your arch-nemesis.

Languages will go by many metaphors throughout this book too: sometimes a fabric that connects us, sometimes a sword, sometimes a tool, sometimes an object of study, sometimes a mountain, sometimes a wave, sometimes magic. It is inevitable. Languages are complex characters.

They were not created by simple creatures.

(cons 'Apple 'Soft)

The word "Applesoft" in "Applesoft BASIC" is a combination of two company names: "Apple" and "Microsoft." Originally licensed by Apple from Microsoft in 1977, the Applesoft license only cost Apple $31,000 (McCracken 2012), but allowed them to ship their Apple II computers when Apple was unable to finalize their own version of BASIC (Isaacson 2011). Eight years later, when the

Applesoft license needed renewing, Microsoft renewed on the condition that Apple would kill MacBASIC (Manes and Andrews 1994) (Hertzfeld 1985), Apple's up-and-coming BASIC programming language, which everyone expected to be more efficient. (Allen 1984)

Indeed, MacBASIC had better benchmarks and more features than Microsoft's BASIC – yet it scarcely saw the light of day and vanished from the world when Apple dropped it. Programmers went on using and learning the old BASIC, oblivious to the fact that language designers they had never met had made a decision they never knew about, quashing language features they had never learned.

These language wars (whose version of BASIC would ship on whose computers) were largely overshadowed by what was seen as the dominating historical force at the time: the hardware wars (whose machines would sit on the desktops of the world). The fact that improving BASIC might improve the lives of the programmers of the time wasn't enough to drive the evolution of the language.

Famous computer scientist Edsger Dijkstra claimed in 1975 that BASIC caused brain damage (Dijkstra 1982):

> It is practically impossible to teach good programming to students that have had a prior exposure to BASIC: as potential programmers they are mentally mutilated beyond hope of regeneration.

It does seem odd *not* to improve something that might cause brain damage. But economic pressures are often stronger than educational ones. For better or worse, this was the first program one author remembers typing into Applesoft BASIC, a few years after MacBASIC's secret death:

```
PRINT "HELO"
```

He was too young to know how to spell "Hello", and too inexperienced of a typist to type out the full traditional "HELLO, WORLD". Nor did he know, at the time, how to turn off the caps lock.

These were his struggles. Far from his mind were the warnings that this very language might cause brain damage. Far from his mind was the story of how Applesoft BASIC had come to be installed on that computer. So it is with most of us. We cannot see languages for what they are until after we have learned them; and we often cannot see the bigger historical picture until long after that.

At some point, brain damage or not, it is too late to unlearn a language. If Dijkstra is right and some languages *can* cause setbacks in one's ability to become a programmer, the only recourse is to hope he is wrong about being "beyond hope of regeneration." Our only choice at that point is to learn *more* languages in hopes of correcting damage caused by previous ones. Let it be stated for the record: This treatment appears to have been successful for the author in question.

For better or worse, the evolution of BASIC was once a strategic part of the early skirmishes between what would become two of the biggest software mega-giants on the planet, Microsoft and Apple. Its existence sparked the origin stories of all programmers who completed their rite of passage on those machines. Yet today, the remnants of those original versions of BASIC remain alive only in the form of online JavaScript-based emulators that allow certain programmers to engage in nostalgic reconstructions of the programs we wrote as children. They are preserved: Software enshrined in software. As tools of the mind, though, they are not wielded as they once were.

Today, Microsoft champions many languages. Microsoft's TypeScript, a super-set of JavaScript, is listed as the 41st most popular language in the world on the TIOBE index. Microsoft's C#, partially inspired by Java, is the 6th most popu-lar language. Apple meanwhile champions languages like Objective-C and Swift, the 10th and 13th most popular languages. The linguistic ecosystem changes so quickly that these numbers will probably be out of date by the time you read them, which underscores the point. Languages are ever changing; what seem like mountains turn out to be tall waves in a shifting sea.

Whether brain damaging or enlightening, we learn these languages, and they make us who we are. Then we learn more, and continue to change.

For some, our first language may have been BASIC. For others, perhaps it was Logo. For others, Scratch. Regardless of our first language, the younger we are when we learn, the less likely it is that we are making an informed, rational decision about which language to learn.

It is not uncommon for everyone in a classroom (perhaps even the teacher) to be using a language without knowing where it came from and why. In that ahistorical context, students sit down to write their traditional first line, bidding their computer to say hello to a multilingual world they do not yet understand.

Tower of Babel

Our digital Tower of Babel is on the one hand quite beautiful, and on the other hand not. It's beautiful because unlike the biblical story of Babel, the legion of languages was not a curse cast upon humanity; it is an act of creation to which we have been willing participants. These languages didn't just happen. We created them – not by accident.

Programs written in these languages run our world – our planes, our cars, our governments, our militaries, our businesses, our charities, everything. An optimist might see it as the opposite of the Tower of Babel story: We *gave* ourselves the gift of tongues to write our edifices into existence.

On the other hand, there are less beautiful aspects of the polyglottic world – not the least of which is that newcomers face a bewildering array of choices the instant they enter the gate. Some of those choices are popular languages like Python and Java. Some are languages designed to make programming easier to learn – like Scratch, Hopscotch, and Snap. The Wikipedia page on "Educational Programming Languages" lists more than 50 languages that were either created for educational use or are used as such. Even the language BASIC (created in 1964) stands for Beginner All-purpose Symbolic Instruction Code – marking it as a language tailored for beginners, which is why it shipped in the 70s on "microcomputers," and then again in the 80s on "personal computers."

Being a beginner coder is a bit like being a hero embarking upon a quest, but then immediately being faced with a fork in the road that goes in more than 50 different directions (or 850 directions, if we look beyond specialized educational languages). It's like the quest to become a coder begins with a meta-quest: which quest to go on; which language to learn.

Confessions

This section is a disclaimer.

The authors of this book are not innocent when it comes to increasing the number of beginner languages in the world. As the architects of a coding education start-up (ThoughtSTEM), they've created a variety of languages with the purpose of making programming more accessible for beginners: *LearnToMod* is an environment and language for creating Minecraft mods; *CodeSpells* is a game where you program your own magic spells using an in-game version of JavaScript; `#lang vr-lang` is a Lisp-like language for constructing virtual reality scenes; `#lang game-engine` is for creating 2D RPG-style games. And that's not even all of them.

Once you've designed one new language, it becomes easier to design more.

While we designers mean well in creating these languages, it's a bit awkward to explain: "Hi, welcome to the land of programming. Sorry there are so many roads here at the entrance. But don't worry! We're making this part more user-friendly by paving these additional roads for you."

Um . . . Wait . . .

Alan Kay, the creator of object-oriented programming and the language Smalltalk, is often quoted:

> Every problem in computer science can be solved by another layer of indirection – except the problem of too many layers of indirection.

Similarly, problems in coding education can be solved with another language – except the problem of too many languages.

This book uses a different method.

Penances

Rather than paving yet another road, we decided to write a book *about* the roads – a book to be read before embarking on any of them.

One of the motivations was to show that the "problem of too many languages" is not a problem at all. It's what makes computer science the powerful and elegant field that it is.

Throughout this book, we'll examine a sequence of increasingly interesting languages, starting from basic ones and ending with ones as powerful as those in professional use today – as powerful as the ones that top the charts, as powerful as those mountains of our day.

There will be plenty of coding exercises – but never in any one language. We'll take the way cooler road.

To be continued . . .

A LANGUAGE WITHIN

Installing Languages

Because of the polyglottic nature of this book, we'll be using a special tool called Racket – a language for creating languages. If you want to run the programs in this book, all you have to do is 1) download Racket, and 2) download our languages. You only need to do these steps once.

If you're ready to do that now, here are the directions. If you're just reading the book cover-to-cover, you don't have to download Racket yet.

Even if you don't download, though, don't skip this section! That goes for any part of the book too: Don't skip. You won't get lost. Above all, we've written this book to be read. Following along on the computer is for bonus points. Whenever the output of a program isn't obvious, we'll print it. This is so you can follow the main ideas whether or not you're following along on a computer.

Exercise

Step 0: Don't be scared to ask for help. If you get stuck installing, please feel free to ask for help at **dont-teach.com/coding/forum**

Step 1: Download and Install Racket. Go to *download.racket-lang.org*. Download the appropriate installer. Launch it and follow directions.

Step 2: Install the "Don't Teach Coding" Package. With Racket installed, you can now launch a program called DrRacket. Do so.
Next, click

```
File > Install Package...
```

In the prompt, type dtc and press enter. Installing this package will take a few minutes.

Lastly, in the lower left-hand corner, DrRacket may say *No Language Selected*. Click that, and select *Determine language from source*. Racket is in polyglottic mode now, which we'll explain in a moment.

Step 3: Write some "Hello, World" programs. The point of such programs is less about printing "Hello, World" than it is about checking to see if everything got set up correctly. So feel free to print whatever you want.

Your DrRacket may look slightly different from the following figure. For example, the version number may be different (in ours it is 7.3). Do not be alarmed; the programs in this book will still work. To write your "Hello, World" program, you simply need to write it your Editor Window (the one that doesn't have the version number). In the following figure, we've labeled the two windows after running the program. Can you guess which window has the program and which has the output?

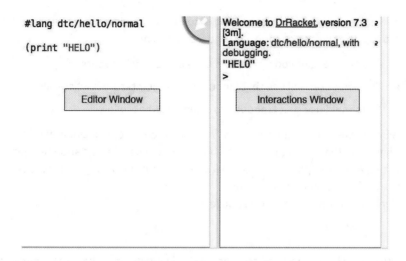

When you've written your program, you need to run it – which we think you will be able to figure out on your own (Hint: Look for the "Run" button). If something meaningful prints out, everything is set up correctly. If something went wrong, feel free to post on the forums.

dont-teach.com/coding/forum

Writing in Tongues

From now on, when there's a code example, we're not going to insert the entire screenshot as in the figure above. Instead, we'll show code examples like this:

```
#lang dtc/hello/normal

(print "HELO")
```

Notice the first line. This will always be there – the so-called "#lang line." It tells human readers *and* the computer the language under which to interpret what follows.

This is how we'll accomplish writing in tongues. Any time you see a `#lang` line at the top of a snippet of code, you know three things:

- That's a piece of code you could type into DrRacket yourself.
- The computer will use that language when it interprets what follows.
- *You* should use that language to interpret what follows.

All code we write will be written for you to read – only incidentally for the machines you type it into. This is not a book about machines. It is about language.

Often, after a snippet of code, we'll show the output. Though it may *look* like code, it will never have a `#lang` line.

Here's the output of the code above.

```
"HELO"
```

The reason for abandoning screenshots is obvious – they take up a lot of room. If we used screenshots for every example in this book, it would either become twice as long or have half as many examples.

Efficient use of space is key.

Kiss, Gift, Poison

Let's try another language.

```
#lang dtc/hello/colors
```

```
(print "HELO")
```

Here's its output:

If you run it again, you might get:

This is a language with some trickiness to it. Whereas in `#lang dtc/hello/` `normal`, the `print` word simply printed the thing that came after it, the `print` word in `#lang dtc/hello/colors` places the thing that came after it onto a randomly colored shape.

Language designers would say:

The syntax is the same; but the semantics are different.

Most books about coding deal with one language, and have just one "Hello, World" example. But this book is about language itself, so we'll see a few "Hello, World" programs in different languages. The point is to give you an intuition for syntax and semantics. We'll define these more formally in the next chapter. When we do, you'll already have absorbed their meanings via linguistic immersion.

Let's look at one more example that has the same syntax as the previous two – but different semantics again.

```
#lang dtc/hello/animation

(print "HELO")
```

Now, when you run the code, something different happens again. The word "HELO" is displayed with an animation every time you run it. We can't print a dynamic picture in a static book, but the basic story is:

HELO → *HELO* → *HELO*

And so on.

The key thing to notice about the last three examples is that we didn't change the code, only the language. The first time we said "HELO" to the world, we used #lang dtc/hello/normal. The second time, we used the language, #lang dtc/hello/colors. The third time, we used #lang dtc/hello/animation. What's interesting though, is that if you look at *just* the code (ignoring the language), you wouldn't be able to tell what language each is written in.

Here are all three programs together:

```
#lang dtc/hello/normal

(print "HELO")

#lang dtc/hello/colors

(print "HELO")

#lang dtc/hello/animation

(print "HELO")
```

They do different things because the word print means something different depending on the language.

This concept arises in human languages, not just programming languages. The English word "gift," in German, means "poison." The English word "kiss," in Swedish, means "pee." And flashing the peace sign on one's forehead, in American Sign Language, means "stupid."

The same words or signs, under different interpretations, are not the same words or signs.

Nova: Va o no va?

A famous (but surprisingly false) example of misinterpretation is the cautionary tale about the Chevy Nova. As the story is told in hundreds of marketing books and business seminars (Aisner 2000), (Colapinto 2011), this car sold poorly in Spanish-speaking countries because the word "Nova" is similar to the Spanish phrase "no va," which translates to "doesn't go." Supposedly, Spanish speakers were concerned that if they bought a Nova, it wouldn't go.

But language isn't always so simple. The Chevy Nova actually sold well in Spanish-speaking countries, meeting or exceeding expected sales numbers in both of Chevrolet's primary Spanish-speaking markets: Mexico and Venezuela (Hammond 1993).

When you think about it, it makes sense. Just as in English, we don't say that a car "doesn't go," in Spanish, it would be more common to say something like "no funciona" ("it's not working") or "no camina" (literally "it's not walking," but a better English translation would be "it's not running"). Furthermore, until 2016, the word "Nova" was used for a kind of leaded gasoline provided by PEMEX – Mexico's state-owned petroleum company (Onursal and Gautam 1997). In terms of word associations, Nova gasoline is more connected to cars than the phrase "no va," which doesn't even apply to cars and isn't even pronounced like "Nova."

This story *is* a cautionary tale – but less about how to market cars than about how language works. It's a reminder not to make assumptions about how words, phrases, or pieces of syntax will be interpreted in a language you do not know. Languages are not simple.

The fact that the Chevy Nova story is so often repeated suggests that we English speakers don't need much convincing when it comes to how others are misinterpreting our words. The reality, of course, is that we are often the ones poorly interpreting the words of others: "No va" being unrelated to cars; and "Nova" being a leaded gasoline.

Hello, Hello, Hello

Programming students confuse syntax and semantics too. One of our favorite trick questions is, "In what language is the following code written?"

```
print("Hello world")
```

Students will raise hands and say things like Python, Ruby, or Lua – all of which *could* be correct. You *could* write this line in those languages. Something would happen.

However, the only truly correct answer is to note that it's backwards to ask, "In what language is this written?" – just as it would be backwards to ask in what language strings of symbols "gift," "kiss," or "Nova" are written. There isn't just one language in which a string of symbols like "gift" has meaning – just as there isn't just one in which print("Hello World") has meaning.

The reverse is also true: The string of symbols "gift" has *no* meaning in some languages (e.g., Chinese or Arabic, whose syntaxes use different symbols entirely). Likewise, there are languages in which `print("Hello World")` has no meaning – in Node.js (a non-browser-based implementation of JavaScript), for example. Running it will trigger an error that basically translates to: "I don't know what `print` means." In browser-based versions of JavaScript (yes, there are many JavaScripts), `print` does have meaning. It will ignore everything inside the parentheses and open a print window. Running `print("HELO")` and `print("Goodbye")` do the same thing for this JavaScript.

In other words: The same string of characters that causes one language to say `"hello"` will cause others to tell you that you've made a mistake, and still others will do something else entirely.

Furthermore (as if it weren't confusing enough), any JavaScript programmer can make *their* JavaScript understand that `print` should display words, rather than triggering an error or opening the print window. Whereas the following doesn't *normally* function in JavaScript the same way it does in Python, Ruby, and Lua – one could *make* it do so:

```
print("Hello world")
```

It's not difficult at all – and we'll cover this very basic form of language extension ("defining a function") later in this book. Many languages allow you to change the basic functionality of certain words, like `print`. Every programming language in modern use allows you to add vocabulary that wasn't there before.

Summing up:

- On the one hand, a program can act differently in different languages.

- On the other hand, two programs that act the same may look different in different languages.

- To make matters more confusing, some programs that don't work at all in a language can be made to work in that language by extending it with new vocabulary.

Syntax even changes between versions. This works in Python 2.7 . . .

```
print "Hello, World!"
```

. . . but in Python 3 it must be . . .

```
print("Hello, World!")
```

Yes, it's true. There are many Pythons. We say this because it often comes as a surprise to our students – even the ones who love Python, even the ones to whom we have already explained that there are many JavaScripts. Python was created in the 90s, and there have been many implementations since: Python, Jython, PyPy, and so on. And of course, there have been many versions *within* each of these Pythons (2.7 and 3.0, for example).

Don't despair, though! The process of becoming a coder is, in part, the process of becoming better at learning new languages – and becoming better at keeping them separate in your mind. It might seem impossible at first. It might seem like programming requires the world's longest cheatsheet. But we humans have an incredible capacity for learning languages and switching among them based on context.

If you're truly bilingual in English and Spanish you will have little trouble switching between them. Likewise, as you become a skilled coder, you'll have no more trouble keeping track of which programming language you're using than you would keeping track of the difference between poker and solitaire. Our brains have tremendous capacity for absorbing new sets of rules – whether they are game rules (like how the knight moves in chess), or grammatical rules (like "Put a comma between salutations, like 'Hello,' and recipients, like 'World'"), or syntactical rules (like "Put a parenthesis after symbols like `print`"), or even meta-linguistic rules (like "Speak Spanish with your mom and English with your dad," or "Use Python for the company's web app but use Bash for your personal shell scripts").

In any event, with our newfound ability to write in tongues, we are ready to begin our journey through a fascinating land – fraught with syntactic perils and semantic adventures.

To be continued...

LANGUAGES WITHOUT

As C-3PO put it:

> I'm fluent in over 6,000,000 forms of communication.

The authors have taught many students and teachers throughout the years. We overhear things.

When we had first launched our company, one 12-year-old student boasted on his first day of a coding summer camp that he was "fluent in six different languages." When asked which ones, he said: "English, Scratch, Java, JavaScript, and a little bit of Python."

"That's only five," one of the camp counselors pointed out.

"Oh, I forgot," he said. "My mom also taught me sign language." He started signing the alphabet with the kind of total confidence that "fluent" 12-year-olds sometimes have.

One of the other kids in the camp inadvertently asked a deep philosophical question, "What does 'fluent' mean?"

"It means you know it," the first kid said, rolling his eyes, as if the question was offensively trivial.

As the coding camp went on, it became clear that his only fluency was in English. His "fluency" in Scratch came from having done an "Hour of Code" at his elementary school. His Java/JavaScript "fluency" came from his father (a full stack web developer) having explained the difference between "Java" and "JavaScript" while showing him some of the JavaScript code he had written for work. His Python "fluency" came from a few hours of online Python lessons with his dad, who had decided that Python was a better first language than JavaScript. His American Sign Language "fluency" boiled down to knowing the words for "hungry" and "milk," and about 15 of the signs for letters of the alphabet.

Still, we learned a lot from this kid. This was the first time we'd heard someone claim to be "fluent" in a programming language – and to so deeply conflate this "fluency" with fluency in natural languages like English and American Sign Language.

As it turned out, this kid had his finger on the pulse of the times. A few years later, from 2015 through 2016, Senate Bill 468 (Florida Senate 2016) was percolating through the Florida state government. The bill was to require the Florida College System to allow high school coding classes to count as foreign language credits. That is, high school students could take a Java class instead of a Spanish class – and the two would be equivalent for the purposes of college admission and college credit.

The League of United Latin American Citizens (LULAC) and the Spanish American League Against Discrimination (SALAD) objected (Clark 2016):

> Our children need skills in both technology and in foreign languages to compete in today's global economy. However, to define coding and computer science as a foreign language is a misleading and mischievous misnomer that deceives our students, jeopardizes their eligibility to admission to universities, and will result in many losing out on the foreign language skills they desperately need even for entry-level jobs in South Florida.

Although the bill was stopped in the House after passing the Senate 35 to 5, the whole attempt suggests how easy it is for 12-year-olds and/or lawmakers to notice that the L-word in "programming language" and the L-word in "foreign language" are, in fact, the same L-word, and to draw conclusions about the two being the same.

Lawmakers in Georgia and Rhode Island have both also recently discussed allowing coding credits to substitute for foreign language credit, as have legislators in Washington, Kentucky, and Virginia. Texas actually *does* allow students to substitute coding for foreign language, provided that the student has attempted the required foreign language class and failed (Galvin 2016).

Tongueless Languages

If you're "in the know" – that is, already a coder – it's easy to laugh. But it's not entirely people's fault. That pesky L-word is literally sitting there, proclaiming that these things – Java, Scratch, Python, Racket, etc. – are all "languages." It's worth asking how that L-word got there.

They weren't always universally called languages. Early computing pioneer Charles Babbage labeled it the "Notation" in the 1840s. In the 1940s Konrad Zuse invented what he simply called "the calculus of plans" (Plankalkül, in German), which we recognize in retrospect as the world's first high-level programming language. Some of the other earliest things we recognize today as languages were simply called "autocodes" by their creators. There were times when people were more reserved about dubbing these pieces of technology "languages."

But in the 1950s, the L-word caught on (Nofre et al. 2014). It began to be included in the names of influential early languages – like ALGOL, developed in the 1950s: *ALGOrithmic Language.*

Today, we sometimes include it in the names of particular languages – like HTML ("Hypertext Markup Language") or SQL ("Structured Query Language"). But largely we don't bother – referring to the entire category of technologies as languages.

There's nothing wrong with that.

We just need to be aware of the confusion this can cause. Students are often unaware of how programming languages differ from those other things that we call "languages" – the ones we are much more familiar with, the ones that have likely been around since the dawn of our species. Likewise, teachers sometimes struggle to articulate their subtle relationships: either overstating their similarities or overstating their differences.

Naming something is a powerful linguistic act. To name something a *language* is a powerful meta-linguistic act. When we do such a thing, it is worth asking why.

The attribution of the word "language" isn't always given as easily as it was to programming languages. In the 1960s, American Sign Language (also called by other names, "Ameslan" and "manual communication") was *finally* formally accepted as a language by the scientific community. Sadly, it took almost a century. People had to fight for it. Powerful people fought against it, as we will see later in the book.

The word, "language," of course, comes from the Latin word for "tongue" (*lingua*). No surprise then that the concept is anchored to speech, sometimes limiting our understanding of other things that might qualify.

Yet, those technologies that are far less "language-y" than American Sign Language or English got the L-word appended without much fuss, pomp, or circumstance. They slipped into the club for free.

Who paid their membership?

As it turns out, mathematicians had adopted the L-word before modern electric computers had been built and before modern programming languages had been designed. The *Principia Mathematica* routinely distinguishes between "ordinary language" (Russel and Whitehead's native tongue: English) and things like "logical language" (their mathematical notations) (Whitehead and Russell 1925). These twentieth century mathematicians were not the first to make such metalinguistic distinctions. It goes back much farther.

Mathematicians had, for centuries, been cultivating their notations while simultaneously and responsibly separating their newly constructed "languages" (as they called them) from the other kind – their native tongues. Augustus De Morgan – famous for his contributions to mathematical logic and algebra, and for being a calculus tutor to Ada Lovelace – wrote of this separation (De Morgan 1849):

> In abandoning the meanings of [mathematical] symbols, we also abandon those
> of the [ordinary language] words which describe them. Thus addition is to be, for
> the present, **a sound void of sense**. It is a mode of combination represented by +;
> when + receives its meaning, so also will the word addition. . . . [N]o word nor
> sign of arithmetic or algebra has one atom of meaning throughout this chapter . . .
> If any one were to assert that + and - might mean reward and punishment, and A, B,
> C, etc. might stand for virtues and vices, the reader might believe him, or contradict
> him, as he pleases . . .

He is saying that the word "addition" is merely imported from English – but when it crosses the threshold between English and algebra, it becomes a "sound void of sense." Even the sense of "addition operates on numbers" is – as he emphasizes – too much to assume. At first, one wonders why he didn't use something like "gorblesnop" if, indeed, he wanted a senseless word. However, to do so for all operations, across all the symbolic languages one might design, leaves the mind juggling many words that have no sense in *any* language.

Programming language designers over the decades have imported other words from English rather than inventing new words: "if," "class," "object," "graph," "interpret," "compile," "execute," "tree," "branch," "library," etc. These do not retain their ambiguous English meanings when used by programmers. They take on a much more technical meaning in "programmer English."

Babbage's Calculus Club

Even before this, as early as 1813, when Charles Babbage was merely a college student at Cambridge – long before working on his Difference Engine or his Analytical Engine – he wrote of what he called "symbolic language," describing such mathematical notations as tools for unburdening the mind:

> It is the spirit of this symbolic language . . . (so much in unison with all our faculties,) which carries the eye . . . to condense pages into lines, and volumes into pages; shortening the road to discovery, and preserving the mind unfatigued by continued efforts of attention to the minor parts, that may exert its whole vigor on those which are more important.

This was written in the preface to a manifesto authored by a small group of revolutionary Cambridge students called the Analytical Society – of which Babbage was a founding member. The group's goal was to bring about a linguistic change in their education system: getting Cambridge to abandon the use of Newton's calculus notation in textbooks and exams, and rather to use the more popular notation in continental Europe – Leibniz's notation.

This might sound trivial or geeky, but it was actually a surprisingly forward-thinking idea. Recall that the debate about who invented calculus (Newton or Leibniz) still smolders to this day. Newton was the Englishman, so one can imagine which side the schools of England were on. Babbage's group was championing Leibniz – the non-Englishman who had invented a notation that many considered superior to Newton's. In spite of their controversial position, however, they were ultimately successful, with the momentum continuing even after the group had been disbanded. Cambridge began to include Leibniz's notation on exams; textbooks were translated; and by 1830, Leibniz's notation was commonplace in England, alongside Newton's. Today, pick up any calculus textbook, and you will find Leibniz's notation for derivatives and integrals, not Newton's.

It is perhaps the first example of an education system's wholesale adoption of one symbolic language only to replace it with another, more popular one. In computing, this is commonplace with the symbolic languages of our day: Before universities taught Java they taught C++ and Pascal (Guzdial 2011); today, more and more are shifting to Python, which is now the most common language taught (Guo 2014). Tomorrow? Who knows?

Babbage's Analytical Society was less about calculus and more about a psychological idea:

that one language of symbols can be a better tool for the mind than another.

Later, he would go on to do what he is most famous for: inventing the Analytical Engine – a machine that could manipulate symbols. This machine would be programmable in a Notation of his invention – a symbolic language. In other words, the career of the father of computing was, from his university years onward, intertwined with symbolic languages, what mathematicians today would call "formal languages." This is a broad linguistic category that includes mathematical notations like the ones of De Morgan and Babbage, as well as modern programming languages like Java and Python.

Between 1837 and 1845, Babbage and Lovelace would pen (using the Notation) the first things that historians consider to be "computer programs" – a full century before the first thing that historians consider to be "computer hardware" would actually be built (Konrad Zuse's electronic Z3 computer, in 1941).

In the 1950s, the designers of early programming languages (many of them mathematicians) would begin to gravitate toward the already-accepted L-word for describing the notations of mathematics. It had been that way since before they were born. Though this fact is probably lost on the average elementary school student learning the Scratch language, the L-word gravitation was less about connecting programming languages to English or Spanish, and more about connecting it to the mathematical languages of people like Newton, Leibniz, De Morgan, Babbage, Russel, and Whitehead.

Today, the programming languages we teach and learn in schools are instantiations of a long and ongoing tradition of language design – one that predates the earliest of the electrical machines on which they run. The machines are by no means the origin of these languages; and to think so would be unfair to them.

Indeed, there isn't even a chicken/egg ambiguity here: Programming languages were built a full century before programmable machines.

Babbage never built the Analytical Engine, in fact. Yes, that machine he is most famous for – the thing that launched the digital age – was never fully constructed. The notation he and Lovelace wielded came from a long tradition of notational design that predated even his *drawings* of that machine – inherited from predecessors like Newton and Leibniz. Babbage's and Lovelace's early programs were comprehensible to others in spite of the Analytical Engine being the stuff of dreams.

Diffs

It's easy to find differences between Java and English, or Scratch and ASL. Let's get most of that out of our system here, so that the rest of the book can deal with what is actually much more interesting: *what these very different kinds of languages have in common.*

In the next chapter, we'll see that, different though they are, programming languages and natural languages actually do have one surprising thing in common: In an fMRI machine, a medical device used in brain imaging, the parts of a coder's brain that light up when they are reading code are the same ones that light up for all human beings when we comprehend natural language.

This was a groundbreaking scientific discovery in 2014 that will be all the more exciting and delightfully puzzling after we have spent the rest of this chapter examining how *different* computer languages and people languages are.

Finite Descriptions of the Infinite

The 3rd edition of the American Heritage Dictionary of the English Language has more than 350,000 words (Soukhanov 1992). The Academic Dictionary of Lithuanian has about half a million (Academic Dictionary of Lithuanian 2005). The online dictionary of the Turkish Language Institute contains more than 600,000 words (Turkish Language Institute 2019). And the online dictionary for the northern and southern dialects of Korean tops out at more than 1.1 million words (National Institute of Korean Language 2019).

Natural languages are big things.

That said, one might argue that the number of words in a dictionary doesn't really denote the size of a language. That's true. The average American high school graduate knows about 45,000 words (Pinker 1994). And although they may know and recognize 45,000 words, the active vocabulary of the average American adult is closer to 20,000 words (Jackson 2011). That's far short of the

350,000 words in the English dictionary. And that's okay. Knowing all of the words in a dictionary is never a requisite for fluency in any natural language. Still, whether you look at the number of words in a dictionary, or something more modest, you see the same thing when you put that number next to the tiny numbers that describe the sizes of programming languages.

Java, for example, has about 50 keywords (Gosling et al. 2019). The thing is, no one learns Java simply by learning the definitions for those keywords. They are merely symbols void of sense – until they are combined with other symbols according to certain rules.

Even these rules, though, are few in number compared to the many grammatical rules of natural languages. Java's rules fit on a single webpage (Gosling et al. 2019). Though their number grows as the language evolves, there have never been more than a few hundred.

Even when we include all the vocabulary and all the grammar rules of Java, we'd be in the low hundreds, whereas our *most conservative* estimation of English vocabulary size is 20,000 ambiguously defined words, plus many (often subtle) grammatical rules. This difference should serve to illustrate that when it comes to natural languages, there's simply more there. A lot more. At minimum, two hundred times more. At maximum, it's hard to even estimate.

Scheme, famous for being perhaps the smallest programming language that human minds can effectively use, has only 5 keywords and 8 syntactic forms. Peter Norvig (current director of research at Google), wrote on the subject, showing in a single blog post that you can re-create Scheme with fewer than 120 lines of Python code (Norvig 2010). This alone should illustrate the smallness of programming languages. You can re-create one inside the other.

The idea of "re-creating Chinese within English" is nonsensical. But how much English would need to be spent to fully articulate the subtleties of the Chinese language – from word definitions to grammatical usages? Definitely more than 120 lines.

Although programmers routinely add new vocabulary to programming languages in the form of "libraries," the small number of built-in keywords are the ones that you get when you download a language from the internet and sit down to write with it for the first time. Indeed, that's what a programming language is: A program that understands *other* programs – provided they are written with a certain set of keywords that are arranged according to a certain set of grammatical rules.

Downloaded Scheme? You now have a program that reads programs. What programs does it read? Any, as long as they use those 5 keywords, combined appropriately with those 8 syntactic forms. That's what it reads, and that's *all* it reads (at least at first).

Let's not underestimate the complexity of programming languages, though. After all, there are only 88 keys on a piano too (and really only 12 tones, repeated across various octaves). Yet the "language" of the piano takes many years to master. Indeed, the number of pleasing ways those 12 tones can be arranged is, for all practical purposes, endless.

Endless too are the number of ways even those 5 keywords of Scheme can be combined. Not to mention, one of those keywords is `define` – which lets you add new keywords. So it's a bit like a piano that has a meta-key that lets you add new keys. Let's ignore that, for now, though.

Languages start small. Yet, in those small spaces, the seeds of infinity are already there. This is a vital quality of all languages – they are "generative." Given sufficient time, fluent individuals can generate an infinite number of new expressions, all grammatically correct, all unique, all meaningful. This applies to both natural languages and programming languages. This connection between the two kinds of languages was articulated by linguist Noam Chomsky.

However, when it comes to programming languages, mathematical notations, and music – their infinite potential proceeds from something undeniably smaller, something small enough to be immediately perceivable as a tool. Sometimes 88 keys. Sometimes 5 keywords and 8 rules.

Bottling the Human Will

The channel of a language is how that particular language is transmitted to other human beings. English and other spoken languages can make use of the vocal-auditory channel – for example, you voice, they hear. American Sign Languages and other signed languages use a physical-visual channel – that is, you sign, they see. Written English makes use of a physical-visual channel too – that is, you write, they see.

In some sense, programming languages are akin to written languages – in so far as they share the same channel. You type, they see.

Furthermore, we can say that they rarely (if ever) make use of the vocal-auditory channel. If you don't believe us, try reading some programs aloud and see if people understand you. We're not saying they'll understand nothing; but it's a guarantee that, very quickly, they'll tell you to shut up and just let them read the source code.

That's certainly one difference – the channel – and a key one. No doubt, the visual nature of programming must belong to any serious discussion about how students learn it. This will come up again later, as we discuss the training of "vision" for skills such as chess.

But before we leave behind the idea of channels, doesn't it feel a bit strange to talk about the "channel" of a programming language? When it comes to programming, there need not necessarily *be* a channel between two human beings. Programs need not be means of communication at all.

True, there is that famous adage:

> Programs should be written for people to read, and only incidentally for machines to execute.

Should. Not must.

We *can* write programs in secret; we can even run them. If the programs we write are never seen by eyes other than our own, this does nothing to remove their ability to move matter in the world. We type programs into a computer, and their story unfolds. The presence of a human mind besides the author's is never strictly required. Once it is running, the laws of physics have already taken over. Such laws operate in spite of our awareness or attention. It is like setting a boulder rolling down a hill – or rather, trillions of boulders, called "electrons."

Indeed, a program can be written and forgotten about, yet still be running and doing things in the world. Thank goodness for that; our digital society rests upon it. Coding wizards write programs that run our airplanes, power plants, cars, systems of commerce, stock markets, and systems of communication. The vast majority of what these programs do is hidden from users – uncommunicated. Only the very tip of the iceberg is made manifest to most – for example, that the planes do not crash, that the stock market keeps humming, that our text messages are sent.

To put it dramatically, program authors may die, yet the programs will not.

When you turn the steering wheel on many modern cars, you cause your car's computer to execute code that helps turn the car's wheels. What that code looks like and what it might have communicated if you read the source code are mysteries. Yet, the wheels do turn. And our society rolls on.

What an incredible difference between programming languages and natural ones. As philosophers are fond of asking: If a tree falls in the forest and no one is around to hear it, does it transmit any information across the auditory channel? Certainly not. If a man speaks his dying words alone in the forest, are his words lost forever? Certainly so. If a dying man writes a message, places it in a bottle and casts it into the sea, do not those words lie inert and dormant until the bottle is discovered? Certainly so.

Yet, if a dying person writes their final program, presses "Run" and perishes, what can we say? Nothing so concrete. We can only shrug our shoulders and say, I need to know more about this story. What is the text of this program that survived, and what computer was it running on, and what network, and was there was any other technology involved? A robotic arm? A self-driving car? A nuclear missile? A great many things might happen after this person's death – their will living on, encoded into a program. It's not a message bottled up; it's a message uncorked and in motion. Motion can be hard to predict.

Still, on real software teams: Programs *are* shared between people. What you write today will be read tomorrow – by you and by others. Small programs, if they're lucky, become big programs that require many people working together, all reading and understanding the same growing piece of text. By one report, in 2016, Google had approximately 30,000 software developers working on a multitude of codebases (Security and Exchange Commission 2014). In these large endeavors, being able to write code that communicates to computers *and* to human beings, who are writing and editing the same textual artifact, is critical.

On the entryway to his school in Athens, Plato is said to have written, "Let no one ignorant of geometry enter." Perhaps upon the school for coding wizards there should be written, "Let none enter here who write programs solely for machines."

Wise coders know this. But the reason we must specify it up front is that we can all fail to do so. It must, therefore, be a practice and a discipline. Not just to write, but to write well, to write clearly, to write for others, to write better over time.

Natural languages are similar in this way. But the difference is still clear: In natural languages, the option of writing them "incidentally for machines" or otherwise never comes up. Freed from that option, we are freed from that temptation.

Machines Anchor Language

Both programming languages and people languages change and grow over time. However, people languages change slowly and seem to have a mind of their own.

Programming languages, on the other hand, change immediately, and only when we allow them to.

Looking back in time at an earlier English can be an odd experience.

```
And gladly wolde he lerne, and gladly teche.
The lyf so short, the craft so long to lerne
For hym was levere have at his beddes heed
Twenty bookes, clad in blak or reed,
Of Aristotle and his philosophie...
```

English didn't always look or sound the way it does, as anyone who has read Chaucer – our "Father of English literature" – can see. Certainly, the English language does change. Still, the above passages are *relatively* intelligible, in spite of being from the 1300s.

When it comes to English, the fact that it *can't* change suddenly is one thing that makes it so useful. We can still look back more than 700 years and understand the messages of the past. We can observe that, today, life is still as short and the craft is still as long as when those words were written. (These words were as true in Chaucer's day as they were in the days of Hippocritus, whom he was probably quoting).

Although we occasionally have to worry about new words like "selfie" popping into our lives or words like "levere" dropping out of it, we do not have to worry that we'll wake up one day, drive to Starbucks, and say "Can I have coffee?" and be met with blank stares. The basic words and grammatical structures we rely on are, thankfully, hard to change in dramatic ways on a large scale. To do so immediately is impossible. Our language is distributed among too many.

Consider for a moment what you would have to do if you *did* want to make a minor but definitive change to English. For example, suppose you wanted to add a word. As a first stab, maybe you could get dictionary writers to insert an entry for your word. That's probably not enough, though. People don't wake up in the morning and consult a dictionary for recent updates and then proceed through the day with the linguistic "patch" installed in their brains. You could try to use the internet to make your word "go viral" – but that is easier said than done. Barring that, you may have to launch a costly worldwide campaign.

Most people who are not giant corporations are unable to launch such campaigns. We mentioned Starbucks previously without having to define it. Starbucks already defined itself for us. Whereas Starbucks successfully added the word "Starbucks" to our language, the quests of the rest of us will be harder. The rest of us sometimes have to band together to make the same kind of society-wide linguistic patches.

By comparison, programming languages are trivial to change. Python was first released in 1991. A version 2.0 was released just nine years later – in 2000. This version went through seven minor version changes, up to version 2.7 – at which point the language was given an end-of-life date of 2015 (which was later bumped to 2020). Although Python 2.7 was scheduled to die, the 3.0 (released in December 2008) is alive and well. And so on. If history is any indication, this version will not be the last.

Suppose you had been an ordinary Python programmer on that cold day in December 2008 when version 3.0 had been released. Suppose you got your morning Starbucks, and sat down at your computer to write some Python code. Would you have been met with a blank stare from a computer that yesterday understood version 2.7 and today understands only 3.0?

Luckily, not. It's perfectly normal for one computer to understand Python 2.7, even though other computers understand 3.0. You can even get your computer to understand either one – whichever you happen to want to use at a given time. This should come as no surprise: Earlier in this chapter, we installed Racket and then wrote "Hello, World" programs in several different languages. Python 2.7 and Python 3.0 are simply different languages – and it's quite easy to have different languages installed on the same computer.

The fact is that programming languages are just software – and as such, they get changed. New versions get released, and old ones die. Whereas people languages are not governed by an authority that legislates top-down changes – programming languages generally *are* governed in this way. Python's creator Guido van Rossum was given by the Python community the title "Benevolent Dictator for Life." It was a joke – but with a grain of truth. Although he voluntarily relieved himself of this title in 2018, he was a major player in the ongoing design and redesign of the Python language for more than a quarter of a century. Although he can't reach into your computer and legislate the version of Python that's installed there – he can (like you) install his favorite version on his own computer, release it to others, and then talk about all the cool features that it has. Others can follow suit and switch. Or they can decide not to – even on a project-by-project basis.

This is exactly what you *can't* do with people languages. You can't just start saying "I'd like a large gorblesnop with milk, please" at Starbucks without immediate backlash – even if you go on to clarify that by "large" you meant "venti." But you *can* create your own programming language and use it all you like without anyone even knowing. It is, therefore, much easier to experiment with new programming languages than it is to experiment with new people languages. A corollary of this is that it is much easier to create multiple versions of the same language, or new languages entirely. We need only create them for ourselves and use them long enough to convince ourselves that they are better. Then, when the time comes to convince others, they can dip their toe into the new language without fully committing – that is, by installing it alongside their other languages so that they can use the new without abandoning the old.

Reading Chaucer shows us that people languages change and drift. But the changes are rarely driven by a single person, or even traceable back to a single person. Shakespeare coined many new English words – like "articulate" and "invulnerable" – but that kind of single-person linguistic contribution is the exception, not the rule.

When linguistic construction by a centralized authority *is* the rule, it is the stuff of nightmares – or dystopian novels like *1984*. The Party's language of Newspeak is designed to limit free thought by redesigning free speech – removing politically undesirable words. Negative words like "bad" are removed in favor of modified positives like "ungood"; new words like "goodthink" are given definitions like "conformance with the Party's ideals." The book meditates on the Sapir-Whorf hypothesis – a hypothesis that suggests the structure of our native tongue limits the space of thoughts we are able to independently explore. If the Sapir-Whorf hypothesis is true, then such a dystopian nightmare is nothing short of state control over people's ability to think.

With programming languages, the situation is reversed: Changes never happen without someone initiating them, and we can almost always trace those changes back to the small number of individuals who initiated them. The whole process of changing a computer language is consciously managed, by small groups or by large ones. The process is not unconscious. In some open source projects, the changes can be publicly discussed by thousands (as was the case with Mozilla's Rust programming language, with more than 2,000 people contributing to the project). All are willing participants in changes to this tool of the mind.

In coding, one reason so many can collaborate is that it's easier to agree on the meanings of things. In a programming language, we can fall back on defining the "meaning" of some word or phrase as "what it makes the computer do." In a natural language, we define the "meaning" of a word or phrase as "what other people will understand."

When it come to meaning, software tends to be more consistent than brainware (or as it is commonly called, "wetware"). In practice this means that if two programmers disagree about what a program means, they don't need to argue about it. They *can*. . . But they can often just run the program and see who is right and who is wrong. Whoever disagrees with the computer is wrong.

What's more, programmers fundamentally agree about this method of settling disagreements. It's part of becoming a programmer – realizing that a program's meaning is defined by what the computer actually does, not by what we thought we told it to do.

With this empirical test to anchor the meaning of programs, we are free to experiment. For example, we can create new languages – knowing that if we create an abomination, we can return to the safety of our last working version. And that last version will have the semantics we all agreed upon at the time.

Consider a phrase like "life is short; but art is long":

Does it ring to you as a lament about the shortness of life? Or is it a celebration about the staying power of art? Does "art" apply to software artifacts? Is life an art? Is art life? The questions of meaning are potentially endless – a single phrase, an infinity of questions.

With a program, the buck stops – computers having only one interpretation. Programmers know this, which cuts down on a certain amount of philosophical discussion from the get-go. A finite number of questions will answer any meaningful question – that is, any question about meaning.

Now That It's Out of Our System

We have just spent a lot of natural language to articulate the differences between computer languages and natural languages. But the truth is that the two are intertwined in ways that are truly fascinating. These are the main motivations for this book.

Yes, computer languages are smaller (in terms of raw vocabulary), and, yes, they use a different channel, and, yes, they don't even need a channel at all necessarily, and, yes, they have precise meanings and do not drift when we create new versions.

But, as we will see, computer languages and natural languages are locked together in a cyclical way. The construction of new programming languages often requires the construction of highly specialized people languages. And the construction of new, highly specialized people languages often arises from the construction of new programming languages.

Furthermore, as we have already foreshadowed, programmer brains process programming languages with the same parts that process natural language. So, perhaps the two kinds of languages are more similar than they appear at first glance.

Their similarities might not always be clear "out there." But the science is clear: "In here," as neurocognitive activities, they are interwoven.

To be continued...

LANGUAGES WITHIN

It is easier to talk about language "out there" than to talk about what happens when our brains process language. Much of that inner process is unconscious, unknown even to ourselves. Many secrets of that gray organ have remained locked inside our skulls, hidden from scientists for as long as science has existed, hidden from all of us for as long as we have existed.

Our attempts to measure something often changes the thing we are measuring – the brain being particularly guilty of this. Throughout history, perhaps more so than any other object that we have yearned to study, the healthy functioning brain has resisted the crude instruments of science: our surgical knives and our microscopes. Such an inconveniently fragile thing – it tends to stop being definable as "healthy or functioning" the moment we start probing it with our instruments.

In 1892, an antique dealer named Edwin Smith bought an ancient Egyptian papyrus more than 15 feet long. Although it was unintelligible to him, it was later discovered to be a medical text from circa 1600 BCE, containing the world's earliest recorded observations about the brain. This "message in a bottle" revealed that the author, an ancient Egyptian surgeon, had made observations related to brain injuries and their adverse linguistic effects – for example, aphasia, the inability to speak.

It's true. The earliest record we have about the brain contains observations about language.

For many centuries, the knife was indeed the scientific instrument of necessity. The Romans used it to cut up the brains of animals. Andreas Vesalius, in the 1500s, used the knife to dissect human cadavers, including their brains – positing that the brain makes use of the nervous system for transmitting both sensation and motion (Vesalius 1543).

In 1861, French anatomist Pierre Paul Broca used the knife to uncover the first evidence that the brains have substructures responsible for different activities of the mind. One area of the brain still bears his name today: Broca's area. It was given to a portion of the frontal lobe of a patient who had, over a period of 21 years, progressively lost the ability to speak and move, but never lost the ability to think or comprehend language. Of course, Broca did not know why until, post-mortem, his knife revealed a lesion at what we now call "Broca's area." Until then, it had not been shown that one region might control language production, whereas others might control comprehension.

As we linguistically wired creatures so often do when we discover something new: We named it. Indeed, as we so often do: We gave it a name that had already been given out. As a result, there is now a region within all of our skulls that bears the name of a French anatomist from the 1800s (for reference: born about a decade after Ada Lovelace).

Knives and microscopes gave rise to many of our named discoveries over the years: lobes, hemispheres, neurons, axons, dendrites, synapses, and so on. More cutting led to the discovery of more pieces worth giving names to. It wasn't until 1964, however, that the first department of neuroscience was founded at the University of California, Irvine. Harvard followed suit a few years later. Today, the field is firmly established in our scientific institutions, and our tools have evolved considerably beyond just knives and microscopes (though it should be mentioned that these tools are by no means obsolete!).

One tool is functional magnetic resonance imaging (fMRI). First used on humans in 1992, fMRI allows us, without the use of knives or saws or metal probes, to peer into the skull, into the brain's inner workings – all with virtually no discomfort to human subjects – save that they must lie still inside of a machine for the duration of the experiment. The subject, however, may speak, listen, read, and perform a range of tasks. All the while, scientists may gather precise spatial data about which parts of the brain are active.

Finally, we could ask questions about how we process language, without worry that our instruments of inquiry would change, damage, or destroy the object of inquiry. And furthermore, we could do it as the subject was in the midst of linguistic acts (actually reading words!) – rather than, as Broca was forced to do, wait for 21 years until a subject had died.

Within the decade, fMRI was being used to study language. If Broca had magically lived more than a century longer, he would have seen the region bearing his name light up on a screen, confirming his life's work. The "lighting up" is a computer's rendering of the fact that the blood near Broca's area is deploying oxygen to the neurons there more quickly than to other areas. The effect can be detected by a magnetic field because oxygenated blood has different magnetic properties than deoxygenated blood. This oxygenation response literally fuels thought: Neurons need the oxygen to fire, and thoughts need neurons to fire.

The combination of knives and modern instruments has allowed humanity to discover or confirm the role of several areas in the brain, further refining our "atlas" of the brain.

We now know of areas that play roles in a range of other linguistic or language-related activities: working memory, word retrieval, object naming, planning, decision making, and so on.

In 2014, scientists showed that areas such as these – language areas – were the ones lighting up when programmers read programs. In 2017, it was confirmed.

Interestingly, this wasn't the first visual-spatial language discovered to do so.

Signed Languages

An obvious question: Do signed languages activate the same parts of the brain as spoken language?

Broca's area is fairly close to parts that control the face (including the mouth), whereas another linguistic region called Wernicke's area is close to the auditory cortex. One might then hypothesize that both regions are specialized for speech. Furthermore, the left hemisphere had often been considered to be for verbal processing, whereas the right was for spatial processing – which raised questions about where sign language processing might occur.

However, studies of deaf signers who have sustained brain injuries have shown that damage to the left hemisphere does inhibit signing ability, whereas damage to the right hemisphere does not (Hickok et al. 2002). This would suggest that sign language is at least processed in the same hemisphere as spoken language.

Localizing it further, damage to the left frontal regions (near Broca's area) results in difficulties with producing signs – just as damage to Broca's area results in difficulty producing words. Damage to the left hemisphere in the temporal regions (near Wernike's area) results in difficulties with comprehension of signs – just as damage to Wernike's area results in difficulties understanding spoken words. Thus, despite the modality difference, each form of language uses the same wetware for similar tasks.

Studies across a variety of techniques (including fMRI) seem to support this, with one meta-analysis (Campbell et al. 2007) summing up the current scientific understanding:

> ... [P]art of Wernicke's region appears to be particularly interested in signed language processing, just as it has been shown to be for spoken language processing using similar experimental paradigms (see Scott, Blank, Rosen, & Wise, 2000; Narain et al., 2003). Thus, this appears to be a language-specific region that is not sensitive to the modality of the language it encounters.... Every neuroimaging study to date reports activation in the left inferior frontal regions for signed language production and planning. Broca's area is always involved, and left hemisphere dominance is always observed.

Regions like Broca's area are now conclusively linked to spoken languages, signed languages, and programming languages.

As is the case in many stories, protagonists occasionally pick up new companions along the way. Our main protagonists are, of course, programming languages. And spoken languages are an old friend. But let us briefly fill in the surprisingly tragic back-story of signed languages, the latest addition to the party. If they share a neurocognitive boat with our protagonists, it makes sense to get to know them.

Silent Battles

Gallaudet University, whose charter was signed by Abraham Lincoln, is a thriving deaf university with over 60 bachelor and graduate degree programs, and even a Ph.D. program in educational neuroscience. Many American high schools offer ASL, counting it as a foreign language (though it sprang up on American soil). As of 2016, ASL was the third most studied language in U.S. institutions of higher education, with approximately 31% of American colleges offering ASL classes (Looney and Lusin 2019). It is becoming more mainstream to see deaf actors signing on television – for example, *Switched at Birth* (2011-2017) – and in blockbuster movies – for example, *A Quiet Place* (2018).

However, there was a time when neither the American public, nor the American scientific establishment, nor American educational institutions considered ASL to be a true language. It was a century of educational darkness.

But let us start at the beginning – a time of growth and prosperity.

For reference, the story starts roughly between the years that Babbage was in university (the 1810s) and ends in the year that the Lisp programming language was released (1960). In other words, while the rest of the world was inventing the computer and the second high level programming language after Fortran, another very different kind of visual-spatial language experienced an arc of its own: It was born, grew into something beautiful, was almost erased from the earth by dystopian educational reform, and was finally saved (in part) by a formal language called Stokoe notation – with just a few keywords and grammatical structures.

ASL students are required to learn the beginning of this story by heart, an educational oral tradition – much like our `"Hello, World"` tradition. You can watch students and experts alike signing it on YouTube by searching for "ASL Gallaudet Story."

As it begins: In the early 1800s, a hearing man named Thomas Hopkins Gallaudet, from Connecticut, traveled first to England and then to France in search of a teacher for his neighbor's daughter, who was deaf. In France, he met a deaf educator named Laurent Clerc, fluent in what is now known as Old French Sign Language. The two of them sailed back to America and, in 1817, founded a school that used sign language for instruction – the first of its kind on American soil. A group of deaf students came from a place called Martha's Vineyard (near Cape Cod) – where unusually high rates of congenital deafness had led to a community of signers – some hearing, some deaf, all signers. Others came from nearby villages in Maine and New Hampshire, bringing their own, independently developed sign languages. Others brought their own "home-signs," developed solely to communicate with family members within their own home. Thus began the evolution of American Sign Language – a melting pot of Laurent Clerc's Old French Sign Language and all of these various indigenous sign languages that had sprung up organically in America prior to his arrival.

All seemed well for half a century. However, after the end of the American Civil War, a counter-movement in deaf education called "oralism" began to emerge. The key players in this movement were neither deaf nor fluent in sign language. Although their reasons were diverse, they were unified in their anti-signing philosophy. Some believed simply that the deaf should learn to speak and lip-read to become more tightly integrated with society – whereas others believed that sign language was an inferior language, a relic of our ape ancestors and "savage races" like the Native Americans and other tribal people (Baynton 1998).

It would be a century before science would show the grammatical structures of signed languages to be as rich and complex as any spoken language.

There would be no fMRI studies to save the day either – not for almost a century and a half.

No, at this time, science was on the dystopian side: The emerging vocabulary of Darwinism had been co-opted by eugenicists, who believed the human population should be improved by discouraging the reproduction of certain individuals with undesirable qualities, such as disabilities or certain skin colors. Many oralists used this same line of reasoning to make their case against sign language. A key leader in the oralist movement – none other than scientist and inventor Alexander Graham Bell – wrote an article called "Upon the Formation of a Deaf Variety of the Human Race" in which he wished to call attention to the problems of the deaf people intermarrying, reproducing, and thus passing their deafness on to the next generation. He ends the essay with the sentence:

> Having shown the tendency to the formation of a deaf variety of the human race in America, and some of the means that should be taken to counteract it, I commend the whole subject to the attention of scientific men.

As it turned out, for Bell, the recommended way to prevent "the deaf race" was to stop using sign language in deaf education. You can't erase a language from a brain without changing the wetware; but you can erase it from the world simply by changing education. And so, Bell – the father of the telephone – also influenced educational establishments to begin silencing that already-silent language. In 1880, there began what is referred to by deaf historians as "the dark ages for deaf education in America" (Winefield 1987).

The dusk began at what sounds, at first glance, like a relatively innocent place: a meeting of the International Congress on the Education of the Deaf. Here, however, it was decreed that the best means of instruction for the deaf was oralism – the teaching of speech and lipreading in classrooms, and the active suppression of sign language. Of the 164 educators who attended that meeting, only one of them was deaf. One of their resolutions was:

> Considering the incontestable superiority of speech over signs in restoring the deaf-mute to society, and in giving him a more perfect knowledge of language.... That the Oral method ought to be preferred to that of signs for the education and instruction of the deaf and dumb.

For three days at that conference, there were presentations from oralism's champion – Alexander Graham Bell. He was deeply affected by his mother's gradual progression into deafness, which began when Bell was age 12. Around this time his father, a famous phonetician, invented a writing system called Visible

Speech: a collection of symbols that described how speech organs should be positioned in order to produce sounds. This was a notation for pronunciation that Bell believed could be used in deaf education, and in which he became fluent at the tutelage of his father. Later, his growing wealth from inventions gave him a platform from which to promote Visible Speech and oralism.

The proponents of sign language – who were not in attendance – could do nothing to stop the conclusions reached. Nor could they stop the worldwide damage that followed. After the 1880 decision, the dystopian conversion of deaf education began: One-by-one, hearing teachers replaced deaf educators such that by 1919 over 80% of educators were neither deaf nor fluent in sign language. Entire schools switched from the manual method to the oral method. Sign language itself was banned in classrooms and other formal educational settings. Students caught using it were punished. Some were forced to wear gloves tied together to prevent the use of signs.

The language was preserved in boarding school dormitories, in Deaf social circles, and through the intentional use of film technology, which arrived just in time. Here is an English-interpreted message in a bottle from a 1913 American film called "The Preservation of the Sign Language" (Veditz 1913):

> We American deaf are now facing bad times for our schools. False prophets are now appearing, announcing to the public that our American means of teaching the deaf are all wrong. These men have tried to educate the public and make them believe that the oral method is really the one best means of educating the deaf. But we American deaf know, the French deaf know, the German deaf know that in truth, the oral method is the worst. A new race of pharaohs that knew not Joseph is taking over the land and many of our American schools. They do not understand signs for they cannot sign. They proclaim that signs are worthless and of no help to the deaf. Enemies of the sign language, they are enemies of the true welfare of the deaf. We must use our films to pass on the beauty of the signs we have now. As long as we have deaf people on earth, we will have signs. And as long as we have our films, we can preserve signs in their old purity. It is my hope that we will all love and guard our beautiful sign language as the noblest gift God has given to deaf people.

And so film technology was used for signed language in the same way that writing systems had been used for spoken languages for centuries: to encode words and thoughts for retrieval by others in the future – messages in bottles. To make words live beyond the ephemeral moment of their birth.

So the battle of language was waged. On the one side, the oralist's Visible Speech writing system was used as a tool to dislodge sign language from deaf education – although this was later abandoned. On the other side, sign language retreated to the shadows while signers turned to the technology of the time to make their linguistic acts less ephemeral – and harder to dislodge. All the while, the battleground was the American education of deaf children.

Visible Speech, lipreading, and phonetic education were not the only linguistic tools designed by non-signers to replace American Sign Language. Many such tools were developed. Manually Coded English is a signed language that borrows English grammatical structures, while mapping spoken words to signs borrowed from ASL. Another system, Signing Exact English has a similar motivation, as does Seeing Essential English.

Oddly enough, these linguistic tools were designed in service of erasing a language that wasn't designed at all: one that evolved naturally – by Americans, for Americans. Whether you saw these new languages as tools or weapons, depended very much on which side of the linguistic trenches you were standing.

The dawn began to break in the 1960s, when linguist William Stokoe revolutionized his field by studying American Sign Language. He was the first to explain what had always been true: American Sign Language was a rich and thriving linguistic system, complete with its own grammar and syntax, worthy of study in its own right, of deep value to those who know it, and of tremendous potential value to any who choose to learn it. He was able to bridge a linguistic gap between ASL and the meta-language of linguistics. His book *A Dictionary of American Sign Language on Linguistic Principles* popularized the name "American Sign Language," permanently displacing other names like Ameslan, manual communication, and sign language.

David Armstrong, anthropologist and former Gallaudet University administrator, said a few days after Stokoe's death in the year 2000 (Armstrong 2000):

> At the time of his arrival at Gallaudet, the sign language used by deaf Americans and now known as American Sign Language (ASL) was generally believed to be a corrupt visual code for spoken English or elaborate pantomime. It and other national sign languages were widely suppressed in educational programs for deaf students, in favor of instruction in articulation and lip-reading. Stokoe proposed instead that ASL was, in fact, a fully formed human language in the same sense as spoken languages like English. He set about devising a descriptive system for the language that could be used to demonstrate this point to other linguists and the general public.

Note this final sentence. Stokoe's contribution wasn't just to *observe* that ASL was a language – not just to proclaim this fact in English. His contribution was to devise a way of explaining that fact with new, different language. In order to do so, he had to invent a new notation.

$$\mathrm{B_\alpha B_\alpha}^{z\sim} \quad \ddot{\cal N}\dot{\cal N}^{\dot{a}\cdot} \quad 3^\perp \quad [] \ \mathcal{J}C^\dagger \mathcal{J}C^{\vee}_\times{}^\cdot \quad \} Y^{\oplus}_{\vee} \quad \mathcal{J}G_\wedge{}^{<v<}$$

$$\mathrm{\bar{B}_\alpha \ \mathcal{J}B_\wedge}^{\psi}_{\mathcal{Y}} \qquad G^\perp \quad B_\wedge{}^{\prime} B_\wedge{}^{\ddagger}_{\vee} \quad D \ \dot{A}^{\oplus x} \quad \underline{B}_{\scriptscriptstyle\mathrm{D}} \ B_{\scriptscriptstyle\mathrm{D}}{}^\perp$$

$$G^{\ni} \quad \wedge\dot{5}^x \quad [] \ \mathcal{J}C^\dagger \mathcal{J}C^{\vee}_\times{}^\cdot \quad X_\perp X_\perp{}^{\ddagger}_{\dot{a}} \qquad B_{\scriptscriptstyle\mathrm{T}} \ V_{\scriptscriptstyle\mathrm{D}}{}^{v\cdot}$$

$$\mathrm{\bar{B}_\alpha \ L}^{\#\cdot} \quad X_\perp X_\perp{}^{\ddagger}_{\dot{a}}$$

Above is the beginning of the classic Goldilocks fairytale, with the ASL written in Stokoe notation. Each "word" is a sign in ASL. Each symbol within each word denotes how that sign is performed (how you hold your hand, the movement of your hand, whether you use one hand or two, etc.)

Consider Stokoe notation, which participated in the elevation of ASL, in relation to Bell's notation, which participated in its suppression. If you ignore this opposition, both are surprisingly similar: One is a notation for how speech organs should be arranged to produce English sounds; the other is a notation for how the hands and fingers should be arranged to produce ASL signs. Both are simply new ways of writing down things that were already known to many.

Both made their impacts. Both have faded into disuse, as if they only needed to exist for a brief moment in history, just long enough to cause change.

Although the fight for Deaf rights and better education for the Deaf is far from over, the dystopian dark ages have ended. Armstrong goes on to say:

> . . . Stokoe's other published works won wide acceptance in the linguistic community and ultimately among educators of the deaf, such that ASL is now widely recognized as an appropriate language of instruction for deaf students and even as an appropriate second language for hearing students in high schools and universities in the United States. Stokoe was also a tireless personal advocate for the linguistic and educational rights of deaf people, often in the face of skepticism or even outright hostility.

Stokoe didn't just elevate ASL, though. He also paved the way for ASL to elevate the study of linguistics itself. After his demonstration that ASL was indeed a language, any serious investigation of "language in general" from that point forward would need to consider signed languages.

Our Strange Citizens of Broca's Area

fMRIs show that a great many things are processed by the parts of the brain that were first identified in the context of processing speech: programming languages, signed languages, spoken languages. Studies have also found that the processing of musical syntax (Kunert et al. 2015) and the processing of simple formal languages known as "artificial grammars" are also processed in Broca's area (Fitch and Friederici 2012).

Teachers and students of *any* language: the science about other languages matters. Each sheds light on the other. They're all in us together.

To be continued . . .

Chapter 2
Beginnings

"A good notation has a subtlety and suggestiveness which at times make it almost seem like a live teacher."

Bertrand Russel

"By relieving the brain of all unnecessary work, a good notation sets it free to concentrate on more advanced problems, and, in effect, increases the mental power of the race."

Alfred North Whitehead

"It is no exaggeration to regard this as the most fundamental idea in programming: The evaluator, which determines the meaning of expressions in a programming language, is just another program. To appreciate this point is to change our images of ourselves as programmers. We come to see ourselves as designers of languages, rather than only users of languages designed by others."

Harold Abelson and Gerald Jay Sussman,
Structure and Interpretation of Computer Programs

A WIZARD'S TALE
The Leap of Faith

The ancient wizard led them up a stairwell. Above them crisscrossed other stairwells, some sideways, some upside down. Nothing obeyed the laws of physics as Henry knew it. Yet Harmony and Rob didn't seem to be bothered.

"The designer was obviously inspired by M.C. Escher," said Harmony.

"Obviously," agreed Henry, so he wouldn't sound dumb.

"Look," said Rob, who had stopped to point over the banister. Below, as above, there were crisscrossing staircases too, each seeming to obey its own local rules of gravity. But Rob wasn't pointing at the staircases; he was pointing at the lines of other students walking up, down, across, or sideways upon them.

There were the Python recruits, walking sideways below them – a line of over a hundred, all following a group of young, hip professors carrying scepters with golden pythons upon them. They were easy to see because they were all sideways with respect to Henry's vantage point. Finally, Henry could no longer bear it. "I don't understand. Why are the stairs all wrong? How is this possible? This is coding school, not *Harry Potter*."

"You don't remember?" said Rob. "It's a simulation. They explained it back at the 'train station.'" He used air-quotes on "train station," which only further confused Henry.

"What do you mean 'train station'?" Henry said.

Harmony put her hand on his forehead. Then she called to the ancient wizard, who was getting quite far ahead of them. "I believe Henry is suffering from simulation-induced amnesia," she said. "He doesn't remember he's even *in* a simulation."

"Come along," said the ancient wizard, not seeming to mind. "While the rest of the students go down, we go up," he said, pointing up the seemingly endless staircase before them. It stretched up infinitely, the two parallel lines of the banisters meeting at a single point somewhere in the dark infinity.

Henry kept walking, not sure why his thighs were burning if this was all a simulation. He tried as long as he could to keep from breathing heavily, but before long, he was panting and sweating. His robes grew damp and gross inside.

He half expected to look up and find that Rob and Harmony were doing just fine, knowing something he didn't know. To his relief, Harmony and Rob were panting as much as he was. Only the ancient wizard seemed unaffected, now even farther ahead.

"Just a bit longer," called the ancient wizard.

"How is he going so fast?" whispered Rob between gasps.

"Different settings," said Harmony. "The simulation treats professors differently."

"They get to code their own rules," said Rob. "Maybe he'll teach us how."

A moment later, they all caught up to the ancient wizard – but only because he had stopped. He pointed at the step beneath him. "This is step 2047, it starts at 0. What I'm about to demonstrate, you mustn't tell the members of the other Houses. We have secrets to protect."

He clapped his hands and disappeared, leaving the three alone. The emptiness in the vast stairwell was suffocating. Above them were no more staircases crissing and crossing; they had climbed higher than the other stairwells. There was only darkness up there. Over the railing, the other staircases looked like tiny threads far, far below. Their heavy panting was all the noise there was.

"Well," said Rob, stepping onto step number 2047, "I'm not scared . . . I think." Trembling, he clapped – and was gone.

Henry said, "Harmony, I'm sorry I dragged us into this. We should have just joined Python like you said."

She took him by the hand and led him onto the magic step with her. "Do you remember what you said to me right before they plugged the cranial links in?"

Henry racked his brain. "I remember getting on the train."

Harmony laughed. "It's safe to say that anything that seems like it's borrowed directly from the *Harry Potter* fandom is actually part of the simulaton. The school has a deal with Warner Bros." She poised her hands, about to clap.

"Wait!" said Henry. "What did I say?"

"You said," she said, "that your favorite kinds of stories are the ones that start *in medias res*. What do you want? Do you want me to explain your own backstory to you? Or do you want to learn to be a wizard?"

Henry peered over the edge of the railing, taking a deep breath, as if he were about to jump. Slowly, he raised his hands, ready to clap.

Harmony counted, "One. Two . . . " They clapped together on "Three."

The Forge

They found themselves standing before a cauldron filled with thick mist. Rob and the ancient wizard were peering in. The room was otherwise bare and small – and doorless. But each wall had a window that looked out upon a vast, emerald landscape – too beautiful to be real.

"Welcome to the tower," said the ancient wizard. "This room is called the Language Forge. It is where the members of this House with no name spend most of their time."

"What's a language forge?" asked Rob.

Harmony retorted, "Isn't the name self-explanatory?"

"Indeed! What a wonderful segue into your first lesson, Harmony," said the ancient wizard. "Our House has no name. Yet, naming things is one of the most powerful linguistic acts a human being can make – wizard or not. With that, let us start at..." He reached his wizened hand into the cauldron. Thick mist covered it. "...the beginning." He pulled his hand out, bringing with it a tuft of mist.

He released the mist into the air at about shoulder height. Henry watched it twist and coalesce, forming into something... A moment later, it had clarified itself. The word beginning floated there, rotating slowly – at times beginning, at times gninnigeb.

The ancient wizard reached again into the cauldron, saying, "All beginnings have an eventual..." He drew his hand out as he said the word, "...end."

This cloud of mist too formed into the word end, or dne, depending on its orientation. He plucked both translucent words between thumb and forefinger and brought them near each other. There was a tiny flash of light, and a small arrow appeared between them. The words began to rotate with the arrow as a unit.

At times, it was:

And at times, it was:

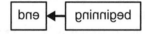

Henry was about to ask what it meant, but the ancient wizard's dark scowl communicated: *No speaking.*

He reached in and said, "Baby shoes," pulling out a tuft of mist that formed into the word baby–shoes. He then said, "Never worn," producing the misty words never–worn. He connected them; a flash; an arrow. Then he said, "For sale," and attached the result to the beginning, forming the chain:

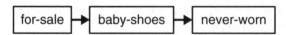

He raised an eyebrow and looked at Harmony. She nodded enthusiastically. He turned his wizened gaze upon Rob, raising an eyebrow. Rob hesitated, but then nodded with careful confidence. Henry's stomach dropped as the ancient wizard raised his eyebrow at him. He forced himself to nod even though he had no idea how any of this related to magic, or wizards, or programming, or computers, or "language itself," or anything they were supposedly here to learn.

The old wizard continued. Reaching into the cauldron, he quickly spoke the words, "Rob born," which caused the resulting mist to form into the word rob-born. He used the same trick to add brothers-born to the beginning of the chain, creating:

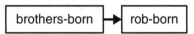

The ancient wizard raised his eyebrow at Rob, who nodded that he understood. Henry too thought he was beginning to understand the ancient wizard's main idea. However, what the ancient wizard did next cast some doubt. He produced the word family-complete. Then, eyes never leaving Rob's, he left that word hanging in the air. He pulled brothers-born and rob-born apart, breaking the chain – arrow disappearing with a flash. Then, he inserted the new part in the middle, forming:

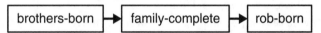

The wizard nodded that he had finished and gently wafted the chain toward Rob. The misty words floated toward him and began rotating in the air near his head. Rob looked wordlessly at the floor. Henry and Harmony tried to catch his eyes, but he didn't look up.

The ancient wizard turned to Harmony. Although she tried to hide it, Henry thought he saw her gulp.

First, the ancient wizard produced the expected harmony-born. Then only-child.

Henry wasn't sure if he felt worse for Harmony or for himself, who would be next.

The wizard spoke softly, so that Henry couldn't hear. But as the mist formed and he attached the word, he saw:

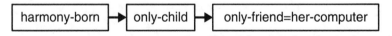

The ancient wizard wafted this chain toward Harmony, who watched it grimly as it rotated slowly beside her. Then she grabbed it, relocating it to a spot where it was not blocking her line of sight. If any of it bothered her, Henry couldn't tell. She was too tough; her face was expressionless.

Henry tried to be tough as the ancient wizard turned to him. He could feel himself sweating simulated sweat drops inside his simulated robe.

The ancient wizard began with `henry-born`. Henry waited with awe and dread to see the plot points to which the ancient wizard would reduce his backstory.

However, he simply wafted the lone word toward Henry.

> henry-born

For some reason, this "chain" seemed every bit as appropriate as Rob's and Harmony's. Perhaps his backstory was best forgotten.

They Slept

With a clap of his hands, the ancient wizard was gone, leaving them alone in the doorless room – windows blocked by iron bars. The cauldron churned, revealing no secrets.

"Well, that was awkward," said Rob.

Harmony was already examining the floor tiles, looking for a way out. Henry's legs felt weak. He crossed to a window and leaned against a wall, inhaling the fresh air from outside.

"I found a trap door," said Harmony. Behind him, Henry could hear the grate of stone on stone. He looked over his shoulder to see that Harmony had pulled up one of the floor stones, revealing a staircase. Peering into a room only she could see, she said, "There are bunk beds. I guess it's our dormitory. Every House has one."

"I don't know about you two," said Rob. "But I'm exhausted."

The three of them climbed down into a dusty bedroom. Candles burned on the bedside tables. Henry brushed dust off of one bed and crawled into it without bothering to take off his robes. Neither Harmony nor Rob seemed to be in the mood to discuss their first day at wizard school. Henry couldn't help but feel that this was all his fault. Maybe he should have chosen Python. Or HTML.

To be continued...

A LANGUAGE WITHOUT

We'll now discuss the design of a language we'll use later. In fact, each subsequent chapter will present a new language – but each is also an evolutionary stage of a single language, like an organism that gains new powers with each new adaptation. Looked at as an evolving thing, our language will, chapter by chapter, become simultaneously more complex, and more powerful.

Simple though it will begin, we hope to underscore: Languages don't have to be complicated to be interesting and useful. In the last chapter, we saw two notations simpler than any programming language. When you compare Stokoe's notation to ASL, or when you compare Bell's notation to spoken English, it becomes obvious that these are just simplified ways of describing things that were already obvious to many. Stokoe's notation described signs using symbols that could be written down and/or printed; Bell's notation described utterances similarly.

Such notations are not the only ways to describe such things. Prior to Stokoe, various books on sign language had already been published – using drawings, photographs, and English textual descriptions. Books and websites today use the same techniques.

What advantage did Stokoe's notation confer? What magic allowed it to communicate with the scientific community? To answer, it's helpful to see both together.

If you want to learn ASL, the photographs are clearer. Video would be clearer still. That said, Stokoe notation does have advantages: For one thing, the symbols can be printed smaller on a page.

More importantly, the notation makes certain details of signs more apparent – especially for non-signers. For example, $\wedge 5^x$ (which describes the sign for "father") indicates that the hand should be shaped as if you were signing the number 5. The small ⌒ indicates where the sign should be performed – in this case, at the level of the forehead. Finally, the × indicates that the hand should touch the body.

Now, knowing just this bit of Stokoe notation, can you determine which of the following two signs have the same handshape as "father" but a different location, and which have a different handshape but the same location?

- ⌒B× describes **Know**

- ᴗ5× describes **Mother**

When it comes to photographs, it can be difficult to see whether two signs share the same handshape. Camera angles hide details. In a video, motion can be an additional distraction. Stokoe's notation abstracts away all of this, so that the *relationships* between signs are immediately apparent.

He used his notation to demonstrate that signs are a combination of physical parameters – just as English words are combinations of phonemes. These parameters are what Stokoe notation makes immediately apparent – whether you are ASL-fluent or not.

The keyword is "immediately." A good notation should make something previously effortful into something immediately obvious. Stokoe's notation helped him reveal to non-ASL-fluent linguists what photographs and videos struggle to – that the language of ASL is a system, one with syntactical and grammatical rules, not a mere collection of gestures and pantomime.

An interesting feature of Stokoe notation is that it reuses symbols that already carry meaning – that is, the symbol 5. When you learn that this symbol more technically means "the handshape you would make if you were signing the number 5," it is easier to remember. That's why programming languages borrow English words, even though they end up meaning something more technical or entirely different – for example, "if," "print," "string," "object," "graph," "stack," "queue," "loop," etc.

Purists like De Morgan may dub these "sounds void of sense," but the reality is this: Brains have trouble dealing with completely senseless things. The more senselessness, the more trouble. It helps to reuse words that do have some sense – even if we plan to alter it. Borrowed words retain an echo of their original meaning, aiding the mind.

Unlike Stokoe's or Bell's notation, however, ours will not be for describing the production of words or signs. Instead, we wanted to design a language that would have immediate communication benefits in this book.

This being a book of stories, with many more to come, it would be nice if we could have a story-shorthand, like:

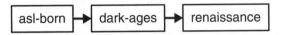

Because of the increasing need to refer to, compare, and discuss stories, we will design a language for describing them. It also has poetic symmetry: In a book that tells stories about language, we begin with a language for telling stories.

We shall use all of the above – the stories, the language, and their combination – to reach a better understanding of human languages, computer languages, and their intersections.

In a deep way, a computer program is a special kind of story: fiction when written, fact when run. Looked at thusly, the computer is a fascinating piece of linguistic technology. It mechanizes the conversion of fictions into facts.

Syntax – Building Materials

Programming languages' syntaxes are usually restricted to letters, numbers, and symbols (things that keyboards produce). But in human communication at large – we use other building materials: vocal sounds, handshapes, body motions, lines on paper, images, and so on.

Our "Story Language" shall use symbols that can be typed on a keyboard. (Later, we will permit images, too.) Keyboards are amazing extensions of the mind, the unsung heroes of the digital age. Once we've become fluent in their use, we hardly notice them. We think; symbols appear. In turn, fluent programmers think and programs appear – at least when the syntax is keyboard-constructable. (Note: In languages like Scratch, where the syntax is largely mouse-constructable, things are different.)

In any event, let's call anything written in our (presently) alphanumeric Story Language a "Story."

> **Definition of "Story."** A Story must consist of a series of Moments. Moments must be separated by Arrows. And between each Moment and Arrow, there must be whitespace (what you get when you press the spacebar, tab, or return keys).

We'll use a capital letter to help us remember that a Story, Moment, and Arrow have been borrowed from English. When we speak of the Story Language, these words are now "sounds void of sense" – mere echoes of their former selves.

Usually, we'll talk about Stories in the context of some language, for example:

```
#lang dtc/story/images

beginning -> middle -> end
```

If you ran that, you'd get:

Note that a Story with one Moment would look like this:

```
#lang dtc/story/images

beginning
```

The image would be:

```
beginning
```

A Story with one Moment is the only kind of Story that has no Arrows. The moment you add a second Moment, you now have a second Story with two Moments.
And one Arrow.

A Meta-Linguistic Meander

Note that sentences like the one above (you know the one) become difficult to make sense of. We could have said:

> The moment you add a second Bloop, you now have a second Story with two Bloops. And one Arrow.

It helps. But take this "antidote" to its extreme, and you get something worse.

> The moment you add a second Bloop, you now have a second Floop with two Bloops. And one Snoop.

Using sounds *truly* void of sense makes it even *harder* to talk about our language. Would-be users would have trouble telling Bloops from Floops and Snoops. It's much easier to tell the difference between Stories, Moments, and Arrows.

When designing a language, we must design the meta-language too. We must teach people, either by definition or example what things like "Story" look like syntactically. We must teach them things like the difference between a "Moment" and an "Arrow." We want users to actually remember what we teach. Snoops', Floops', and Bloops' interweavings are hard to follow, their relations soon forgotten.

Yes, the art of designing a language and the art of teaching are intertwined. When designing tools for minds, we must understand how minds will wield them *and* how they will learn them in the first place.

When teaching others a language, we have at our meta-linguistic disposal: 1) Our shared natural languages, 2) Whatever words we successfully add to our shared natural languages.

For the latter, there are two options, each with a different cognitive friction that psychologists have names for. If we make up a soup of Floops and Bloops, we increase what psychologists call "cognitive load." If we borrow words from our shared language (even if we capitalize them), we create "linguistic interference." Teachers and students of language experience this one daily: It's when a student's knowledge of their native language interferes with their comprehension of the language they are learning.

Students of coding will encounter both of these – a lot. Stay on the road long enough and your mind will inevitably feel the load of manufactured words like "thunk," "monad," and "y-combinator." And you will feel the interference of words like "actor model" – which is not an actor who also has a career in modeling – or "map reduce" – which is not to make a map smaller – or "code smell" – which is not how one smells after a long session of coding.

Borrowed senseful words and manufactured senseless ones are respectively like Scylla, the many-headed sea monster, and Charybdis, the bottomless whirlpool. Oops. That analogy was hard to parse; let's use the standard anological notation instead.

```
sense-full words  :  sense-less words
                  ::
  Scylla, the many    Charybdis, the one
         hungry  :    dark
     somethings       nothing
```

That is, we namers must choose between names that carry too many meanings and those that do not carry any. One of our most powerful spells has a casting cost: To name something, we must lay down one of these two cognitive traps.

Back to Syntax

We're not quite done defining our syntax. We've defined "Story" in terms of "Moments" and "Arrows," but we've a bit more work to do.

Moments may be written with any symbol you'd want except a whitespace. Weird-looking Moments are okay.

```
$t@rL0RD -> ____hello____
```

There's one combination of characters that a Moment definitely *cannot* employ, though. This is not a Story, because it violates the rule that a Moment cannot be an Arrow (–>).

```
-> -> -> -> ->
```

Is this a Story with no Moments at all, and only Arrows? Is it a Story with some moments that *look* like Arrows?

It's neither, because neither of those fit our syntactic definitions. Syntactically wrong Stories are not Stories. Allowing –> to be a Moment *or* an Arrow is an ambiguity that leads to more confusion than it's worth. In English, it's okay for words to have multiple meanings. But in a language that only has a three things – Stories, Moments, and Arrows – it's a bit lazy if we can't manage to cleanly separate things.

Note that you *can* use the characters –> *within* a moment, like so:

```
a-> -> b-> -> c->
```

It's not easy for the eye to read, but if it's broken onto multiple lines, the Moments and the Arrows are clearly different:

```
a->
->
b->
->
c->
```

This produces a perfectly good Story image

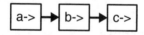

Lastly, there are no spaces allowed in Moments. If we permitted spaces, something as simple as a -> b could be interpreted as either one Story with two Moments, or a Story with one Moment that has spaces inside. Because Moments can have the characters –> *inside* them, the space around the Arrows is the only thing that unambiguously tells us when –> is to be seen as an Arrow.

Whitespace is part of the syntax. Negative space matters.

Semantics: "When your eyes see this, do this with your mind..."

Defining semantics is where we use language and meta-language to describe what syntactically correct Stories *mean* – how to think about them, how to move your mind when you see them.

For intuition, you can assume (for now) that the Arrow indicates time – as in "time's arrow." You can further assume (for now) that the Moments represent periods of time, or events, or stories, or anything that can be placed on a timeline. More precisely, if a Moment comes after another in a Story, the author of the Story is trying to say that that Moment is after the other in time.

Consider:

```
brothers-born -> family-complete -> rob-born
```

If we re-order the Moments it becomes chronologically untrue, but still a syntactically correct Story – just as sentences in English can be grammatically correct and still untrue.

```
brothers-born -> rob-born -> family-complete
```

Note that Moments are a bit like algebraic variables. They can be anything, as long as they obey the syntactic rules. What they *mean* is largely based on context – just as the variable c has no inherent meaning in algebra, unless it is explicitly given one. Einstein made it the speed of light. Luckily, variables can be reused.

A good analogy would be analogies themselves, for which there exists a common notation.

```
a : b :: c : d
```

We need not know what a, b, c, and d mean in order to know *something* about them. Anyone who has learned the notation could express their relationships in an English sentence.

The bits of syntax that really matter are the : ("is to") and : : ("as"). They form a four-part grammatical structure into which we can plug whatever we want. The Arrows serve a similar structuring purpose in Stories.

We can even plug in a blank (a kind of negative space) to ask readers to fill it in.

```
teacher : students :: programmer : _____
```

(Note: computers is the obvious answer, but it's wrong. We'll give the correct answer in the final chapter.)

In any event, what we're trying to show is that it's common for notations to contain symbols that help your eye find structure. The structure helps interpret everything else. By way of an analogy, the colons and double-colons are to the analogy language as arrows are to the Story Language.

```
(":" and "::") : analogies :: "->" : Stories
```

We're not just being meta and abstract for no reason here. Reflect for a moment on what your brain must be doing in order to parse a weird self-referential analogy like the above – the matching of parentheses, the assigning of meanings to things like quotes, to unpack the meaning from groups of symbols nested within other groups of symbols, nested within other groups of symbols. What part of your brain do you think would light up in an fMRI during that process?

Our eyes are able to segment the visual field using certain syntactic "beacons." The colons and double-colons are the beacons of structure in an analogy, and the Arrows are the beacons of structure in Stories.

In other programming languages, other bits of syntax serve analogous purposes.

Exercise

Two of the following are not syntactically valid Stories. The rest are fine, even though some of them may have meanings that are cryptic or even ones that express falsities. Can you root out the syntactic imposters in less than 20 seconds?

Go!

```
henry-goes-to-school -> henry-has-an-awkward-day

henry-has-an-awkward-day -> henry-goes-to-school

-> henry-wears-the-hat -> ->

X -> Y -> Z
```

```
henry -> harmony -> rob

henry -> henry -> henry

%$%% -> 330d33 -> 1LLAx -> G -> PoTaTo

and that's -> a wrap
```

The answers are given by the following Story:

```
Y -> Y -> N -> Y -> Y -> Y -> Y -> N
```

Checking Assumptions

Moments are permitted to be arbitrary words open to interpretation. Many of the exercises in the next section will involve assigning particular meaning to particular Moments, so that, say, cat -> rotate might be a program that produces a rotated image of a cat.

But as a mental exercise, a kind of discipline, let us spend a moment going through the act of rigorously checking our assumptions. It is a discipline that can serve students well as they venture out to learn their first programming languages (far more complicated than the Story language thus far).

Not assuming is the one antidote we have for linguistic interference. It works well as a preventative vaccine, too. The more we practice approaching a formal language without assumptions, the more we approach De Morgan's ideals.

If you were at the beach and found a washed-up bottle labeled Story, which happened to contain a paper on which was scrawled the Story:

```
he-saw-her -> he-ran.
```

This could mean that he ran from her *because* of what he saw. Or it could mean that he saw her on Dec 31, 2047 and then, for unrelated reasons, he ran for Congress in the year 2117. Subsequent Moments in a Story are not necessarily caused by any previous moments. They can be. But you can't assume this. If you do: That's linguistic interference coming from the fact that "story" is senseful.

Furthermore, the first "he" may not even be the same as the second "he," or they may not be people at all. They could be cats. Or the first "he" might be a cat, and the second one an avatar in a futuristic simulation. Or the entire phrases "he-saw-her" and "he-ran" might be coded messages for something we cannot venture to guess – no more than we could guess what X and Y mean.

We Have a "Language." Now What?

Stokoe didn't just create a notation, then sit back and wait. His notation was a tool, which he used *in conjunction with* and *embedded into* standard English. Our humble Story language will do its work similarly – embedded within the larger context.

As we'll see, not only can you embed the Story language into English text, you can also embed it into other programming languages. And so on. In a later chapter, we'll embed our Story Language into an even more powerful language. And then we'll do the same thing again in the final chapter. Like Russian dolls.

This is actually a unifying principle of the written medium (code or otherwise); the surrounding context shapes our reading of the surrounded text. It's true at the level of English words in sentences, sentences in paragraphs, and so on. It's true at the level of blocks of code within other blocks of code within other blocks of code. It's even true at the boundaries between English and code: The English text that surrounds bits of code tell you why those bits matter, and how you should read them – as you've already seen.

To be continued...

A LANGUAGE WITHIN
Cats

Consider these programs – identical except for their language.

```
#lang dtc/story/images

cat -> rotate

#lang dtc/story/cats

cat -> rotate
```

They both produce images, too. Respectively:

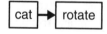

And:

In other words, the second produces a rotated image of a cat; whereas the first produces an image of the story that describes *how* to produce a rotated image of a cat.

Out of context, the story `cat -> rotate` can be variously interpreted into English:

- A cat was born. Then it rotated.
- There once was an image of a cat, and then it was rotated.
- First you must take a cat, and then you must rotate the cat.
- The computer loads an image of a cat from a file, and then it transforms that image by rotating it 45 degrees in memory to produce a bitmap of the result, which it displays to the screen.

And so on. Stories always have multiple interpretations. But when you give a Story to the computer, and tell it to use `#lang dtc/story/image`, you are instructing the computer to use a particular interpretation – under which certain Moments have pre-defined meanings. The word `cat` no longer retains its generic English meaning. It refers to precisely *this* cat:

There are many cat-related words in `#lang dtc/story/cats`, each with its own meaning.

`#lang dtc/story/cats`

`first-viral-cat`

This single-Moment Story produces:

This is a blurry frame from the very first cat video ever uploaded to YouTube (in 2005). Cat video technology improved over the early 2000s, however, resulting in our present golden age of viral cat videos.

The YouTube cat was not the first to be immortalized on screen. If you use the symbol `edison-cat`, you'll get a frame from the first cat video in all of history – shot in 1894 by Thomas Edison. No doubt, his decision to film two cats boxing was one of his most inspired moments.

So, for example, you could give this Story to the computer, telling it to load Edison's cats:

```
#lang dtc/story/cats
```

```
edison-cat
```

This produces:

Or you could tell a more complex story, involving a rotation:

```
#lang dtc/story/cats
```

```
edison-cat -> rotate
```

Note that longer Stories are acceptable too:

```
#lang dtc/story/cats
```

```
edison-cat -> rotate -> rotate
```

Given what you know about how `#lang dtc/story/cats` works, you can probably guess that the English translation of this code is something like:

```
Load an image of Thomas Edison's cat.
```

```
Then rotate it.
```

```
Then rotate it again.
```

Exercise

Run the above program and see if your prediction is correct. Then, write a Story that produces an upside-down picture of `cat`.

`#lang dtc/story/cats` has other cat starter-images that you can use. You could try to guess, as if they are Easter Eggs. However, we've done what most programmers do when they release a language: We've produced a bunch of meta-language about our language. You can find this so-called "documentation," which lists all available cats, along with any relevant cat-historical notes at

dont-teach.com/coding/docs

Exercise

Use the above documentation to help you to produce an upside-down image of the oldest known image of a cat – older even than Edison's!

Note that documentation pages like the above are the concrete instantiation of that abstract quotation from Edsger Dijkstra (Dijkstra 1982):

It is a severe mistake to think that the programmer's products are the programs he writes . . . the written program text is only the accompanying material . . .

The code with which we created #lang dtc/story/cats is just the accompanying material for this book, not even important enough to print. The documentation pages likewise outrank the source code – which would be nearly valueless if it did not accompany these materials. As programmers, we should not *only* produce programs in some computer language; we should also be able to explain those languages – using, of course, more language.

Still, the documentation is not the only way to teach/learn a language – and indeed is generally used as a reference, not as a primary tool. In general, a well-made language also follows a set of logical rules, so that if you begin to grasp a rule, you can infer how to construct programs (or in this case, valid Stories) that you have never seen before. This aids the mind – linguistic interference harnessed for cognitive good.

Exercise

Write a Story that describes how to produce a tiny, upside-down image of the world's oldest known drawing of a cat. Make an inference from the fact that shrink, like rotate, is defined in #lang dtc/story/cats.

We implemented #lang dtc/story/cats in such a way that you can insert your own images at the beginning of the Story – much like being able to insert your own character into a story.

Here's a Story of a cat being flipped upside down and shrunk.

-> rotate -> rotate -> shrink

Some might be tempted to ask, "Doesn't this break the syntax rules? Aren't Moments only supposed to be alpha-numeric characters?"

Yes. `#lang dtc/story/cats` breaks the rules. Who cares? Languages evolve to meet the needs of the times. Most would agree that the world needs a language into which one can embed images of cats. It's the twenty-first century.

Exercise

If you have a cat, create a Story that describes how to rotate it 270 degrees and tint it green. Acquire a cat if necessary, or borrow a cat image from the internet to complete the exercise.

Hint: This is how one would tint the author's cat red.

 -> `redify`

To insert an image in DrRacket, put the cursor where you want the image to go, press the "Insert" tab, and click "Insert Image . . .".

Linguistic interference can be harnessed for good, such that occasionally you can guess what might be valid in a language ("if `redify` works, does `purpleify`?"). Languages that have this quality will often have a higher level of learnability, because learners can leverage the existing intuitions about meaning. In this case, you are able to combine your knowledge of different color words "green," "blue," "red," "purple," etc., with your knowledge of what the suffix "-ify" means in English, with your knowledge of what a previously learned word (like `redify`) means in `#lang dtc/story/cats`.

However, there is always a limit to how much you can analogically transfer from your native language to a programming language. Here, for example, is a Story that might *look* like it should work, and yet it does not – illustrating a critical point: That `#lang dtc/story/cats` does not understand all Stories.

 -> `rotate-left` -> `enlarge` -> `frame`

That's because some of the following words have no meaning in this language: `rotate-left`, `enlarge`, and `frame`. There's no reason why they *couldn't* have meaning. They just don't. It's because we (the designers) chose not to put those vocabulary words into this particular language. If you invent your own cat language one day, you can add your own vocabulary.

As you may have noticed, all Stories accepted by `#lang dtc/story/cats` must start with a cat. This is hardly a restriction of Stories in general – just an extra restriction imposed by `#lang dtc/story/cats`.

This restriction is an illustration of the more general principle: What you can say in a computer language will often feel like a highly restricted version of what you can say in your native language. Restrictions can feel unpleasant or oppressive at first. But sometimes the unrestricted nature of natural language makes it harder to get things done. There's so much you can express. Sometimes smaller languages like `#lang dtc/story/cats` can make for sharper tools. When there's less that can be said, we can sometimes find what we want to say much more quickly.

To be productive within a smaller language, you'll have to internalize the rules that govern how that restricted language works. Different languages will have different vocabulary and grammatical rules. These might even change on you when someone updates the language, or when you voluntarily augment your language with someone else's vocabulary words (known as "importing a library," or "requiring a package," or "using a framework"). However, on the bright side: You'll have documentation pages to teach you the lay of the land in any new linguistic territory. And you have your own wetware – wired over millions of years of evolution to learn languages.

You will get better naturally. It may, however, help to know that to improve as a programmer, you shouldn't just focus on learning languages; you should focus on improving your general ability to learn new languages. We'll discuss the science of learning how to learn in Chapter 3.

Stories and Back Stories

The Iliad is famous for beginning *in medias res*, or in the middle of things. By the time Homer's poem begins, the Trojan War is already in its final year. Bit by bit, we get information about events leading up to the war and the nine years of siege that occurred prior to the start of the story through flashbacks – little stories within the story.

The classic murder mystery has a fascinatingly nonlinear shape, too, beginning after the murder has been committed. The rest of the story is about discovering the story of the murder – a meta-story wherein a detective, by profession, must uncover backstories. The final moment: Who dunnit? Experiencing such a story is to see two stories unfold together: the present-tense story of the detective's human struggles, and the past-tense story of violence unpunished. One dead body; one living hero.

Another nonlinear gem is the famous six-word story (sometimes misattributed to Hemingway):

For sale: baby shoes, never worn

The "real" story – or backstory – is never stated. Your mind must reconstruct it from these six words that, presumably, tell the end.

Given the flexibility of our understanding of stories, does the Story language *need* to remain so chronologically restrictive? What if we freed it from these final semantic shackles?

There's nothing syntactically preventing us from using the Story language to tell nonlinear stories. We need only abandon our intuitions that the Arrow represents time's arrow. We must come to view it as a symbol void of sense – a mere separator for Moments, which themselves imply whatever chronology they wish. We must come to view the time's arrow metaphor as a once-useful, now-obsolete form of linguistic scaffolding. The right-pointing Arrow must now become merely a sign-post for the eye, guiding it rightward. The Moment-to-Moment ordering becomes strictly textual, not chronological. It becomes at its core a Story about how the reader's eye should move.

Because there is nothing preventing us from liberating Stories from the cognitive tyranny of the chrono-centric worldview and because there is so much to be gained, let us proceed. It will pay dividends later, when we begin to apply the idea of a Story in ever-more subtle ways within larger programs.

Let us get a feel for flexibly switching between linear and nonlinear Storytelling. On the one hand, *The Iliad*'s linear story (beginning with its backstory) could be described with this Story:

```
#lang dtc/story/images
```

```
1-abducted -> 1000-launched -> 10-years -> 1-horse
```

Output:

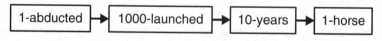

On the other hand, the experience of reading *The Iliad* might be a different Story altogether. Depending on the reader, perhaps:

```
#lang dtc/story/images
```

```
9th-year -> 1-abducted? -> 1000-launched?! -> 1-horse
```

Output:

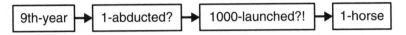

Then again, if we look anew, that nonlinear Story is actually also a linear one. The historical events, jumbled, yield the non-jumbled discovery moments experienced by the reader who reads in the traditional linear way through a text. It's as if linearity is a matter of perspective. The Story above *is* chronological, yet from the perspective of a different hero: the reader, hero of their own story.

Thinking flexibly about the chronological order of ideas turns out to be a common cognitive task for coders. Users of your software are the heroes of their own stories, too (we call these "user stories" in software engineering). They are your readers: the ones who interact with your code. The story of how a user will navigate your web app or how another programmer uses code you've given them is a story that skilled software writers are capable of keeping in mind.

Your story awareness will sometimes need to extend downward too – into the machine. Your code's text might not match up linearly with the story of what the computer does when it runs that code. The process of jumbling up code on purpose, by feeding it into another program, is known as "compiling" – the transformation of your code as written, into code written differently, perhaps unrecognizable to you by comparison. Compilers are programs that make it easier to write for human minds, by allowing us to incidentally send our program on a quest to be transformed repeatedly until ready to be understood by machines. This entire quest, transformation after transformation, can finish in a flash.

The moral is that we've many story levels above and below us. Luckily, our species has a knack for telling complex, multilayered stories – and for understanding them. Coders simply need to bring these human skills with them, and keep them sharp.

Exercise

The story of a murder might be:

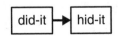

The Story of the detectives solving the murder mystery might be:

Pick a movie, book, or short story.

Write two Stories: 1) the linear Story beginning with the back-Story, and 2) the linear reader experience Story.

Exercise

For this story "For sale: baby shoes, never worn," write 1) a Story that describes it linearly, and 2) a Story that describes what the reader experiences when reading it, the Moments of discovery of the eye.

Ab(stract)

The use of the word "abstract" as a verb is more common in computing than it is in everyday English. To understand its meaning, let us recall the Latin roots of the word "abstractus": "trahere" meaning "to drag, draw, or move" and "ab" meaning "away." Literally, it means to drag something out or away.

In computing, to abstract is to remove detail. Programming languages are a tool for this very thing. They are not for describing the world in exhaustive detail. More the opposite: They are tools that allow us to build abstractions of reality – truths with distracting details left out.

Abstraction deletes distraction.

What separates a skilled coder from a novice is their ability to abstract away the complex details of something, "dragging away" the simple truths into something that can be written concisely. A good story may be long, textured, and complex; but a good Story is an abstraction of a story – short because it reduces events of the story into concise symbols, and because it uses as few of those symbols as possible. For these exercises, challenge yourself to write the perfect Stories – long enough to contain everything necessary, but short enough to contain *only* what is necessary. This is an exercise in efficient communication.

A Story does not describe stories in great detail – but rather captures the essence in a minimum of visual space. For these exercises, treat Stories like a specialized form of literature – much like a haiku. You must abstract them down to their bones.

Exercise

Write a Story that describes **A Wizard's Tale** thus far. Write a Story that describes how you think it will end – or write an alternative ending if you already know how it ends.

Do this exercise once with purely textual Moments. Do it again with image Moments found from the internet.

Exercise

Write the Story of ASL in a nonlinear way. Choose the moments that matter to you – so that your Story reflects the parts that *you* think are most important.

Do this exercise once with purely textual Moments. Do it again with image Moments found on the internet.

Shortest Path: Dijkstra to You

Below is a Story told in photographs of famous computer scientists, each of whom was a Ph.D. advisor to the next.

Exercise

All computer science education is part of a history, threads of ideas, passed from teacher to student. The computer scientists above are, in order from left to right: Edsger W. Dijkstra, Nico Habermann, David Notkin, and William Griswold.

One of the authors' own Ph.D. advisors was William Griswold (plot twist!).

Use the documentation to help you re-create the above image. That's **part one** of this exercise.

Part two is add a missing image: your own.

Although reading this book won't get you a Ph.D. in computer science, if you count this book as a teacher, there's a chain of teachers that starts at Dijkstra and leads to you.

Hint: You can get an image of the cover of this book if you read the documentation page. You'll have to supply an image of yourself, though. By the end, you'll have a 5-part Story. That way, you can ask your students to append their pictures onto the chain. And so on.

And we invite you to post your results on our forums! If you have a different educational back-Story, with different teachers to highlight, post that one, too. We'll organize the whole teacher chain project at **dont-teach.com/coding/forum**.

During his lifetime, Dijkstra gave the world a multitude of quotes that are self-contained gems. He had quite a knack for distilling (or should we say "abstracting"?) the essence out of the complex cognitive work of being a programmer. If it seems coincidental that many of his quotes sound like they could describe the content of this book – well, you now know it's not a coincidence. We all owe intellectual debts to the teachers who came before us.

Here are just a handful of the gems Dijkstra is famous for.

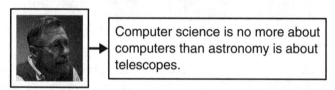

Computer science is no more about computers than astronomy is about telescopes.

If you were wondering why we are many pages into this book and haven't bothered to mention motherboards, CPUs, and RAM, it is because people like Dijkstra championed a different way – a more linguistic way. The way we think about the thinking we do as computer scientists – these meta-cognitive insights get passed down.

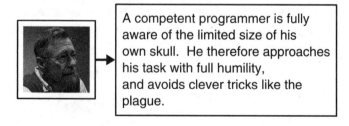

A competent programmer is fully aware of the limited size of his own skull. He therefore approaches his task with full humility, and avoids clever tricks like the plague.

Code is a tool of the mind. During the act of wielding that tool, coders must be aware of our own thinking, and our own cognitive shortcomings – for it is effortless to type another key, write another line, believing we are expressing ourselves precisely, when in fact we are mis-thinking in ways that have external manifestations: bugs.

The lifelong process of growing as a coder is to learn to write in ways that reduce the ways we mis-think, and therefore the number of bugs we produce.

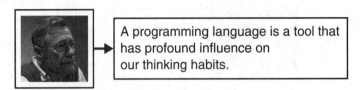

A programming language is a tool that has profound influence on our thinking habits.

Here, he seems to invoke the Sapir-Whorf hypothesis – the one that says our worldviews and cognitions are influenced by our language – but he applies it to programming languages. His position on this matter sheds some light on his position regarding the damages that BASIC can cause.

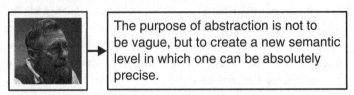

The purpose of abstraction is not to be vague, but to create a new semantic level in which one can be absolutely precise.

From our newfound precision flows our ability to capture truths that others can only speak vaguely about. It gives us the ability to write in ways that others cannot, at semantic levels that others cannot understand, for they are levels of our own creation.

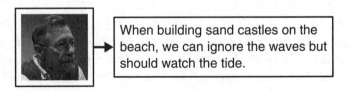

When building sand castles on the beach, we can ignore the waves but should watch the tide.

Abstraction deletes distraction.

Exercise

This one is not easy.

Skim ahead in this book and see if you can figure out how to create images like the ones above (ones with multi-line moments and spaces). Make one like this, filling in the blanks with an important lesson you learned from a teacher, and filling in the first Moment with a picture of that teacher:

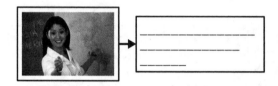

Yes, that's right – we're encouraging you to break the rules. No one says you have to read a book in the linear way it seems to want you to. Jump forward and see if you can steal the knowledge from the future. Like Prometheus: Snatch fire from the gods.

Or read the documentation page.

Either way, if you can't figure it out, that's okay. Just come back later.

Do the best you can on this exercise using what you've learned thus far. Get as close as you can to the image above, using the languages you know. Then just continue reading. By the end of the book, you'll know much more, and your vocabulary will be greater.

Exercise

This one is intended to be completable (with the help of the documentation page) after you finish the book. It is placed in the middle as a kind of meditation – a way to reflect on what you knew at two different points in your educational story.

Whether it is your first or second time here, we want you to meditate on what kind of vocabulary must necessarily exist in a language that allows you to produce an image that contains 1) smaller images, 2) English text, and 3) code. Writers of a program like this (as, perhaps, you know – if it is your second time here) would need words and grammatical structures that interweave all three of these into a single piece of code.

The task is to produce the following (except with the blanks filled in).

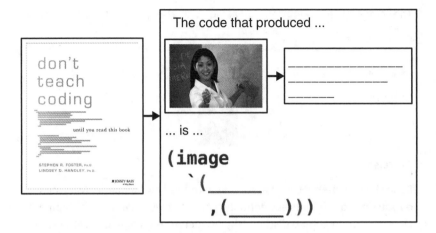

Note that when you see a blank in a coding assignment, that blank may be abstracting away a single line, or many.

How long do you hypothesize the code will be? How complicated does the story need to be?

A Brave New Syntax

We must now learn a new syntax. It cannot be avoided: This is a book about language itself. We cannot dally for too long on any stop along the road. We shall now introduce the next evolution of our language, named #lang dtc/story+/images.

Instead of A -> B -> C you can write (A B C).

It saves visual space because the Moments are separated by fewer characters. The Arrows were becoming mere sign-posts for the eye anyway, so the eye that knows the way no longer needs them.

Here is a Story that we've seen before, but written in the new syntax. Both #lang dtc/story+/images and #lang dtc/story/images have the same semantics – differing only in which Story syntax they understand.

```
#lang dtc/story+/images
```

```
(cat rotate rotate)
```

Outputs:

The same is true, analogically speaking, with `#lang dtc/story+/cats`.

```
#lang dtc/story+/cats

(cat rotate rotate)
```

Outputs:

Exercise

Redo the exercises in this chapter, but with this new language. Ask yourself, do you find your fingers accidentally typing arrows between each Moment? Or is your brain able to distinguish between these languages with relative ease?

This is the syntax that we'll use in Chapter 3, when we begin nesting Stories within Stories. Using parentheses to mark the beginning and end of Stories will actually help us with that.

More broadly speaking, the world of computing is and will continue to be one of many languages. Syntactic flexibility comes to those who practice, those who squint to see past the superficial differences between programs like the following — until finally they all seem to say the same thing.

```
print ("Bonjour")
(print "Hello")
echo "Hola"
console.log ("Ciao")
System.out.println ("Namaste")
std::cout ≪ "Salaam"
```

Syntax is something coders train their eyes to see beyond — to the meaning behind the symbols. Over time, we stop struggling to see, and the words we read seem to simply direct our thoughts effortlessly. With practice, a great many syntaxes can come to direct our thoughts in similar ways.

This is an internal journey of cognitive growth that anyone who has learned to code has experienced firsthand. Only recently, though, have scientists begun to uncover the mysteries of this story as it plays out in the brain inside an fMRI. We'll examine these findings momentarily.

To be continued...

LANGUAGES WITHOUT

The terms "computer language," "programming language," or "formal language" may connote that they are alien and inhuman – and indeed, sometimes they are such abstractions of everyday language that they hardly feel friendly, inviting, warm, or human.

Yet, between natural languages and formal languages, only one of the two was a conscious human invention. They were made by humans, to help other humans do jobs that help other humans.

What we're driving at is that the creation of "un-natural" languages is a natural process. As natural language evolved, so did our ability to craft new languages: more precise ones, ones that abstract more away, ones that aid the mind differently.

It comes as a surprise to many of our students that the co-evolution of natural and formal languages is as old as language itself. Yes, at the very dawn of written language, we were already using it to craft new, more precise forms of written language – forms that diverged further and further from natural speech, acquiring specialized syntax over time.

We know this, in part, from clay tablets unearthed in ancient Babylonia – thousands of years old, yet covered with mathematical notations and algorithms. The evolution of written language and the invention of formal language – both are part of the story of humanity and one of the weirdest things we've done if you look at the big picture of human history: How our knack for written language led us to create machines we could control with our writings; how our knack for building tools led us to create tools we can write to; how we made written language into a tool for creating new linguistic tools; how our knack for telling stories led us to create devices that could make stories translated into formal languages come true.

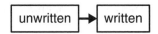

This Story (shorter even than the one supposedly written by Hemingway!) is precisely long enough to illustrate the two grand moments in the history of language. There was the time before the written word (often called "prehistory") and the time afterward – in which we currently reside.

Granted, this two-Moment Story abstracts away the transitional period, hiding it and implying it within the Arrow. Perhaps it would be clearer to expand that arrow into a Moment of its own:

This transitional period was a "moment" that lasted a few thousand years, and in which various writing systems sprang up: in 3400 BCE, in ancient Mesopotamia, in 3100 BCE in Egypt (possibly independently), in 1200 BCE in China (possibly independently), in first century BCE in Mesoamerica (probably independently) (Houston 2004) (Daniels and Bright 1996) (Martínez et al. 2006).

From studying what remains of these writing systems, linguists have constructed a timeline for how such systems were developed. Although the systems themselves use different symbols and rules from each other, the abstract developmental stages of these systems can be illustrated with this general Story:

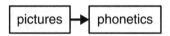

Or if we wish to reify the transition between:

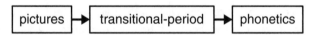

In other words, early writing systems began with a vocabulary of pictures, where the symbols looked like the objects or ideas they represented. These symbols gradually began to represent words (i.e., sounds for things), not just the things themselves. And finally, they began to represent sounds (void of sense) that could be used to construct senseful words – much like the letters in this book.

Each of these stages, and even the substages within, are like miniature lessons in abstraction. Take simply the `pictures` Moment in the evolution of a writing system. In the Stories below adapted from (Wallis and King 1908), we can see how early writing systems transitioned from more detailed drawings to more abstract ones.

Here the symbol for **star** begins like a nova, but implodes into a symbol.

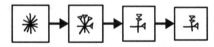

Here the symbol for **circle** and **sun** makes one half-hearted attempt to become more circular before deciding to abstract itself into something else entirely.

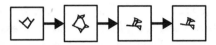

Here, details in the symbol for **rain** are washed away.

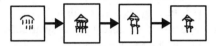

And finally, the symbol for **fish** shrivels to a mere skeleton.

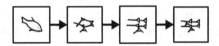

Without such abstraction, these writing systems would not have been so easily etched into the clay tablets we find today. Abstraction, shortening, simplifying: These are powerful tools. Abstraction operates at the level of symbols as well as the level of stories.

In English, we have 26 letters in the alphabet, but we have many more words. Only needing to learn 26 symbols and their sounds is certainly easier than needing to learn a new symbol for every word. The early versions of Sumerian cuneiform had 1,500 symbols for 1,500 different words and required scribes to go to *edubba* ("tablet-school"), where they typically studied for 12 years to learn to write (History on the Net 2019).

Systems with a very small set of building blocks (e.g., humble languages like Scheme, or humble instruments like the piano) can still achieve great expressivity through combinations. This idea of "expressing a lot by combining a few" is such a useful tool in modern language design that we should have no trouble believing that it was just as useful during that key transition so many thousands of years ago: from pictorial writing systems to phonetical ones.

The Unwritten, Unwritable Backstory

We have begun our story *in medias res*. That transitional period from a planet without writing systems to one filled with them is the middle of a Story with two major Moments:

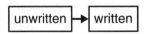

And what a strange Story it is, only half-knowable. Its first Moment, by definition, predates history – describing a time in which stories were lost. Scientists estimate that our species has been capable of speech for at least a hundred thousand years, with the most extreme estimates placing the event closer to our shift to bipedalism 3.5 million years ago (Uomini and Meyer 2013). However, the millions of years of lost stories may as well be denoted simply as `unwritten`, an abstraction of a million-year mystery into a single symbol. We can say little more than this: The stories told during this time have vanished into the air. For this was a time characterized by languages whose only medium of transmission was the air itself – a treacherous place for words, a place with high risk of eternal death.

Speculation about how language evolved during this period was banned in 1866 by the Linguistic Society of Paris, due to the fact that we simply had no way of gathering evidence for our speculations – placing the whole discussion outside of the realm of science. Today, however, studies of neurolinguistics in primates may hold some clues. Our old friend Broca's area, for example, has homologues in primates. Their analogous neurons have been found to fire when they hear a sound associated with a previously performed action (Kohler et al. 2002). Also, Broca's and Wernicke's homologues both become active in some monkeys when they hear other monkeys' species-specific calls (Gil-da-Costa et al. 2006); and Broca's homologue becomes active when chimpmanzees perceive other chimpanzees signaling – that is, begging (Taglialatela et al. 2008).

Although we have no records of the stories told in the `unwritten` period, the evolutionary backstory of the human brain can be guessed at by examining primate brains – helping us piece together the next best thing. Stories told by early *homo sapiens* are lost forever – less so the story of the organ that tells stories, the organ that existed throughout the `unwritten` Moment and persists throughout `written` Moment, the organ that we teachers are trained to train, the organ that makes us human.

Perhaps some clues to our brain's mysterious powers are locked within the very grey matter itself, and that of our relatives. Perhaps we will one day peer inward to squint backward.

Three Old Friends: Language, Math, Algorithms

The written word catalyzed a cascade of linguistic innovations that led us all the way to the computing era. To discuss such matters, let us give names to some key Moments within the `written` period, in particular the ones that are crucial to computing as we know it.

Let us begin with the time before electricity, in which almost every necessary linguistic ingredient for algorithmic language arose within the span of a few thousand years after the invention of writing, each catalyzing and accelerating the next:

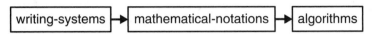

The above Story can be taken as a large arc, beginning with the invention of writing systems in ancient Mesopotamia 3300 BCE, proceeding to mathematical revolutions of Euclid circa 300 BCE, and culminating with early treatises on the subject of algorithms circa 820 CE by Persian scholar Muhammad ibn Musa al-Khwarizmi (from whose name the word "algorithm" derives).

However, it would be impolite to the people of ancient Mesopotamia to ignore the fact that they created all of these things, too, including algorithms, before the Bronze Age fell apart: a much shorter arc – with all Moments occurring in the Mesopotamian states between 3000 BCE and 1600 BCE.

The complexities of Mesopotamian trade and commerce were enabled by the use of arithmetic, algebra, and geometry. Indeed, the civilization of Sumer, located in what we now call Iraq, is estimated to have had a population between 0.8 and 1.5 million. To put this in perspective, this would have made it just slightly less populated than large American cities like San Diego, San Antonio, Phoenix, or Philadelphia. Wherever there are large numbers of people, there are large numbers of things that people care about: food, buildings, roads, animals, pottery, wood, stone, clothing, jewelry, roads, and so on. And whenever there are large numbers of things that people care about, it helps to have cognitive tools for dealing with large numbers of things, their acquisition, construction, sale, etc.

One such tool, as useful then as now, was mathematics. The Sumerians wrote their multiplication tables out on clay tablets. They knew how to calculate the areas of triangles and the volumes of cubes, which enabled them to do the necessary calculations for building their buildings, temples, storehouses, cisterns, and ziggurats.

By the year 1800 BCE, their clay tablets included mathematical advancements such as algebra, fractional numbers, quadratic equations, and cubic equations. They were even familiar with the Pythagorean theorem – beating Pythagoras by over a thousand years (J. J. O'Connor and Robertson 2000). One tablet approximates the square root of 2 to better than 1.41421. If you want to see how close they were, try running this Story – not so different from rotating a cat, syntactically speaking.

```
#lang dtc/story+/cats
```

```
(sqrt 2)
```

Their number system was based on the number 60 (rather than 10). This may seem like a strange way of defining numbers – and yet, their influence is the reason that today we divide our hours into 60 minutes, minutes into 60 seconds, and (it's hypothesized) even our circles into 360 degrees. When modern brains do arithmetic related to time and degrees, our minds are manipulating numbers not so differently from ancient minds.

All of this we have concluded from 400 clay tablets that were unearthed in the regions that were once ancient Babylonia, and which have been dated to between 1800 and 1600 BCE. On the one hand, it is easy to conclude that the writing system of the ancient Mesopotamians is simply what allowed us to "look back in time" at their mathematics, as if each of those 400 clay tablets were messages in bottles, sending information thousands of years into the future. However, the writing system of the ancient Mesopotamians didn't just *allow us to know* about their mathematics – it is what *enabled them to do* their mathematics in the first place. It was both.

Mathematics, one of the greatest tools of the mind, has since the Fertile Crescent been one enabled by writing down thoughts in precise ways. Do we know this because they wrote this fact down? Did they carve in cuneiform the self-reflective sentiment "Thank goodness we invented writing, for it enabled us to do mathematics?" No. And yet, we know it all the same, because we know today how the brain works.

Whether you're a neuroscientist or not, any educated adult has learned this first-hand: The brain's ability to perform calculations increases by orders of magnitude when it can store calculations on paper. Consider, for example, the largest two numbers you can add together in your mind. Can you add together 2 + 7 in your mind? Probably. What about 67 + 98? Possibly. What about 345 + 799? Most of us would have to think about this for a bit. What about two 4-digit numbers? That's when we tend to grab our calculators. What about two 10-digit numbers? Most of us wouldn't trust ourselves with this one. Everyone has a threshold where they begin to make too many mistakes to be confident in their answers.

Although we have limits on the amount our unaided minds can calculate, with the benefit of writing down the numbers, it becomes unclear what the limits are.

Given enough time, enough paper and pencils, and enough motivation for doing mind-numbing calculation, most mathematically educated people could add up gigantic numbers. If someone offered you a million dollars to do the following calculation on paper, could you do it?

9102394059843223588893845 + 994933845222144999934822111

Probably. Would it be boring? Yes. Would it be cognitively feasible using pencil and paper? Without a doubt.

Now, we're not saying performing this calculation in your mind is *impossible*. We're just saying that with the benefit of written notation, you simply don't have to. The notation for numbers and the addition algorithm you learned in grade school make it unnecessary to train your brain to do mathematical gymnastics.

There's a general principle at work here, that we should give a name to. It will reappear.

Extended Mind

Andy Clark and David Chalmers introduced this idea with a thought experiment in 1998 (Clark and Chalmers 1998). To paraphrase:

Suppose Otto and Igna are traveling separately through the same museum. Now, suppose that Otto has Alzheimer's disease, and (aware of his condition) has written down directions in his notebook. Igna, however, can remember the directions. Both of them are able to navigate the museum with ease – Igna consulting her memory, and Otto consulting his notebook. Chalmers and Clark give a name to what Otto is doing: Namely, his mind has been "extended" to include his notes as his memory.

They go on to suggest that many things in our environment can serve the purpose of extending the mind. Indeed, such extensions are quite normal – something we all do, something intrinsic to how minds work.

Unless Mesopotamia was somehow stuffed with mathematical savants, their writing system is what enabled them to do mathematical calculations, write down the results of those calculations, invent new ways of calculating, and so on. With writing, their minds extended, becoming capable of thoughts previously unthinkable.

The true hero in this early surge of mathematical creativity was the invention of symbols for expressing concepts like numbers, quantities, angles, multiplications, divisions, squares, roots, triangles, circles, areas, volumes, and so on. It was the invention of procedures that involved the manipulation of the above as linguistic objects, and (more importantly) objects of thought. The true hero was written language – a language designed for mechanizing the discovery of truths previously unknown.

Yes, cuneiform allowed them to write stories like the *Epic of Gilgamesh*, one of the earliest works of fiction. But fictions only take a civilization so far.

Algorithms of Antiquity

Donald Knuth – famous for his seminal multivolume work *The Art of Computer Programming* – wrote an article on Babylonian algorithms in 1972 (Knuth 1972), in which he gives the following English translation of a cuneiform tablet dating back to the Hammurabi dynasty between 1600 and 1800 BCE. The parentheticals are Knuth's explanations.

> I invested 1 maneh of silver, at a rate of 12 shekels per maneh (per year, with interest apparently compounded every five years).
> I received, as capital plus interest, 1 talent and 4 manehs. (Here 1 maneh = 60 shekels, and 1 talent = 60 manehs.)
> How many years did this take?
> Let 1 be the initial capital.
> Let 1 maneh earn 12 (shekels) interest in a 6 (= 360) day year.
> And let 1,4 be the capital plus interest.
> Compute 12, the interest, per 1 unit of initial capital, giving 12 as the interest rate.
> Multiply 12 by 5 years, giving 1.
> Thus in five years the interest will equal the initial capital.

As Knuth notes, these algorithms tended to use specific numbers, rather than abstracting away the specifics into variables. However, he does find the following example, with no concrete numbers to be found:

> Length and width is to be equal to the area.
> You should proceed as follows.
> Make two copies of one parameter.
> Subtract 1.
> Form the reciprocal.
> Multiply by the parameter you copied.
> This gives the width.

Interestingly, many of these algorithmic tablets ended with a customary phrase:

> That is the procedure.

It is reminiscent of "Q.E.D" – the abbreviation of the Latin *quod erat demonstrandum* which was a translation of a Greek phrase that served as a beacon to end ancient Greek mathematical proofs – a signpost that the quest for truth is complete. At the end of Mesopotamian algorithms, "That is the procedure" has the same feel.

These ancient algorithms are sequences of commands asking the reader to perform various actions in pursuit of new knowledge. Some of those are arithmetic actions, but some are actions of the body or actions of the mind. Note the command to "make two copies" and then to later "multiply by the parameter you copied." Other tablets instruct the reader to essentially "keep this number in your head."

These algorithmic tablets would have served to extend the mind, allowing anyone who could read and do basic math to perform a complex series of calculations to find the areas and volumes of things, or the number of *maneh* and *shekels* owed. Whereas Otto used a notebook to extend his memory, allowing him to navigate a museum, the Mesopotamians used algorithms baked into clay to navigate territories of the mind – able to arrive at destinations that would have been previously impossible. Like Ariadne's thread, the written algorithm keeps the mind tethered and oriented within the labyrinth of possible thoughts.

Just as we can, with Otto, ask "where is the memory?" and answer "partially in the notebook," we can ask a similar question with the ancient Mesopotamians. When an ancient merchant performed a calculation related to his investments, where is the calculation happening? Part of it, certainly, is happening in the merchant's brain. For example, we know already that Broca's and Wernicke's regions would have activated while reading the tablet. Numerical operations tend to light up different regions: the parietal and prefrontal regions (Friedrich and Friederici 2013).

However, it would be unfair to the tablets and the writing systems to give the brain all of the credit. If the merchant scratches some symbols into the dirt or wet clay, then he has stored some information in the external world for later retrieval (much like Otto with his notebook or Dumbledore with his pensieve). And what of the algorithmic tablet itself? A merchant who has not committed the algorithm to memory must reference the tablet at each stage in order to know what to do next. Just as Otto's notebook aided his navigation through the museum, the merchant's tablet aids the navigation of his mind through complicated mathematical territory. Should he forget where to direct his mind next, the tablet will remind him. Should he become lost, Ariadne's thread leads the way back.

The mind of the merchant proceeds from task to task, performing each to completion before moving on.

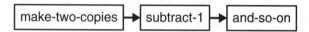

And so on: Moment by Moment. At the end of the Story, the merchant knows something he did not know before.

The connection between algorithm and Stories is not coincidental. Indeed, the connection between algorithms and stories isn't either. A tablet containing the *Epic of Gilgamesh* would also have directed the mind, only differently.

The difference? Unlike literature, algorithms attempt to direct *all* minds to the *same* result, via the *same* process, every time, without fail. To do so, they almost always assume an extended mind – that is, equipped with paper and pencil. Literature does not usually assume such extensions.

Writing, mathematical notation, and algorithms are linguistic technologies that have the power to augment minds, giving them powers that they did not previously have. Every such algorithmic tablet was like a sorcerer's stone that could give new abilities to whoever possessed it. Furthermore, each stone could be copied by a scribe and distributed to others. These were the stones upon which that cradle of civilization was built – not just the boring ones that lay dormant in their walls, streets, bridges, or ziggurats.

One written mark at a time. One tablet at a time. One idea at a time.

Unlike ideas in the air, the ideas in clay can be more easily examined, refined, combined, discussed, improved, and edited over time. New versions of old ones can be produced. One wonders if novice scribes in their 12-year tenure at scribe school might have asked questions of their teachers, like, "Why do we have so many tablets? And why do many say similar things in different ways?" We hear a reformulation of that question every day from novice programmers: "Why do we have so many languages? And why do they allow us to say so many things in so many different ways?"

A Brief Story of Stories

We swim in a river of language. It began somewhere in the first Moment of that grand story:

In that time before writing, minds could speak, or perhaps sign, or gesture. In this way, minds could send words toward the eyes and ears of other minds.

The word was a powerful thing, even then. It was enough to define us as human, enough for the genesis of early cultures.

Then, in the fertile crescent, we began to put words into clay, imbuing them with a new power – the potential for immortality.

Words, when moving from one mind to another, could now take longer rests, baked or even buried. This alone – writing – was enough to launch civilizations.

In Chapter 3, we will see how the next act of linguistic sorcery began: the use of the written word to control machines. The mechanization of language.

To be continued...

LANGUAGES WITHIN

What was happening in the brain of a Babylonian merchant as he performed an algorithm written on a clay tablet? Was there a slight oxygen differential in the areas of his brain that we now call Broca's or Wernicke's areas? We cannot take an fMRI machine backward in time. However, evolution tells us that the structure of human brains has moved forward in time largely unchanged since the times of ancient Babylon. In the Darwinian story, a few thousand years is but a moment.

In 2014, scientists first began putting programmers into fMRIs, trying to unlock the puzzle of how brains process programming languages. It was a natural thing to do. We've been putting people in fMRIs since the 90s, slowly mapping out how the brain processes various kinds of linguistic activities: speech perception, semantic retrieval, sentence comprehension, incomprehensible sentence processing, word learning, word retrieval, sign language perception, sign language production, artificial grammar processing, etc.

In this 2014 study, scientists took a group of computer science students and, one by one, placed them into the bed of the fMRI. They were given a series of programming tasks that could be performed with a minimum of bodily movement. Getting an accurate scan requires the subject to be as immobile as possible. They were able to see small snippets of computer code reflected on a mirror at eye-level. The subject could respond by pressing buttons on a response box with their index finger.

Keeping bodies still is easy. Brains remain in motion, though. A key challenge in fMRI is to detect activity *only* in the parts of the brain that activate in response to the thing being studied – in this case, "program comprehension." However, during the process of program comprehension, many parts of the brain may become active. Some of these may have little to do with the task being studied. Simply lying down and looking at a program in a mirror might activate regions related to lying down and looking at mirrors. Not to mention, random thoughts may pop in. Minds can wander. Brains rarely obey instructions to do "nothing but the task at hand."

In an infamous 2010 study, a dead salmon was placed into an fMRI and shown pictures of human faces, some in happy social situations and some in unhappy ones (Bennett et al. 2010). The salmon showed distinct activation patterns when shown the photographs. Although the dead fish did not respond when asked to characterize the "emotional valence" of the situation in the photographs, the fMRI did detect measurable and statistically significant Blood Oxygen Level Dependent (BOLD) signal patterns in the brain and spinal cord while photographs were being displayed.

If a dead fish's brain can behave unpredictably, a live human brain can, too. Therefore, fMRI studies must take certain precautions to prevent false positives. Namely, subjects are generally asked to perform at least two tasks – one of them being the experimental task and one of them being the control task. To sort out the case of the dead salmon, one of its tasks might be seeing the happy photographs, and the other task might be seeing the sad ones.

Conclusions would then be drawn by comparing the two tasks to see how the BOLD response *differs* – with parts that stay the same being ignored. You delete the same and keep the difference.

Thus, the more similar the tasks, the more likely the fMRI will pinpoint the regions of the brain that are specific to the cognitive process that you're actually trying to study. In the dead fish (or, as the study called it, the "post-mortem Atlantic salmon"), there were no detectable differences between the task of examining happy photos versus the task of examining sad photos. This would suggest that the post-mortem Atlantic salmon did not, in fact, have insight into human social dynamics.

The computer science students in 2014 were given two similar tasks. The control task involved looking at source code to find simple syntax errors. The comprehension task involved predicting what the program would do. The idea is that finding syntax errors requires less comprehension than prediction does, yet it still requires the same motor functions: looking at source code in a mirror, clicking a button with your index finger, and so on.

The following code has a syntax error in it:

```
#lang dtc/story/cats

cat -< rotate -> redify -> rotate -> shrink
```

So does this one:

```
#lang dtc/story/cats

caT -> rotate -> redify -> rotate -> shrink
```

So does this one:

```
#lang dtc/story/cats

cat -> rotate -> red ify -> rotate -> shrink
```

Here's a tricky one:

```
#lang dtc/story/cats

cat -> rotate -> redify -> rotate -> stink
```

We suspect that if you have worked even briefly with the dtc/story/cats language, you can see that the detection of simple syntax errors often requires nothing more than scanning the code until some oddity "jumps out" at you. The more you've worked with a language, the quicker your eyes will land on the bits of syntax that disobey the rules. This is a critical skill in programming, to be sure. However, it is a task that should feel (especially if you've done the coding exercises in this chapter) distinctly different from what your mind does when it predicts the output of a Story. In other words: The process of finding typos in Stories is different from running through Stories in your mind. It's one thing to notice that the symbol caT doesn't look right; it's another thing to see a cat photograph in your mind, then rotate it, then turn it red, then rotate it again, then shrink it.

If you're curious about what's going on in your brain when you do one versus the other, Dr. Janet Siegmund and her team did, too – prompting them to run that historic 2014 fMRI study (Siegmund et al. 2014). Because our brains can be left or right lateralized, the team recruited left lateralized participants only for this study. Here's what they found:

> ...for comprehending source code, five different brain regions become activated, which are associated with working memory (BA 6, BA 40), attention (BA 6), and language processing (BA 21, BA 44, BA 47)...

Brodmann area 44 in the left hemisphere also goes by the name Broca's area. It's our old friend – which, in your own brain, may have just flickered with activity when you read the familiar words "Broca's area." Her paper goes on to say:

> Our results indicate that, for learning programming, it may be beneficial to train also working memory, which is necessary for many tasks, and language skills, as Dijkstra already noted.

Here she references Dijkstra's famous statement that:

Besides mathematical inclination, an exceptionally good mastery of one's native tongue is the most vital asset of a competent programmer.

Here we find all three language friends mentioned in a single epigraph: mathematics, programming, and natural language. Dijkstra wrote this in 1975 – in the same essay in which he observed that BASIC caused brain damage to students.

It makes sense that Dijkstra, quite the mathematician himself, prized mathematics over mastery of the native tongue. He served as a professor of mathematics in the Netherlands, making many deeply important mathematical contributions during his career. It also makes sense in terms of history: the entire field of computer science was born from the field of mathematics. In 1837, mathematician Charles Babbage invented the first mechanical computer, earning him the title "Father of the Computer." Mathematician Ada Lovelace wrote one of the first programs for Babbage's machine. Later, mathematician Alan Turing developed many of the foundational ideas in theoretical computer science, even mechanizing mathematics to break German codes during World War II.

Given the history of computer scientists who viewed the field as being born from mathematics (turning a blind eye to the fact that mathematics was born from natural language), we can forgive Dijkstra his subtle biases.

Another confirmation of programming comprehension activating Broca's area arrived in 2017. Scientists placed another batch of participants into an fMRI, but gave them three different tasks.

- In one task, participants were asked to perform a "code review," which entails reading a message describing a change made to a codebase, along with the changed code itself – with differences highlighted.

- In the second task, participants were show code along with an assertion that they needed to identify as true or false – requiring the participant to comprehend the code to evaluate the assertion.

- In the third task, participants read English prose unrelated to code altogether, but which included some "track changes" style edits, like those you might make in a word processor, and which visually and conceptually resemble highlighted code differences you might find in a code review (as in the first task).

Consider the differences among these three cognitive tasks – the third was already widely known to activate language portions of the brain (reading arbitrary English prose); the second had in 2014 been surprisingly shown to also do this (comprehending source code); and the first interweaves the two (reading English *about* changes being made to code).

Some of the obvious findings were (1) that the brain activation patterns in each case were distinct – meaning that the brains of programmers reading source code don't look *exactly* like the brains of programmers reading messages about code or arbitrary prose, and (2) the activation patterns were more similar between the two code-related tasks.

The fascinating finding was that the skill of the programmer was correlated with greater *similarity* between the code comprehension and English prose reading tasks. As the paper puts it (Floyd et al. 2017):

> The inverse relationship between accuracy and expertise suggests that, as one develops more skill in coding, the neural representations of code and prose are less differentiable. That is, programming languages are treated more like natural languages with greater expertise.

Consider that for a moment as you look at this program:

```
#lang dtc/story/cats

cat -> rotate -> redify -> rotate -> shrink
```

The claim is: as you become better and better at programming, your brain will become more and more capable of processing the above program and the following prose in the same way.

```
First, we take a photo of a cat and rotate it.
Then we color it red and rotate it again.
Finally, we shrink it down.

That is the procedure.
```

Does it sound believable to you that your brain will one day process both similarly? If you did the programming exercises in this chapter (even in your mind), then this process has already begun, and you may already be able to feel it. You can likely conjecture that this process will continue, with you gradually acquiring the ability to understand more and more formal languages with the same fluency that you understand English.

Acquiring fluency is a process that should be familiar to anyone who has learned a new language to some degree of success. Words, grammar, and symbols that, at first, look alien begin to become more and more familiar. And eventually, you simply understand. The language in which a story is written becomes less and less relevant as you become more and more fluent. You simply see the story, not the language.

As Siegmund and her colleagues put it (Siegmund et al. 2014):

> [Our] research will have a broad impact on education, so that training beginning programmers can be improved considerably. Despite intensive research (e.g., Technical Symposium on Computer Science Education, Innovation and Technology in Computer Science Education), it is still rather unclear how and why students struggle with learning programming. With a detailed understanding of the cognitive processes that underlie a developers' every-day task, we might find the right recipe to teach any student to become an excellent software developer (e.g., by including training language skills, since our study showed a close relationship to language processing). . . .
>
> Eventually, we hope to find answers to heatedly discussed questions, such as "How should we teach programming?" or "What makes a programmer excellent?".

Foreign Language: A Friend, Perhaps a Mentor

In Florida, lawmakers tried to allow high school Java to replace high school Spanish. One interpretation of the recent science, however, suggests that the exact opposite would be smarter.

Learning the difference between one's novas and *no vas* might be more related to Java skill than anyone expected, prior to the Siegmund study. We know that the mastery of one foreign language makes mastering other foreign languages easier (Klein 1995) (Grey et al. 2018); could it be true that mastering a foreign language makes learning a computer language easier?

This is an open question in science today.

Our money is on yes, though. It is well known that learning a second (natural) language has a variety of cognitive benefits: better memory, better critical-thinking skills, better concentration and multitasking abilities, better problem-solving skills, and better listening skills (Marian and Shook 2012). Creativity and mental flexibility are also enhanced (Dijk et al. 2018) (Gullifer et al. 2013).

Furthermore, a study of 853 participants in Edinburgh University showed that cognitive advantages are gained regardless of the age that you learn a second language (Bak et al. 2014) – busting the common (and silly) myth that only young children can or should learn second languages.

The cognitive benefits from learning a second language seem to be exactly the ones that make good coders great: better memory, stronger critical thinking skills, improved concentration abilities, enhanced problem-solving skills, and so on.

Dr. Siegmund calls for coders to "train language skills." What better way than learning languages?

But life is short. Suppose one doesn't have time to study Spanish before coding. Can coding teachers still find ways of teaching computer science that leverage the decades of scientific research on Second Language Acquisition theory? We discuss this in Chapter 3.

Zapping Broca's Area

In artificial grammar learning studies, scientists make up entirely new, but very simple formal languages, with their own (designed) grammatical structures. In the learning and producing of these artificial languages, Broca's region is (as should be no surprise by now) also active in fMRIs (Fitch and Friederici 2012). In 2010, it was shown that transcranial direct current stimulation of Broca's region helped people learn these artificial grammars more quickly (Vries et al. 2010). That's right, zapping Broca's region seems to have benefits in language learning.

If that sounds like science fiction, keep in mind that PubMed currently returns over 4,000 results on transcranial direct current stimulation. This is a topic under investigation, already having gained significant momentum. In 2014, Radiolab did a podcast called "9-Volt Nirvana" on the topic.

The technique is non-invasive and seems to have observable positive effects even in healthy individuals – for example, improvements in working memory (Ke et al. 2019). Will we one day hook students up to brain stimulators while they learn to program?

That day is probably far off. Don't try it at home.

However, this line of research suggests something crucial: That Broca's area isn't just "what lights up" when you do language; but rather, it may play a key role in the language acquisition process itself.

Note that transcranial direct current stimulation is thought to work by increasing the firing ability of neurons in the "zapped" regions *during* the zapping period. When this is done during practice sessions, gains are observable in the long term.

So even if such a thing were to be shown to work with languages more complicated than artificial grammars – it would be less of a sudden "I know kung fu" technology, and more of an "I can practice kung fu more effectively" technology.

More Monkey Business

Broca's area is also active when we observe other human beings doing "meaningful action" – for example making meaningful gestures (Grèzes and Decety 2001). Even in chimpanzees, the area that is homologically equivalent to Broca's area activates when they produce gestures or utterances for the purposes of communication with other chimpanzees (Taglialatela et al. 2008). Furthermore, it activates in human beings, even when we don't see real hands doing the gesturing – like when we see the shadows of hands that look like moving animals (Fadiga et al. 2006). (Yes, in 2006, scientists asked people in an fMRI to watch shadow puppets.)

This line of research leads to at least one hypothesis about the origins of language – that language arose shortly after the evolution of bipedalism (as many as 4.2 million years ago), and began as hand gestures. According to the theory, this gestural proto-language evolved into more complex gestures, began to incorporate sound, and ultimately (after millions of years of linguistic evolution and change) came to be spoken languages (Rizzolatti and Craighero 2004).

Others, such as Noam Chomsky, believe the moment was more recent and happened more quickly (Bolhuis et al. 2014).

Either way, everything we know today points to a tremendously flexible wetware for making meaning across available modalities. A few special regions in the brain help make linguistic sense of a great many things: hand gestures, sounds, grunts, spoken words, sentences, symbols scratched in clay, algorithms on clay tablets, hand shadows, symbols on a computer screen, or snippets of code.

To be continued...

Chapter 3
Middles

Meta-Jedi: What did the meta-Jedi say to the Jedi?
Jedi: What?
Meta-Jedi: Meta-force be with you.

↓

Meta-Teacher: What did the meta-teacher say to the teacher?
Teacher: What?
Meta-Teacher: I never meta-teacher quite like you.

↓

Meta-Jokester: What did the meta-jokester say to the jokester?
Jokester: What?
Meta-Jokester: "What did the meta-jokester say to the jokester?"

A WIZARD'S TALE
Purgatory

One of the cool kids shoved into Henry, causing him to spill cafeteria milk from the goblet he was bringing to his lips. It mixed in with his mashed potatoes and green beans, making them gross. But before he could turn and protest, the ancient wizard, who was sitting across from him, raised a finger and said, "It isn't real."

"It feels real," said Henry, face flushing as he watched the cool kids high fiving each other. Rob patted his shoulder as he munched on mashed potatoes.

"Reality is a simulation," said the old wizard.

"What Henry means," clarified Harmony, "is that although we're in a simulation, it still hurts to be harassed on a daily basis. The feelings are real."

"*Are* your feelings real?" asked the ancient wizard. "Chemicals cause feelings – a neuro-chemical simulation."

Finally, Henry could take no more. "It's been months!" he exploded. "All you do is talk in riddles and teach us about 'abstractions' and 'notations' and 'language' and 'brain regions.' All the other kids make fun of us. That's *real*. Their words are real."

The ancient wizard sighed. "So . . ." he said slowly, even sadly perhaps. "You want to learn to code . . ."

Henry glanced at his friends. Harmony was biting her lip, and Rob was pretending to be interested in stirring his mashed potatoes with his fork. "Yes," said Henry. "We're ready. I know we are."

"Then so it shall be," said the ancient wizard. "If you are truly ready, when I next see you, you shall begin working with real code." With that, his eyes slid back into his head, showing the whites. His avatar's idle animation – an infinite loop of beard scratching – kicked in. Teachers were allowed to enter and exit the school at will.

"That was easier than expected," said Rob, through a mouthful of potatoes. "Any chance he'll teach us Python?"

As if saying the word "Python" was a cue, the cool kid bumped into Henry from behind, causing him to spill another gulp of milk destined for his mouth. This time, Henry sprang to his feet and faced his nemesis.

Before Henry could say anything, the cool kid interjected: "This is Crabbe," he said, then pointed at his other friend, "and this is Goyle."

"Couldn't you think of something more creative?" said Henry, going on the attack. "You took that straight from *Harry Potter*."

The cool kid got in Henry's face, saying, "Yeah? Well, we *like Harry Potter*, okay? Don't pretend you don't. I mean, look at you. Do you really expect people to believe you three look like your avatars in real life?"

Before he could stop himself, Henry put his hand to the lightning scar on his avatar's forehead – a decoration hundreds had selected during character creation. If he had known how popular it would be, he might have chosen something different.

Rob was about to respond, but Harmony cut him off, "Please, please!" she said. "Can we *not* fight about trivialities, like who likes *Harry Potter* more? We all care about fundamentally the same thing. Right? Coding. That's what matters."

The cool kid nodded, and for a moment, it seemed like all was well. He extended a hand to Harmony. "You're right. I'm sorry I've been mean to you all these months. When I first saw you, I wrongfully labeled you as 'the uncool kids.' Thus, when you were accepted into the most interesting and mysterious of the houses, I found myself feeling inferior. That led me to make snide comments and bump into you daily for . . ." He pretended to check his watch. ". . . 12 weeks and 2 days straight. But I realize now . . ." His voice quieted. "I was wrong to do all of that."

His hand still hung in the air. Cautiously, Harmony extended her hand. Henry, started to say something. But it was too late: The moment before their hands touched, the cool kid blurted, "Wanna fight a duel?" Before Harmony could withdraw her hand, he grabbed it and shook once, triggering the simulation's gesture detection system. A voice from on high – the computerized voice of the simulation – declared: "Duel accepted!"

Descent

Harmony jerked her hand away with a gasp. They had been forbidden from dueling. It was not "part of the curriculum in this House which has no name." The ancient wizard's eyes were blank and white, though. He would not be coming to their aid.

The cool kid laughed and gave a high five to his buddies. "I *told* you I could get them to do it." To the entire cafeteria, he announced, "The No Namers are dueling Python!"

It was chaos. Suddenly everyone was on their feet. Goblets and cafeteria trays fell to the floor. Mashed potatoes squished beneath boots and stuck to the bottoms of robes. Within seconds, a thick circle of enthusiastic people had formed around them and their table. The ancient wizard just sat there, eyes rolled back, scratching his beard. People stood on the tables to get a better view. One by one, their own eyes began to roll back into their heads as they went into spectator mode, avatars idling.

The computer voice overhead announced: "Battle commencing in 5 . . . 4 . . ." The cool kid joined hands with his henchmen. Their eyes immediately rolled up into their heads, and they simply stood there, holding hands and breathing – avatars in "idle" mode. The voice paused the countdown: "Three versus three mode enabled." Then it continued: "3 . . . 2 . . ." Rob and Henry lurched to grab Harmony just in time. "1!" said the voice.

Henry's vision went blank as his eyes were jerked involuntarily into his head, triggering the simulation within the simulation.

Suddenly, they were in-game. And the battle had already begun. It was a classic game of multidimensional wizard chess – which, among its many differences from normal chess, always begins *in medias res.* A flying enemy knight swooped in, carrying what looked like a light saber, and sliced off Henry's arm – but Harmony healed him with her queen. Rob made a gesture that positioned twenty of his rooks in a giant circle around them. "How do they already have laser knights?" cried Rob over the sound of the explosions all around them.

As they huddled behind a rook that was shaking from the brutal onslaught of exploding pawns bombarding the other side, Rob and Harmony began to discuss strategy. But Henry knew it was hopeless. The Python gang had been collecting scripts for their pieces for months. There was no way the three of them, who had been forbidden from coding, could win. But even in his moment of despair, it was as if he heard the ancient wizard whispering, "Simulations within simulations, within . . ."

Suddenly, Henry stood up, unafraid. "Reality is a simulation," he said, as Rob and Harmony shouted for him to get down. "Don't you see? It's not about this duel. It's about looking cool. They challenged us to one game, but they're really playing a different game – one with social points." He locked eyes with Rob, then Harmony. "Let's beat them at *that* game."

He exited the simulation, and found himself back in the cafeteria. Rob and Harmony's avatars came to life beside him. All around were the idling avatars of the others, like zombies. In front of them were the idling cool kids. Everyone would still be in-game for a few minutes – as long as Rob's rooks remained standing.

Henry wondered what retaliation would be fitting. He could smear mashed potatoes on their faces; there was plenty on the floor. Or he could tie their shoelaces together; it would be fun to watch them tumble to the ground in front of everyone. He knelt down at the feet of his arch nemesis, still not sure if he was going to grab mashed potatoes or reach for the laces – or perhaps both, if he was fast enough. But when he got there, he happened to glance over at the old wizard, still sitting calmly at his chair, eyes white, scratching his beard. Henry could almost hear him say, "Reality is a simulation."

Suddenly, Henry stood up, unafraid. "We're in the wrong simulation," he said, turning to his friends, holding out his hands. "Don't you see?" They took his hands. "Follow me," he said, biting his left molar as if he was crushing a capsule, then he swallowed. His vision was already going dark as it dawned on Harmony and Rob that he had triggered the Exit School gesture. "Please," he said, growing weak. "I think I finally understand. Follow me . . ."

Ascent

A moment later, he was gasping for breath and sitting up on his bed in a long room lined with beds. He pulled the cranial link out of his skull and the IV out of his arm and sat up. There were Rob and Harmony, lying on beds on either side of him. They were still asleep, still plugged in. Their faces looked only vaguely like their avatars. Anxiously, he waited to see if they would wake up.

Seconds turned to minutes. He pulled his hospital gown closer and pulled his knees to his chest, feeling cold and alone. The long row of sleeping students stretched out to both sides of him – a row of people breathing softly, a row of beds extended into apparent infinity on both sides. The rack of servers that ran the simulation took up the entirety of both long walls, extending into that dark infinity as well.

A moment later an old woman in scrubs appeared, emerging from a door between two server racks. "You're out, I see," she said, making a note on her clipboard. "Well, come along."

Henry glanced at his friends. "Could we . . . could we just wait a few more moments?"

She looked at her watch and shrugged, then stood there in silence, making notes on her clipboard. Henry gripped his fists tight, holding his breath that they would awaken. But they didn't.

"You know," she said. "Time passes slower in there relative to here. What feels like a minute for someone plugged in might be five minutes or even ten out here. It depends on the complexity of what's being simulated. So – it's possible they're still thinking it over. It's possible those rooks are still holding on."

"Wait . . ." said Henry. "How did you . . ."

"Remember," she said. "Reality is a simulation."

Henry's jaw dropped. "*You?!*" he said, incredulous. "*You're* the ancient wizard!?"

"It depends on the simulation," she said.

At that moment, Rob gasped, then Harmony. They began coughing and lurching. Harmony yanked her own cranial link out, while the woman in scrubs assisted Rob. Henry was speechless.

"Come along," said the old wizard, "the source code awaits."

To be continued . . .

A LANGUAGE WITHOUT

(Stories (Within Stories))

The Moments in Stories have, thus far, been simple symbols: strings of alphanumeric characters or images. In this chapter, we expand the definition of a Moment by allowing Moments to be Stories themselves.

As a literary device, stories within stories have been around since (at least) ancient Egypt. One papyrus scroll, currently housed in a museum in Berlin, brings to us just such a story, from somewhere between the eighteenth and sixteenth century BCE – the same period in which were written the Babylonian mathematical tablets we discussed in the previous chapter. The scroll tells five stories of magic and miracles; but each story is told by a character in the "frame story" – one of the sons of King Cheops, members of his royal court. In one substory, a magician creates a crocodile out of wax and orders it to eat people; in another substory, a man parts the waters in a river; in another substory a wizard reattaches the severed heads of a goose and a bull.

Whereas the papyrus is perhaps the oldest known example of a nested story, one of the most famous is the collection of Middle Eastern folk tales "One Thousand and One Nights." In the frame story, Scheherazade courageously and with full knowledge makes the dangerous choice to marry a king whose public practice is to behead his wives the day after their wedding night. Indeed, he had already done so with many others. Scheherazade, however, is a cunning storyteller and believes she can use her powers to save other women and herself.

She keeps the king's dopamine loop engaged the entire first night with a story that almost (but not quite) finishes by the break of dawn. Essentially, she finishes with a . . .

To be continued . . .

And so, the king spares her life (as she had planned), wanting to hear the rest of the story. The next night, Scheherazade skillfully finishes the first story and begins the second. So it went for 1,001 nights (and 1,001 stories), during which time she skillfully uses stories to entertain and educate the king, subtly altering his moral fabric. By the end of the larger frame story, she has reprogrammed him – saving her own life and those of others.

Shakespeare wrote many plays within plays as well. In *Hamlet*, several actors perform a play about a murder which bears resemblance to the murder of

Hamlet's father – an attempt to elicit a reaction from Claudius, whom Hamlet believes to be the murderer. Likewise, *A Midsummer Night's Dream*, *Love's Labours Lost*, and *The Taming of the Shrew* all contain plays within the main play.

As a literary device, the nested story is quite common – so much so that the concept has its own Wikipedia article ("Story within a story"). Stories within stories, plays within plays, plays within films, television shows within movies, songs within songs, games within games, and so on. Literature is full of such stories. The history is long and rich, playing out again and again across cultures, across genres, across languages, across centuries, and indeed across millennia.

What we will concern ourselves with in this chapter are programs nested within programs: Stories within Stories.

In this chapter, the subject of nested Stories serves two purposes: It takes us one step closer to a language with the full power of a modern programming language, and it gives us a powerful analogy for the inherently self-containing nature of programs and the machines that run them. An operating system, for example, is a program that runs other programs. Some of those programs (like your web browser) will run other programs. And so on. Software nests software which nests software.

Some of Scheherazade's stories too contained other stories, which themselves contained other stories. The limits in literature are whether the increasingly deep nestings are comprehensible and enjoyable. We are under no corresponding obligation to entertain our software, however, and are free to create intricately nested systems of deep complexity.

Similar examples are everywhere along the road to becoming a coder: programs that evaluate other programs, programs that launch other programs, machines that contain other machines, languages that embed other languages, languages for creating other languages, and so on. But it's important to remember that mathematics and computer science didn't invent these ideas. The reality is, we've simply made into science what our linguistically inclined species has done for millennia.

Indeed, nesting of stories is a fundamental part of the human experience.

We are all heroes in our own stories, after all – our own *frame* stories within which we encounter, read, see, hear, play, or watch stories about other heroes. Every story we encounter is nested within our personal frame stories.

Within a Story, until now, we could not easily write about other Stories. But by the end of this chapter, we will have this ability. Let's get to work by naming the two types of Stories we've seen so far in this book. By the end of this chapter, we will have the ability to place either kind of Story inside the other.

The first type of Story has Moments that describe what the computer is supposed to do. In other words, the Story is "evaluated" or "interpreted" by the computer: The computer makes the Moments "come true."

```
#lang dtc/story/cats
```

```
cat -> rotate -> redify
```

You can tell this story is interpreted because it *does* something. What comes out when you run it looks nothing like the Story you typed in. It produces something else (a tilted image of a red cat). The result at the end is evidence that the Story *happened*; it wasn't just written.

But we have also seen the other kind of Story, whose moments are not interpreted for their meanings. Rather, the whole Story is simply transformed into an image:

```
#lang dtc/story/images
```

```
cat -> rotate -> redify
```

Output:

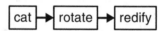

The output is just an image version of the text. It could have been any Story, really, and the results (abstractly speaking) would have been the same.

When a Story isn't meant to be interpreted, any symbols for Moments will do. The symbols don't require any particular meaning. For example, this won't work in the cat language.

```
#lang dtc/story/cats
```

```
dog -> rotate -> redify
```

But it's still a perfectly valid Story if we leave it uninterpreted:

```
#lang dtc/story/images
```

```
dog -> rotate -> redify
```

Thus far, however, the only way to make a Story get interpreted is to tell the computer to use a language that interprets the story (like dtc/story/cats), instead of one that leaves the story uninterpreted (like dtc/story/images).

However, let us introduce a notation that gives us both abilities: the ability to note that a story should be interpreted, or not – but in the *same* language. Doing so will begin to forge a language greater than the sum of its parts – permitting the expression of ideas that weren't expressible in either language separately, the expression of ideas that are only expressible as Stories about Stories.

In the last chapter, we began to abstract the Arrow symbols out of our code. This may be confusing at first, but as our language becomes more complicated, we're going to need the extra space, along with the syntactic ability to mark both the start *and* end of Stories.

We have already introduced this alternative syntax with the dtc/story+/image language, for uninterpreted Stories.

```
#lang dtc/story+/images

(cat rotate redify)
```

For interpreted stories:

```
#lang dtc/story+/cats

(cat rotate redify)
```

This syntactically paves the way for a much deeper change.

We now introduce #lang dtc/frames/cats in which both kinds of stories can be written. Furthermore, Stories of either kind can serve as frame Stories for either of the other kind.

But let's not go too fast. First of all, interpreted Stories look syntactically the same as in the story+ language. They haven't changed a bit.

```
#lang dtc/frames/cats

(cat rotate redify)
```

This still produces a red cat image:

What's different is that we'll now use a special symbol when we want the computer to leave a story uninterpreted.

```
#lang dtc/frames/cats
```

```
`(cat rotate redify)
```

That's all. That little backtick is all we need to mark a Story as uninterpreted. This makes it easy to change an interpreted story to an uninterpreted one, or vice versa.

Note a small difference from before: Now, when we leave a Story uninterpreted, it is *really* uninterpreted. The language doesn't even turn it into an image. It just leaves the text exactly the way it is. The language returns the Story as typed:

```
`(cat rotate redify)
```

Don't worry, though. There is still a way to create images of Stories in this new language. We can use the `image` frame Story with an uninterpreted inner Story.

```
#lang dtc/frames/cats
```

```
(image `(cat rotate redify))
```

This program is a Story with a Story inside. The "frame Story" begins with the Moment `image` – which has a special meaning (like `cat`, `rotate`, and `redify`). It instructs the computer to perform the Story of turning another Story into an image. In this Story-in-a-Story, the outer Story has two Moments: `image` and the entire uninterpreted story `(cat rotate redify).

When the above is interpreted, the output is the familiar:

Let's zoom out and look at the Story that produced the image above, but converted to an image itself:

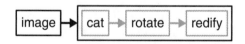

You can probably see that the cognitive complexity has increased. What would have been a standalone Story in the last chapter is now but a Moment in a different Story. The distinction between Moments and Stories has broken down – removing a syntactic barrier that was keeping programs in the last chapter simple. Abandoning simplicity yields both expressive power and cognitive difficulties – a sword with a double edge.

We've seen the above Story in code, and as an image. What about as an English story? Here are a few possible interpretations:

```
Picture, in your mind, if you please,
    the Story whose Moments are cat, rotate, and redify.
```

```
Once upon a time, a computer turned the following story into a
picture:
    `(cat rotate redify)
```

```
Computer! I hereby command you to make the story `(cat rotate
redify) into an image
    by placing arrows between each Moment and rendering the
result to the screen.
```

```
The wizard waved her magic wand and transformed a Story about
rotating and redifying a cat into an image of a Story about
rotating and redifying a cat.
```

Order Word

We want to call attention to one interesting thing about the above story, namely that the Moments might seem backward if you are used to English word order. You might expect to see the moments swapped:

```
#lang dtc/frames/cats
```

```
(`(cat rotate redify) image)
```

This does match the grammatical structure of: "The Story `(cat rotate redify) becomes an image." However, this program will not run. It isn't how we implemented #lang dtc/frames/cats.

The #lang dtc/story+/cats, on the other hand, *did* match English word order: "take a cat, rotate it, and turn it red," or (cat rotate red). Why then did we choose to deviate from this pattern in designing the dtc/frames/cats language?

Partly, it is because there are linguistic traditions in computer languages, and we wanted you to see languages in this book that follow these traditions because you are likely to see them again (e.g., in Python, Racket, Ruby, or Java). One such tradition is to put the verb at the beginning, followed by noun-like things. You've already seen this with programs from Chapter 1:

```
#lang dtc/hello/normal
```

```
(print "HELO")
```

Or:

```
#lang dtc/hello/animation
```

```
(print "HELO")
```

It is common in coding to put the verb first – following the English convention for the imperative voice (giving orders). When we command, we place the verb at the beginning and omit the subject.

Run the marathon. Eat the apple. Tell the story. Open the gate. Power the dynamos. Print "HELO". Image the story.

Although "run," "power," "print," and "image" can all function as both nouns and verbs – the interpretation when they are at the beginning of a sentence (or the beginning of a Story) is that it is an imperative verb.

Although we can certainly make computer languages that permute this order (as we did with the dtc/frames/cats language), it is less common. We did this with cats in the last chapter to make Stories more like stories. We wanted the cat to be like the hero, introduced at the beginning of the Story. We wanted the cat to be undergoing a series of transformations in each subsequent Moment. We felt this would be a good way to leverage your understanding of English stories to help you understand the cat language's semantics.

As for putting the verb-y Moment first, if it seems annoying that in one chapter you learned one convention and then it was changed on you in the very next chapter – welcome to the multilingual landscape of coding.

Easing the Transition

To ease the transition, we actually designed our new language to work both ways, at least when it comes to cats. This . . .

```
#lang dtc/frames/cats

(cat rotate redify)
```

. . . does the same thing as the following Story within a Story:

```
#lang dtc/frames/cats

(redify (rotate cat))
```

In this latter Story, the "frame Story" and the inner Story are both interpreted. Your intuition from the language of arithmetic can be helpful: Any sub Stories must be interpreted first for the framing Story to come to completion. You can think of redify as a command to turn *something* red – that something being the output of the sub Story, (rotate cat).

A few English interpretations that preserve the order of the words in the above Story might be:

```
The computer shall redify whatever image it gets
   after interpreting (rotate cat)
```

Or:

```
You're going to redify something, but before you
   do that, you need to rotate a cat.
   That rotated cat is what you redify.
```

Or:

```
Once upon a time, the redification of a rotated cat occurred.
```

These may be a bit more verbally cumbersome (and harder to make interesting) than "A cat goes upon an epic journey in which it rotates and becomes red – forever changed from that point onward." But the alternatives aren't bad, as long as you have accepted that the purpose of computer languages is not to match your native language precisely – but rather to abstract *away* from your native language ideas that can be written in very few characters and packed into a small amount of space. Sometimes a computer language will be designed to match your native language; sometimes it will be designed to be consistent with other computer languages. In either case, the intention of the designer is usually to make the language easier for you to learn and remember.

Magic Tricks

To return to our main idea here (Stories (within Stories)), it is worth noting that the new Story (`redify (rotate cat)`) is a Story with a Story inside of it, whereas the original was simply a flat Story (`cat rotate redify`). This is the first time in this book that we have seen an interpreted Story within another interpreted Story.

To better understand that Story in a Story, let us take that Story (`redify (rotate cat)`) and view it as an image:

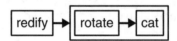

In order to produce this image, we used a Story within a Story within a Story. But the inner Stories were both uninterpreted:

```
#lang dtc/frames/cats

(image
  `(redify (rotate cat)))
```

(You are probably seeing, by now, that the number of Stories-within-Stories can be determined by counting the number of parenthetical statements (like this one (or this one)) inside the program).

If we wanted to turn the above story into a picture, we simply wrap it into another frame Story, and make the inner Story uninterpreted:

```
#lang dtc/frames/cats

(image
  `(image
     `(redify (rotate cat))))
```

Note that the output may seem to be missing one of the Moments (the first `image`). However, that outermost Moment was the one that *produced* this image.

The outermost frame Story will always be missing – for that is the Story that, by "coming true," created the image of the nested Story.

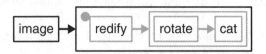

Here's one more level of framing, using the same pattern:

```
#lang dtc/frames/cats
(image
 `(image
   `(image
     `(redify (rotate cat)))))
```

Output:

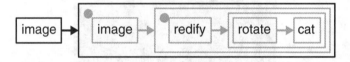

Every time we want to turn an interpreted story into a picture, we need to add another frame Story... Then, this too becomes a Story that can only be turned into a picture if we add yet *another* frame Story around it. You're seeing, in syntax, the exact effect that can be rendered visually in pictures like these (Yau 2019):

This is part of a series of nested paintings in which each person paints the last person's photograph and then (to create the frame image) photographs themselves holding the painting. It's a beautiful modern instantiation of an artistic motif.

The original 1904 advertisement that gave the visual effect its name (the "Droste effect") contained a single iteration.

We'll see more such tricks in the exercises in the next chapter. For the moment, let us pivot to the next obvious language feature. Above, we put uninterpreted Stories inside of interpreted ones. However, we shall also add the dual of that feature: to splice interpreted ones into uninterpreted ones.

To see how splicing works, consider this uninterpreted Story:

```
#lang dtc/frames/cats

`(redify (rotate cat))
```

In this language, the output for a Story like this is exactly what we put in. That's what "uninterpreted" means when you take it to its logical extreme. It means: "Don't give me any meanings." It means: "I mean what I mean."

The computer's response, then, is basically:

```
`(redify (rotate cat))
```

But when we add a comma in the nested Story, we are able to escape out of the uninterpretation and interpret *that part only*.

```
#lang dtc/frames/cats
```

```
`(redify ,(rotate cat))
```

So, the result is an uninterpreted Story containing an actual rotated cat. The cat has been spliced in:

```
`(redify            )
```

Remember that naming this is critical, so it's best not to think of those symbols as the "backtick" or the "comma." It's better to call them the "don't interpret" symbol and the "do interpret" symbol (or the "escape" symbol). Why would you call it a comma if it is being used in a completely different linguistic sense? We chose the backtick and the comma because these symbols have been used in this way in the Scheme programming language for many years, and we wanted to stick with a well-known language's syntactic conventions while illustrating the concepts in this chapter. Theoretically, we could have chosen any set of symbols, though.

It can be helpful to think of the backtick as a mark that is high on the line – like someone raising their hand, saying, "Hey, wait. Don't interpret anything in this Story." And the comma is like someone lowering their hand, saying, "Actually, I changed my mind. *Do* interpret this inner Story."

Let's cover a few more examples, to get a feel for how we can now mix and match both kinds of Stories, one inside the other, inside the other, inside the other, like Russian nesting dolls.

That is how large programs are built – out of smaller ones.

The three Moments in the story below are given by escaped, interpreted stories. At least one of those interpreted Stories has another interpreted Story within it. Oh, and there are pictures of cats involved.

Compare the story below to the English paragraph above. They both serve their purposes. But when it comes to economy of space, the code wins. It expresses a surprising amount in a surprisingly small space. A good notation for an abstract concept should almost always be shorter and more visually clear (to people fluent in the language) than the human language interpretation. That's the whole point of designing a new language in the first place.

```
#lang dtc/frames/cats

(image
 `(,(cat)
   ,(rotate cat)
   ,(redify (rotate cat)))))
```

Here's a Story of cats throughout history.

```
#lang dtc/frames/cats

(image
 `((cat)
   (edison-cat)
   (first-viral-cat)
   (authors-cat)))
```

Which produces the rather uninteresting image of a single frame Story, each of whose moments is actually a Story with its own single moment.

cat → edison-cat → first-viral-cat → authors-cat

Here is the same Story, but with Moments that are "escaped." By interpreting those inner Moments, we get a much more visually interesting output.

```
#lang dtc/frames/cats

(image
 `(,(cat)
    ,(edison-cat)
    ,(first-viral-cat)
    ,(authors-cat)))
```

Output:

Here is a Story, where all the cats are sideways.

```
#lang dtc/frames/cats

(image
 `(,(rotate (rotate cat))
    ,(rotate (rotate edison-cat))
    ,(rotate (rotate first-viral-cat))))
```

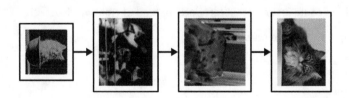

We can use the same trick to tilt the whole thing.

```
#lang dtc/frames/cats

(rotate
 (image
  `(,(rotate (rotate cat))
    ,(rotate (rotate edison-cat))
    ,(rotate (rotate first-viral-cat)))))
```

Output:

Or, if we could just rotate it leftward instead of rightward . . .

```
#lang dtc/frames/cats

(rotate-left
 (rotate-left
  (image
   `(,(rotate (rotate cat))
     ,(rotate (rotate edison-cat))
     ,(rotate (rotate first-viral-cat))))))
```

Output

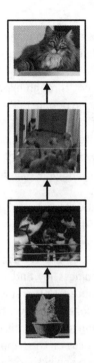

Admit it. When we started this chapter by saying that we were going to augment our language with the ability to put Stories within Stories, you didn't expect to be making towers of cats.

Languages are infinite things. Sometimes we create a language, begin to explore its infinite possibilities, and find ourselves surprised. Our languages are larger than we are.

So it goes, though. The ancient Mesopotamians didn't realize the full ramifications of their linguistic innovations either. Did the first person to mark a clay tablet with a meaningful symbol realize that this was the Moment that history would begin? Did the first "coder" to write down instructions on a clay tablet realize they were doing something that would, by the twenty-first century, be mechanizable? New forms of written expression can be powerful in ways unfathomable to their creators.

To be continued...

A LANGUAGE WITHIN
Implicit Learning

There are two ways to learn a second language – implicitly and explicitly – and some argue that only one of them is worth focusing on (Krashen 2013).

Implicit learning is the kind of learning that all children experience as they acquire their native tongues – not through explicit instruction about grammar rules. Rather, they learn by hearing people talk and seeing people sign.

We'll begin with a series of exercises that ask you to write code that you haven't been taught how to write yet, in a language that we haven't mentioned until this point. This style of exercise is designed to facilitate implicit learning. It asks you to perform a task in a language that you don't know. You're supposed to guess, and get things wrong.

The act of attempting is what will teach you. How, you ask?

You'll attempt something, and if you get it wrong, the computer will tell you. Maybe you'll get an error, or maybe it just won't do what you wanted it to do. Either way, you'll change your code and try again. Then, when it finally works, you'll experience a burst of happiness, joy, and dopamine. Then you'll repeat the cycle. As you program the computer; it programs you too.

People who claim to have "taught themselves to code" are people who learned to enjoy and employ that learning loop. Try; fail; try; fail; try; fail; succeed.

A tip we give our students: Focus on the happiness at the end. Students who take the red error messages personally tend to become bitter and frustrated. Programming fluency into our brains is a long road. Bitterness at the beginning can jeopardize the journey.

Animation

Read through the exercises even if you're not doing them. Run them in your mind.

Exercise

Type in this code.

```
#lang dtc/frames/animations

(animation
  `(1 2 3))
```

Now write similar code but with the numbers reversed.

Yes, you could write:

```
#lang dtc/frames/animations

(animation
  `(3 2 1))
```

But what if we told you that reverse was a word in the language? Could you use that instead – along with a nested (story (story (story)))?

That would be the way cooler way.

Why? Because you would be asking the computer to shoulder the cognitive burden of reversing the numbers.

Exercise

```
#lang dtc/frames/animations

(animation
  (range 20))
```

Make it animate up to 20 and then back down to 0.

Hint. Use the documentation.

Meta-hint. This is the last time we'll give hints about using the documentation. Skilled coders always have documentation pages open while working in a language they don't know.

They do it because they are skilled; and they are skilled because they do it.

Before you run the following, try to imagine what will happen. Make guesses, picture the output in your mind, then see if you are right. If you're wrong, ask yourself why. Make this a habit of mind.

```
#lang dtc/frames/animations

(animation
  `(cat edison-cat first-viral-cat))
```

```
#lang dtc/frames/animations

(animation
  `(,(cat)
    ,(edison-cat)
    ,(first-viral-cat)))
```

```
#lang dtc/frames/animations

(animation
  `(,(rotate (cat))
    ,(rotate (edison-cat))
    ,(rotate (first-viral-cat))))
```

Exercise

Make an animation of 8 frames, with a single cat image rotating clockwise. It should rotate a full 360 degrees, in 8 jumps.

Exercise

Make an animation of 8 frames, with a single cat image rotating counter-clockwise.
Use rotate-left.

Exercise

Make an animation of 8 frames, with a single cat image rotating counter-clockwise. Do not use rotate-left. Remember that two rights don't make a wrong, but six rights (in this language) do make a left.

Exercise

Walk animation:

```
#lang dtc/frames/animations

(animation
  `(,(cat-walk 1)
    ,(cat-walk 2)
    ,(cat-walk 3)
    ,(cat-walk 4)))
```

Make an upside-down animation of a cat walking.

Hint. You can't rotate an entire animation, but you can rotate each Moment of a Story (each frame of the animation).

Exercise

In the code from the previous exercise, reduce the animation speed by half.
   Hint. Double each Moment.

Exercise

```
#lang dtc/frames/animations

(animation
  `(cat ,(rotate (cat))
    edison-cat ,(rotate (edison-cat))
    first-viral-cat ,(rotate (first-viral-cat))))
```

That is basically a sequence of flashcards. But it goes by really fast. By adding a duplicate of each Moment, you can make each image last longer – essentially, slowing the flashcards down.

One final note. Remember that, in most languages, the whitespace doesn't matter to the syntax – which means you can use whitespace as a tool to communicate your intent. Many programmers have strong opinions about how you format your code.

We'll let you form your own tastes.

You could write the above like this, making it extremely difficult to read:

```
#lang dtc/frames/animations

(animation
  `(cat ,(rotate (cat)) edison-cat ,(rotate (edison-cat)) first-viral-cat ,(rotate (first-viral-cat))))
```

Or you could align your code to aid the eye:

```
#lang dtc/frames/animations

(animation
  `(cat            ,(rotate (cat))
    edison-cat     ,(rotate (edison-cat))
    first-viral-cat ,(rotate (first-viral-cat))))
```

Napoleon's Risky Maneuver

Here is an image of what could easily be a Moment in a chess Story. Indeed, the first Moment of every such Story:

In this section, we'll present a Story of the first few moves of a historic chess match between Napoleon Bonaparte and a chess-playing "machine" called the Turk, in 1809. The story behind the Story is that, playing white was Napoleon and playing black was the "machine" – which, in fact, had a chess master named Johann Baptist Allgaier hidden within the table beneath the chess board. From within, Allgaier could manipulate the arm of a mechanical wizard that appeared to be playing against Napoleon. It is one of the greatest hoaxes of all time, an illusion that fooled people worldwide in its 84 years of touring exhibitions throughout Europe and America.

The hardware's reconstruction shows us that it would have looked like this (Wikimedia 2009):

Amazingly, we can also reconstruct that famous game, move by move, because each was recorded – written down and transmitted through time. We now transmit them to you, via a programming language. The `#lang dtc/frames/animations` contains vocabulary words for conjuring an image of any position from that historic game:

```
#lang dtc/frames/animations

(image
  `(,(napoleon/turk 1)
    ,(napoleon/turk 2)
    ,(napoleon/turk 3)))
```

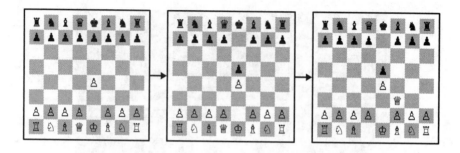

In only the third Moment of the game, it is hard to tell who is winning – though Napoleon's choice of advancing his queen early is a signal of things to come. It is an aggressive move – but a risky one. Perhaps he underestimated his wizard opponent.

Exercise

Find out how the game ends by running the following code and watching the Story animate to completion. In the final Moment of the game, whose king is in checkmate?

```
#lang dtc/frames/animations

(animate (napoleon/turk))
```

The point is that games and Stories are related. Configuration of physical things (pieces, squares, cards, dice, boards, tokens, etc.) – these are the syntax of games. For many such games, the configuration of these syntactic items completely expresses the state of the game at any given time. Thus, each Moment of a Story describing the game can simply be an alphanumeric description of how those physical things are configured.

In chess, we only need to know where the pieces are in relation to the 64 squares. This sort of abstraction describes any moment in chess. Exactly how Napoleon shifted in his chair and scratched his head, exactly what Allagier pondered while secretly playing against the Emperor of France from within a box – these details have been lost to history. But the abstraction of the game remains – the list of Moments that shows the Story of the board, the Story of those 32 black and white pieces on those 64 squares.

The following produces an image of the fourth move of the game:

```
#lang dtc/frames/animations
```

```
(napoleon/turk 4)
```

Output:

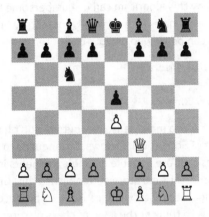

The image is but a Moment in a larger Story.

However, we wish to reveal one secret beneath the surface. This image Moment was actually created from a 64-Moment Story that describes where all of the pieces on the board are.

```
#lang dtc/frames/animations
```

```
(napoleon/turk-raw 4)
```

If reasonably formatted for the eye:

```
`(R _ B Q K B N R
  P P P P _ P P P
  _ _ N _ _ _ _ _
  _ _ _ _ P _ _ _
  _ _ b _ p _ _ _
  _ _ _ _ _ q _ _
  p p p p _ p p p
  r n b _ k _ n r)
```

Consider this algorithm: Settle your eyes in the top left square of the chess board; now begin writing the first letter of each piece that you see as you scan across each row in turn; ending with the square in the bottom right. You would see a Rook in the top left square. Then, a Knight (which is traditionally given the letter "N," because the King outranks it). Use uppercase letters for black and lowercase for white pieces. And so on.

A Story produced by this algorithm can be cumbersome to look at. Turning it into an image with `image` gives a chain of 64 moments, which is too large to be printable, but which can be viewed on your computer.

```
#lang dtc/frames/animations
```

```
(image (napoleon/turk-raw 4))
```

The output is not easy to make sense of – but we don't have to. We only need to know that this sort of Story is what allows the language to produce the human-friendly chess images that are suitable as single moments in the larger Story of a game. The `image-chess` frame story accomplishes this. Giving `image-chess` a different piece-configuration Story will cause it to produce a different image. These images allow us to think at the level of chess pictures, while the software "thinks" at the level of a 64-Moment-long alphanumeric Story representation of piece configurations.

Thus, with a single frame Story change, we can go from producing something unprintable to something crystal clear.

```
#lang dtc/frames/animations
```

```
(image-chess (napoleon/turk-raw 4))
```

When we play or watch a chess game, we think of the story more like: Napoleon moves his pawn, the Turk responds, etc.

That's a correct story. There are other correct stories, too. As a coder, it behooves us to learn many ways of telling Stories – many ways of abstracting the truth from a situation. There are many ways of looking at stateful systems like games, and many different ways of telling stories about them. One kind of story may come more naturally to our minds – that is, those phrased in sentences with subjects, verbs, and objects: "Napoleon moves the pawn," "Turk moves the other pawn," etc.

Equally true is the other story: "The pieces are configured like this," "Now they are like this," "Now they are like that," etc.

Those with high levels of story flexibility can switch between either worldview at will.

Noughts and Crosses

What do you think this Story is about?

```
`(_ _ O O X X _ _ _)
```

Does your eye prefer the code like this?

```
`(_ _ O
  O X X
  _ _ _)
```

And of course, to make it even more visually clear, create an image like this.

```
#lang dtc/frames/animations

(image-tic-tac-toe
 `(_ _ O
   O X X
   _ _ _))
```

Exercise

What happens when you nest an uninterpreted tic-tac-toe story inside of an interpreted frame Story that begins with image-chess?

Try this and assess the results:

```
#lang dtc/frames/animations

(image-chess
 `(_ _ O
   O X X
   _ _ _))
```

Now, try this and assess the results:

```
#lang dtc/frames/animations
```

```
(image-tic-tac-toe (napoleon/turk-raw))
```

What other constructions can you make in `#lang dtc/frames/animations` that look syntactically valid, but still cause the computer to produce an error when the program runs?

Sometimes Stories can be grammatically correct – but semantically silly. It like a nonsensical English sentence:

```
The cat's loom smashed the Luddites rooks in ancient Egypt.
```

The mind has the ability to make up meanings for such sentences – perhaps by imagining an alternative universe wherein the sentence might be uttered. We would not, however, want computers to make up their own sense for things while they are automating the planes and stock markets of the world. We will discuss this in the final chapter.

Round Stories; Square Frames

The moral of the errors above is that a frame Story and its nested Stories will often need to match. There are few frame Stories that can handle *any* sort of nested Story, regardless of its shape and structure.

The `image` frame Story is one such power Story; it will create an image out of almost any nested Story. The `image-chess` frame Story, however, will only create images out of Stories of a certain shape – one that describes where chess pieces are.

The Story `'(_ _ O O X X _ _ _)` cannot be nested in a frame Story beginning with `image-chess`. Likewise, Scheherazade could not have told a 5-minute story to her sociopathic husband. The nested stories *had* to last all night. They *had* to end on a cliffhanger. Otherwise, she would have died, and she would have failed in her mission to save others.

In coding, as in literature, frame stories and their substories must match – meaning that writers of nested Stories must understand which matchings make sense and which do not.

We see this broad concept at the level of programming languages themselves. Java reads in text and runs it. But it can't read just any text. If you try to load up a Racket program, Java will crash. If you try to load Java in Python, Python will crash. If you try to load a `#lang dtc/story/cats` program in the `#lang dtc/frames/animations` language, then `#lang dtc/frames/animations` will crash.

If you tried to nest a tic-tac-toe master inside the mechanical Turk, would it have been able to play chess against one of the greatest military commanders of all time? Would it have been able to play correct chess at all?

Exercise

Make an animation of a tic-tac-toe game that ends in a draw.

Hint. First, use `image-tic-tac-toe` to turn each game state into an image. Then combine all of those image Moments into an uninterpreted story that you can nest within `animate`.

Exercise

Make an animation of a chess game that ends in checkmate in under 5 moves.

Hint. Search the internet for "Fool's Mate" or "Scholar's Mate."

To be continued . . .

LANGUAGES WITHOUT

Illusions of Mind

The mechanical Turk was not a true automaton – but rather a clever illusion. What appeared to be a machine containing human intelligence was really just a machine containing a human. By being erected around a human grandmaster, it was no more a chess player than a room in which a grandmaster might happen to be sitting. You could write your chess moves on paper and pass them under the door to such a room, and the grandmaster within could pass their moves back to you. The idea that you are playing against the room is but an illusion – one that requires a mind on the other side of the door.

Yet, for an illusion, the mechanical Turk was prophetic. Within two hundred years, an IBM computer called Deep Blue was beating the world's reigning chess champion, Gary Kasparov. Sitting across a typical wooden chessboard from Deep

Blue's facilitator in 1997, Kasparov played 6 games, losing three, winning two, and drawing one. After each of Kasparov's moves, the facilitator relayed the move to Deep Blue via a computer keyboard; after Deep Blue's response, the facilitator would make the move on the chessboard for Kasparov and the world to see.

It was not unlike Napoleon's match against the Turk – in which Napoleon reportedly sat at one chessboard, while the Turk was displayed in a roped-off area nearby (Ewart 1980). The owner of the Turk (a man named Mälzel, owner of the automaton, collaborating with the hidden grandmaster) relayed moves between the two chessboards.

But in 1997, there was no illusion. Deep Blue contained no flesh-and-blood human beings. At its heart was no mind – but merely software. Deep Blue was just executing instructions written by flesh-and-blood human beings. Those instructions, as written by the IBM team of programmers and grandmaster chess players, are what vanquished the greatest chess mind of the time. This too was prophetic of things to come. Today, no human chess player stands a chance against software.

IBM gets the credit for that moment in history – but to give them all the credit would be to ignore thousands of years and billions of person hours spent in pursuit of a single human endeavor: Making the world around us do things that, previously, only the mind could do. It is a story that begins even before the dawn of history – before writing.

When exactly it began, amidst the darkness of prehistory, it is impossible to say. Quite ancient it is, though: a magic of the mind requiring no tools of stone or even of wood. It requires the fingers alone.

Dactylonomy: Digits to Digital

American education systems generally ban finger counting at an early age. Although the value of this is debated by scientists (Moeller et al. 2011), it is a cultural norm that is hard to shake.

Finger counting by adults can be a sign of a mind that is not sufficiently trained to keep a socially acceptable amount of computation internal. While it makes sense to teach children their numbers while referencing their fingers and toes, there is legitimate fear that continued reliance on fingers as a mnemonic aid while learning arithmetic might lead to bad habits and weak skills.

This isn't true in all countries, and it hasn't been true throughout all of history. The act of using fingers to do mathematics is one of the oldest and perhaps the first "technology" for externalizing mathematical computations – with the dactylonomist storing numerical digits in the configuration of their... well, digits.

It is no coincidence that the word "digit" refers to our fingers and toes, but also to technologies like the "digital computer" and to sweeping historical phenomena, like the "digital age" or the "digital revolution." The language we use for today's technology hides the historical importance of finger counting in plain sight. In the late 1400s, English began to borrow the word "digit" from Latin (dictionary.com 2019) – where it meant "fingers" or "toes" and also "number below 10" – due to the fact that people can (and do) indicate such numbers on their fingers.

References to finger counting in ancient texts suggest that the practice is extremely old and was passed down by oral traditions, making it older than history itself, much older than writing. In one of the oldest known Egyptian texts, the *Book of the Dead*, it was recounted that the ability to count upon one's fingers was required by Aqen, the ferryman of the netherworld (Neugebauer 1969). He would challenge the souls of kings who wished to cross, asking if they knew the numbers of their fingers, and the appropriate reply (according to the *Book of the Dead*) was to recount a rhyme that paired Egyptian number vocabulary to the digits of both hands. This particular reply was one of many "spells" that a "magician" needed in the afterlife.

As Agarwal puts it in *Creators of Mathematical and Computational Sciences* (Agarwal and Sen 2014):

> Today every young child is able to count small numbers on his fingers, say up to 10, and learns the abstract concepts of addition and subtraction. In antiquity, counting was considered a talent as mystical and arcane as casting spells and calling the gods by name.

Although the abacus ushered in a powerful alternative externalization (for much bigger numbers), the art of finger counting did not die. Its persistence is analogous to the persistence of the spoken word in the face of the written word's invention. New technologies do not always make the old obsolete.

Arab thinkers wrote about finger counting – including methods for representing more numbers than just 10, as well as algorithms for doing more than addition and subtraction (i.e. square root approximations) (Bloom 2002).

Scholars have uncovered and translated various Arabic pedagogical poems that detail how to perform such mathematical magic, written in verse and rhyme to facilitate learning (Oaks 2018). What good, after all, is an algorithm for doing advanced arithmetic, if it cannot be learned? Oral tradition, poetry, and the written word came to the rescue – the state-of-the-art tools of the time for passing along such the knowledge of how to compute upon one's fingers.

In the year 725, a monk called the Venerable Bede penned a treatise called "De computo, vel loquela per gestum digitorum" (Giles 1843) – which translates to "On Computing and Speaking with the Fingers." It described how to form handshapes for numbers up to 9,999. His same methods, modified slightly, were reprinted more than half a millennium later in a 1494 text by Luca Pacioli – the *Summa de arithmetica, geometria, proportioni et proportionalita*. It was the most comprehensive mathematical text of the time – the first to describe double-entry bookkeeping, earning the author the title the "Father of Accounting." Why was the art of dactylonomy still being used in the late 1400s? More modern methods existed. The abacus had been around since the second century BCE, and the use of writing to do arithmetic was well known.

Our analog digits do have one magic power that paper and pencil lack: The calculations leave no trace. Those who have learned the art of dactylonomy can close their eyes, wiggle their fingers in what looks like an arcane spell, performing additions, subtractions, divisions, multiplications, square root approximations, and more – all with a high degree of accuracy and not a single lasting change in the environment around them. The fingers serve as storage – but only temporary, ephemeral storage. It was the original "digital storage," a safe and private place *because* of its ephemerality.

It is a strange kind of sign language – certainly capable of communicating one's mathematical thoughts to other fluent practitioners. But its true value seems to be less about others, more about oneself, more about aiding a certain kind of cognition. This sign language is a tool of the mind.

The art of dactylonomy is by no means lost to antiquity either. In the 1970s, American schools began to pilot an initiative to teach Chisanbop – a finger counting system invented in Korea. The method is an application of abacus-based arithmetic to the fingers, allowing the numbers 0 through 99 to be rapidly manipulated on two hands. Although many teachers were enthusiastic about the results, the initiative was dropped.

Perhaps this was done too hastily, however. In 2011, scientists began to once again question the traditional aversion to finger counting (Moeller et al. 2011). Recent research indicates that an awareness of one's fingers is an early predictor of numerical ability in children. Even adults when doing mental math inside an fMRI have been shown to activate neurological circuitry related to finger motions (Soylu et al. 2017). In 2017, at least one study showed that finger training for children can increase mathematical ability (Jay and Betenson 2017).

This being a book about teaching coding, we will not weigh in on the debate about dactylonomy. Rather, the debate itself serves to illustrate a deeper point – one that is less about mathematics and more about the relationship between the mind, the body, the external world, where a "computation" happens, and how that has changed throughout history.

A historical lens is key.

Computations that happen in software today once happened in the minds of yesterday. As educators in the age of software, the decisions we make about what computations to teach to the minds of today must always be informed by what the programming languages of tomorrow will be capable of.

Luckily, understanding the history of externalization is the key to understanding its future. For it has a kind of momentum to it.

Externalization

Dactylonomy may have been the human race's first-ever example of externalizing a mathematical operation – quite possibly predating even the use of "written" externalizations like tally sticks, the oldest of which is a baboon fibula that archaeologists call the Ishango bone (Wikimedia 2007), a calculating device that dates back to somewhere between 18,000 and 20,000 BCE, from a small fishing community buried beneath a volcanic eruption in Africa.

The marks on that bone have lived millennia longer than the fingers that marked it. Whatever finger shapes meant numbers for ancient humans shall be an eternal mystery.

Marks on the Ishango bone are *unarguably* externalized, whereas the finger shapes of dactylonomy are harder to classify: Handshapes are externally visible, but they are internal, too. The mind (from the inside) must *will* the fingers to maintain a certain shape; and you may not stop willing it lest the numbers evaporate.

The act of maintaining a handshape requires attention to tension in specific muscles. Your nervous system is engaged. Attention and working memory are being expended. Relax, and the storage is cleared. Though more ephemeral than marks upon clay or bone, dactylonomy is an externalization that works today as it did in Africa 20,000 years ago: The handshape, once established, can be maintained while not consciously thinking of the number anymore. The number is "at hand" – but not occupying the mind. Indeed, maintaining a handshape takes very little cognitive effort at all – something you can prove to yourself whenever you want: Arrange your hand into an arbitrary shape, then read a passage of a book, watch TV, or carry on a conversation. None of these should be demanding, cognitively speaking. You could safely forget the number, go about your business, and simply look at your hand to remind yourself.

Dactylonomy aids computation via the same mechanism that writing does: It decreases cognitive load. It frees up a kind of space that scientists have called "working memory" since approximately the 1960s (Miller et al. 1960). In 1956, George Miller published one of the most important and widely cited papers in psychology: "The Magic Number Seven, Plus or Minus Two: Some Limits on Our Capacity for Processing Information."

The concept Miller presented is well-known today, but to summarize: The number of "things" the average person can hold in short-term memory is somewhere between 5 and 9 ("7, plus or minus 2.") Some call this "Miller's Law" – implying that it describes certain physical limits of the mind. Indeed, all minds do buckle under the load of complex computations. We all have limits; and we all dream of transcending them.

Luckily, there are at least two ways to increase human performance beyond the apparent limitations of Miller's Law. One is "chunking," in which a person is able (over time) to combine many things into only one that needs be kept in working memory. We will discuss this in the next section. The other is our present topic: The storage and manipulation of information in the environment – including the very, very local "environment" of one's own fingers.

Technologies that facilitate storage and retrieval of numbers include dactylonomy, paper and pencil, tally sticks, the abacus, the calculator, and others. Storing of numbers in the environment *aids* the mind, but it doesn't allow it to fully relax while actually doing arithmetic. Some of the mind's precious resources must still be spent on the calculation. The numbers might be in the environment, yes, but what of the act of multiplying them together? Minds must keep track of the fact that a multiplication is being performed, whatever the current sum-so-far is, what additions remain to be done, and so on.

In the mid 1600s in France, the idea of removing even these burdens from the mind caught fire in a way that never really stopped.

The Spark of the Pascaline

In 1642, Blaise Pascal, a 19-year-old child math prodigy whose father was a tax supervisor, began building calculating machines. Pascal's devices were capable of storing numbers and actually adding or subtracting them automatically, using only the motion of gears, not the motion of the mind. It was a groundbreaking discovery that prompted King Louis XIV to decree a sort of patent on May 22, 1649:

> The main invention and movement is this, that every wheel and axis, moving to the 10 digits, will force the next to move to 1 digit and it is prohibited to make copies not only of the machine of Pascal, but also of any other calculating machine, without permission of Pascal. It is prohibited for foreigners to sell such machines in France, even if they are manufactured abroad. The violators of the privilege will have to pay penalty of 3 thousand livres.

In other words, Pascal – then only $19 + 1649 - 1642$ years of age – was given total control over any calculating devices made in France. He used this privilege to produce about 50 calculating machines, selling 20 of them. But the devices were not particularly easy to produce, and eventually Pascal busied himself with other things – for example, philosophy.

Still, the Pascaline was like a spark. It inspired Leibniz in 1672 to begin working on an improved calculator (called the "stepped reckoner") capable of multiplication and division. This was an obvious next step. The Pascalines could "do" multiplication – but only as repeated addition – meaning that the Pascaline operator multiplying $397 * 13$ would need to understand what multiplication means: that they must use the Pascaline to add 397 to itself 13 times, collecting a larger and larger sum. It was a loop to be executed by the mind, an algorithm to be learned. Simple though multiplication might sound, it still required that valuable resource: working memory.

The Pascaline could store the numbers and the addition operations, but part of the multiplication task still burdened the mind – and the fact that the human mind was still burdened by such a petty thing was what burdened Leibniz's mind. He wanted to make multiplication and division just as simple – just as mindless, just as mechanical. He achieved this in 1694 with a machine that looked like this:

More influential to computing, however, were the projects that Leibniz was *not* able to complete during his lifetime. What he built and what he imagined were centuries apart, if not more. He envisioned a world where mechanized processes would perform operations of the mind far beyond multiplication and division. In his words, he envisioned (Leibniz 1666):

> ... [A] general method in which all truths of the reason would be reduced to a kind of calculation. At the same time this would be a sort of universal language or script, but infinitely different from all those projected hitherto; for the symbols and even the words in it would direct reason; and errors, except those of fact, would be mere mistakes in calculation.

The Best of all Possible Languages

In a few short sentences, Leibniz foresaw much of our world today. The "reduction of reason to calculation" sums up the technological trend over the next few centuries: Increasingly sophisticated calculating devices would snatch up tasks (and eventually, professions) that once required human reason, leading to the software explosion that we are still in the midst of.

Then again, his most ambitious dreams are ahead of us still. It is unclear whether they represent a finish line for software or a line we will asymptotically approach but never reach. He imagined a "sort of universal language or script" that could mechanize thought – an optimistic description of computer languages even by today's standard. Then he goes on to add *additional* design features (Loemker 1976):

> [S]ome kind of language ... by which all concepts and things can be put into beautiful order, and with whose help different nations might communicate their thoughts and each read in his own language what another has written in his, yet no one has attempted a language or characteristic which includes at once both the arts of discovery and judgement, that is, one whose signs and characters serve the same purpose that arithmetical signs serve for numbers, and algebraic signs for quantities taken abstractly. Yet it does seem that since God has bestowed these two sciences [discovery and judgement] on mankind, he has sought to notify us that a far greater secret lies hidden in our understanding, of which these are but the shadows.

Leibniz was perhaps also the first language designer to grossly underestimate the time it would take to complete their project, and perhaps also the first language designer to experience "scope creep" – envisioning a language that can express all human concepts, can be legible across all cultures, and can lend itself to mechanically verifiable calculation.

Dijkstra lightheartedly teased him for this (Dijkstra 2001):

Like modern computing scientists, he invented impressive names for what had still to be invented, and, for good reasons not overly modest, he called his system no more and no less than "Characteristica Universalis." And again, like modern computing scientists, he grossly underestimated the time the project would take: he confidently prophesied that a few well-chosen men could do the job in five years, but the whole undertaking was at the time of such a radical novelty that even the genius of Leibniz did not suffice for its realization . . .

Leibniz did bend his genius to the task, however, wrestling with one of the hardest parts of language design – balancing its richness of features with its learnability:

[Let] the first terms, of the combination of which all others consist, be designated by signs; these signs will be a kind of alphabet. It will be convenient for the signs to be as natural as possible – e.g., for one, a point; for numbers, points; for the relations of one entity with another, lines; for the variation of angles and of extremities in lines, kinds of relations. If these are correctly and ingeniously established, this universal writing will be as easy as it is common, and will be capable of being read without any dictionary; at the same time, a fundamental knowledge of all things will be obtained. The whole of such a writing will be made of geometrical figures, as it were, and of a kind of pictures – just as the ancient Egyptians did, and the Chinese do today. Their pictures, however, are not reduced to a fixed alphabet . . . with the result that a tremendous strain on the memory is necessary, which is the contrary of what we propose.

Classically optimistic, Leibniz imagines a written-yet-visual language that is instantly comprehensible regardless of culture or prior training. He imagines that it will have a small number of symbols, so that they can be easily memorized. And he imagines that it will allow for lines and layout to express relationships in a richly visual way. Given this feature set, we can forgive ourselves for not living up to Leibniz's optimism. No race of mere humans could. Still, we have perhaps not done badly: Although we have not created one universal language, we have created many highly specialized ones.

We had come far enough by the year 2000, that Dijkstra could see in the science of computing the ongoing progress toward Leibniz's dream (Dijkstra 2001):

Parts of Leibniz's Dream became reality, and it is quite understandable that this happened mostly in Departments of Computing Science, rather than in Departments of Mathemetics [sic]. Firstly, the computing scientists were in more urgent need of such calculational techniques because, by virtue of its mechanical interpretability, each programming language is eo ipso [*sic*] a formal system to start with. Secondly, for the manipulation of uninterpreted formulae, the world of computing provided a most sympathetic environment because we are so used to it: it is what compilers and theorem provers do all the time! And, finally, when the symbol manipulation would become too labour-intensive [*sic*], computing science could provide the tools for mechanical assistance. In short, the world of computing became Leibniz's home; that it was my home as well was my luck.

At this point, looking back upon history, it should be clear where the momentum was heading after Leibniz – directly toward the world as we know it today. The word "computer" once meant a *person* that computes. It was a literal job title until the mid-1900s. Today, of course, it has come to refer to the machines themselves, which have taken on the tasks that previously could only be performed by burdening human minds. The centuries between Leibniz's calculator and today were marked by increasingly advanced machines that could perform more and more tasks that had once required minds. Some were delightfully simple and powerful – such as the slide rule. Some were feats of mechanical engineering – that is, the differential analyzer, which could solve differential equations in 1927 without the use of electricity.

Indeed, Leibniz's calculator (taken as point A) and his dreams (taken as point B) give us a conceptual line L (for "Leibniz") that helps unify the history of computing that came before Leibniz and the history that came after, making Leibniz himself something of a historical and philosophical midpoint between primitive computational activities like dactylonomy, tally sticks, and mechanical calculators and our modern ones that we call "computers," the ones with which we communicate via "language or script." Leibniz communicated with his calculator by turning dials to input numbers and then pulling a crank to add or subtract; repeated additions (multiplication) or subtractions (division) required the additional use of a dial. It would not be many years until you could feed into a computer something that looked like a script. But history dutifully followed that line L: With the machines of the world evolving through many years of mechanical user-interfaces, punch card-based systems, and so on before we would finally arrive at the modern developer experience: Where we write programs of all sizes using all manner of languages and effortlessly execute them upon whatever machines we wish, to solve all manner of human problems, and even to create tools that eliminate entire categories of problems.

The mechanization of language and thought for the betterment of all mankind – Leibniz's dream.

Let us jump backwards and look for that line L more carefully this time. If we look closely, we see that the trend toward getting our environment (via machines) to perform tasks on behalf of our minds is matched with a parallel trend – the line L (perhaps for "Language" as well as "Leibniz") in which we create new ways of interacting with those machines, configuring them, reconfiguring them, and eventually writing instructions directly into them. The machines became increasingly programmable – with that programmability culminating, finally, with computer languages as we know them today – which allow us to draft massive, multilingual textual artifacts to control our machines. From the twiddling of fingers which stored numbers in prehistoric times to the twiddling of fingers which sculpt computer programs today, the wizards of the human race have always employed our physical digits and the best-known magic of the day for making the world do storage and calculation on the mind's behalf.

Automatons

Meanwhile, the trend toward externalizing the work of minds was never just about numbers, but also about art and animation.

Mechanisms such as pulleys, steam engines, hydraulics, and other mechanical engineering techniques were known in ancient Greece – many being leveraged for entertainment, for example, theater and the Olympic games. Of the island of Rhodes, Pindar wrote an oft-quoted verse that conjures for us today a picture of automata that have long since returned to dust (Wheelwright 1837):

```
The animated figures stand
Adorning every public street
And seem to breathe in stone, or
move their marble feet
```

These odd stone puppets may have been powered by water that moved gears, thus producing the illusions of life. Unlike Pascalines or stepped reckoners, however, the motion of gears within these animated figures produced no "answer" or "result" in the mathematical sense. Whereas the Pascaline's gears moved mathematical symbols, the Olympic figures' gears moved limbs of stone. What they both had in common is that they both captured, in mechanisms and gears, something that would previously have required a human mind's attention and working memory.

The Olympic figures moved in a way that would have required a human operator within – a kind of puppeteer hiding in every animated figure, on every public street. Instead, the configuration of gears allowed the puppeteer to be deleted. To change the motion of these automated puppets, an ancient Greek "coder" would have had to encode the new desired movements into new gears, then presumably open up their stone chests and surgically swap certain innards for others. Now, with a new instructions encoded in new gears, the stone figures would breathe and march to a different rhythm.

It is unlikely that the mechanical engineers of Rhodes accomplished their illusion by hiding real, human puppeteers within their automata. The recovery of mechanisms of tremendous complexity and craftsmanship, like the Antikythera mechanism, gives us little doubt today that the Greeks were capable. Its interacting bronze gears could simulate the motions of the sun and moon, the constellations of the zodiac, automatically calculating the dates of solar eclipses and the dates of the four-year Olympic games. The device was dated to 87 BC, but devices of similar complexity would not be created again until centuries later.

In 850 A.D., the Arab work called the *Book of Ingenious Devices* described 100 devices, some of which are recognizable precursors to codeable machines. Consider these three and ask yourself what they all have in common:

- A fountain that could be configured to spray water in artistic alternating patterns.
- A water-powered organ that could play music encoded upon cylinders with raised pins.
- A steam-powered flute player that could also play music encoded upon cylinders.

In the case of the flute player, as the cylinder turned, raised parts could lift various holes in the flute, changing the pitch (Koetsier 2001). Here we begin to see evidence of machines with clear codability. All that was required to recode such a flute player was to swap out some of the innards of the machine – in the case of the musical automata, this would have been a cylinder whose raised parts were code for musical notes, and whose positions upon the cylinder encoded when those notes would play. The pegs reached up like fingers – a metaphor apt in two ways: 1) they mechanically play the part of fingers upon the flute; 2) they are digits of information in this system.

After having circulated throughout the Arab world for almost 400 years, the *Book of Ingenious Devices* inspired a similarly titled book, *The Book of Knowledge of Ingenious Mechanical Devices* – which described not only how such devices worked, but how to build them. This book carried on the tradition of programmability in its machines, describing one "band" of four automata that shared a boat and would play a variety of musical instruments as the boat circled a moat. The drummer could be coded by adjusting pegs that controlled its beat.

Of particular note when it comes to automations is the Canard Digérateur, or the Digesting Duck – if only for the fact that it produced neither music, nor mathematical result – but simply poop. It could walk around, "eat" grain, and (appear to) defecate digested versions of what it had just eaten. In spite of producing nothing nearly as useful as the result of a mathematical calculation, the compelling illusion of the duck brought joy to many and was famous enough that Voltaire dramatically proclaimed that without the Digesting Duck "you would have nothing to remind you of the glory of France." It contained a reservoir of dyed, mushed up plant matter that was released at intervals after the duck began to eat. Presumably the animation could have been recoded to poop out whatever could fit in its reservoir – from water, to liquid mercury, to real duck poop – simply by swapping what was contained in its storage. Whether its inventor Vaucanson ever did so, we don't know.

This creator of the crapping duck was assigned by the chief minister of Louis XV to begin investigating the weaving industry, with the hope of creating an automated loom. He was the first to begin designing looms that could be programmed with punch cards – a script encoded as punched holes.

The loom language can be seen punched into the cards above the machine (Wikimedia 2019):

Jacquard's loom was inspired by Vaucanson's original design. It was the worldwide rise of automation like Jacquard's in industries like weaving that simultaneously turned weaving into unskilled labor and launched what we call today the First Industrial Revolution. The word "drawboy" used to mean a literal boy who perched atop a loom and would pull up threads physically; it came to mean part of a power loom that performed the same function automatically.

Weavers who sat closer to the ground who once needed to bear in mind the details of the pattern they were weaving now found themselves under considerably less cognitive load – and not in the good kind of way. Their minds were soon to be unemployed.

King Ludd

By the year 1811, the Luddite movement began in Nottingham – named after a fictitious leader Ned Ludd, who supposedly lived in the forest like Robin Hood. The movement would have laborers smashing machines such as the Jacquard looms – which they viewed (not altogether wrongly) as the reason for their loss of livelihood. Although the violence had largely subsided by 1816, the height of the movement saw times in which there were more British troops fighting their own Luddite citizens than fighting Napoleon in the Napoleonic wars (Hobsbawm 1964).

Yet as the fighting subsided, the progress of automation did not. As Chris Trueman puts it (Trueman 2015):

[The power loom] ended the life style of skilled weavers. In the 1790's, weavers were well paid. Within 30 years many had become labourers in factories as their skill had now been taken over by machines. In 1813, there were only 2,400 power looms in Britain. By 1850, there were 250,000.

We find for the first time an automaton that seemed to take on a life of its own – not in the sense of getting up and marching around on its own marbled feet, and not in the sense of being able to play chess on its own, but rather in the sense that automation itself "went viral" and no one who wanted to stop it could stop it. A line of human effort that had previously been about animating the marching of statues and the playing of instruments now became about animating the movements of tools once animated by skilled laborers – creating unstoppable economic momentum.

The ideas that would lead to codable machines finally began to come to life in a global way in the 1800s. In the ancient world, the marriage of crude writing systems with clay tablets helped launch history itself and the civilizations that followed; in the 1800s, we begin to see the marriage of crude writing systems with machines, launching a wave of historical change that we are still very much in the midst of.

The holes in the punch cards of a Jacquard loom may look like cuneiform script to the modern programmer, who is used to seeing words in their native language flicker out at them from the midst of the other structural symbols:

```
#lang dtc/hello/animation

(print "Hello")
```

But this is simply a difference in language – not a difference in fundamental approach. There's no law of nature or physics or computers that says computer code must be easily comprehensible to humans (though there may be certain laws of the mind that make some such languages easier to comprehend, learn, and wield than others).

In the late 1800s, Charles Babbage was so inspired by the explosive idea of reconfigurable looms that he would use the idea of punch cards to build upon the dream of Leibniz – proposing a calculating device unlike any the world had seen.

Ada Lovelace, Babbage's collaborator and correspondent, put it more poetically and insightfully than Babbage ever did, saying

> The Analytical Engine weaves algebraical patterns just as the Jacquard-loom weaves flowers and leaves.

It is unclear whether Lovelace ever encountered Leibniz's writings on the topic. Yet, the ambition and optimism in her own writings seem to echo that of Leibniz a century before, only now more firmly rooted in the reality of her time (Lovelace 1843).

> [The Analytical Engine] might act upon other things besides number, were objects found whose mutual fundamental relations could be expressed by those of the abstract science of operations, and which should be also susceptible of adaptations to the action of the operating notation and mechanism of the engine...
> Supposing, for instance, that the fundamental relations of pitched sounds in the science of harmony and of musical composition were susceptible of such expression and adaptations, the engine might compose elaborate and scientific pieces of music of any degree of complexity or extent.

Today, of course our programming languages can easily capture the notions of pitch, harmony, and rhythm. Of course we can program computers to create elaborate pieces of music. Of course we can. Yet Lovelace saw this in the 1800s. The machine wasn't even built, and yet she seemed to clearly see something deeply beautiful about that unborn machine – something that coding students today seem to miss, even with vastly more powerful descendants of those machines in their very pockets. She saw that these machines were, in some ineffable way, a bridge between mind and matter (Lovelace 1843):

> The Analytical Engine does not occupy common ground with mere 'calculating machines.' . . . In enabling mechanism to combine together general symbols, in successions of unlimited variety and extent, a uniting link is established between the operations of matter and the abstract mental processes . . .

Furthermore, the link between the physical machine and *language* did not escape someone as discerning as Lovelace (Lovelace 1843):

> A new, a vast and powerful language is developed for the future use of analysis . . .

As Doron Swade puts it in a documentary on Ada Lovelace (Fuegi et al. 2003):

> Ada saw something that Babbage in some sense failed to see. In Babbage's world his engines were bound by number . . . . What Lovelace saw – what Ada Byron saw – was that number could represent entities other than quantity. So once you had a machine for manipulating numbers, if those numbers represented other things, letters, musical notes, then the machine could manipulate symbols of which number was one instance, according to rules. It is this fundamental transition from a machine which is a number cruncher to a machine for manipulating symbols according to rules that is the fundamental transition from calculation to computation – to general-purpose computation – and looking back from the present high ground of modern computing, if we are looking and sifting history for that transition, then that transition was made explicitly by Ada . . .

Leibniz and Lovelace were well aware of the vast potential for symbol manipulating machines. Today, that vastness is proven to us time and again, with every new disruptive technology, with every new job created, with every old one destroyed, with every industry that rises or falls because of software. A "vast language," Lovelace called it.

But today, we describe it simply as "software" – written in thousands of languages, or one vast one, depending on how you choose to look at it.

The Song for the Luddites

The Luddite movement officially only lasted from 1811 to 1816. But the ideology of distrust for technology never died. Lovelace's father, the poet Lord

Byron, wrote his "Song for the Luddites" in 1816, when Lovelace was a baby (Byron 1832):

```
As the Liberty lads o'er the sea
Bought their freedom, and cheaply, with blood,
So we, boys, we
Will die fighting, or live free;
And down with all kings but King Ludd!

When the web that we weave is complete,
And the shuttle exchanged for the sword,
We will fling the winding-sheet
O'er the despot at our feet,
And dye it deep in the gore he has pour'd.

Though black as his heart its hue,
Since his veins are corrupted to mud,
Yet this is the dew
Which the tree shall renew
Of Liberty, planted by Ludd!
```

Lord Byron died when Ada was only eight, after having been absent for most of her life. It is unclear whether she foresaw that the "vast language" unifying "the operations of matter and the abstract mental processes" would be capable of causing massive societal change – not all of it enthusiastically accepted by those affected. The Luddite movement failed to stop the oncoming wave that we now call the First Industrial Revolution, and with the benefit of hindsight we should not have expected it to. We know how powerful a force automation is.

Today, Amazon's Mechanical Turk – named for that very "machine" that Napoleon once attacked with a risky queen maneuver – is a giant software system with not just one person inside, but half a million people across almost 200 countries, with about 2,000 of them being active at any given time. Whereas the first Turk could play one game of chess every now and then, the other is a fire hose spitting out 2,000 mind-hours of work per hour. The tasks are diverse: "Choose which picture contains a bird," "pick the twitter post with the most left-leaning sentiment," "read the following paragraph and highlight any grammatical errors," and so on. At pennies per task, many minds can be instantaneously employed – their various answers programmatically aggregated, checked against each other, mined for data, and so on.

When we look at Amazon's Mechanical Turk compared with the kinds of automated machines of the past, it is easy to think that this must be (for good or ill) some kind of pinnacle of automation. However, it's better to see it as we saw Leibniz's stepped reckoner, or Pascal's Pascaline. Not as an end point – but as a middle point. In this world of software, the relationships between mind and machine will only grow more complex – with minds and machines working with other minds and other machines, in an elaborately woven software-driven world.

Some of the work done on Amazon's Mechanical Turk is used, for example, to train machine learning models to do those tasks automatically. This is software automating the production of software. It does so by automating the process of distributing work to human minds, automating the collection of data produced by those minds, and automating the training of machine learning models. These models, once produced, become new threads to be woven into the larger system. And so on.

Whereas the Analytical Engine could weave algebra as the loom weaves trees and flowers, our world today weaves together minds and machines in intricate patterns of automation. Anyone who can code can take part in the weaving process. Anyone who can code can build upon that computational infrastructure from the comfort of their home, coffee shop, or library. Anyone with a few dollars to spare can buy programmable human labor or cloud-computing services. With the punch cards we call programs, we can weave those softwares and services together to create new softwares and services. Those become new threads to be woven in. And. So. On.

"And so on" – a phrase that, in this context, wraps up an infinity of possible stories to be written in the vast shared language that Leibniz and Lovelace wrote of – the vast shared language that we as a global society are only beginning to figure out how to teach effectively and ethically, at every echelon of education.

It is a "new" kind of writing, capable of crafting stories that provide global benefit, but also of uprooting lives and livelihoods at greater and greater scales. On the horizon, for example, is the imminent unburdening of millions of minds in the transportation industry, as we write software increasingly capable of driving vehicles. The cars of today are like the looms and chess-playing illusions of yesterday.

The song of the Luddites will be sung and resung, in some form or another, as long as the world continues to write its future with code.

To be continued...

LANGUAGES WITHIN
The Machine Within

Working memory, attention, time. These are the scarce resources of the mind. To err is human. Or the corollary: To be human is to have access to such limited mental resources that we are doomed to err continuously.

When it comes to working around these limitations, the tens of thousands of generations of human minds that came before us have discovered two major techniques, from which a great many technologies have been born:

- **Distributing Cognition**. Using our environment to extend the activities of the mind in such a way that we get the results we seek, without the investment of memory, attention, or our own time. This was the subject of the last section, where we followed the line L all the way to the modern, programmable machines which are recursive Leviathans of mechanically managed complexity.

- **Enhancing Cognition**. Training our brains. This is the subject of this section.

Crudely speaking, the distinction is simply which side of the skull/skin barrier the change happens. It's all a matter of prepositions: The automata of ancient Greece were *beside* us on the streets, the mechanical Turk was *in front of* Napoleon (or all *around* the grandmaster within), the Pascalines were *next to* the accountant that used them, and the cloud is *all around us* today.

Things like dactylonomy, though, are always *within*. Training your brain to do mental mathematics would mean making a change *within* yourself. Indeed, anything that we call "learning" today falls into this broad category of internal change. The effect of the change? That which requires working memory today is intuitive or automatic tomorrow.

"Learning" is such an innocent word. "Instilling long-term changes in our own wetware" – less so. Learning is a noninvasive, natural process – yet it seeks to create irreversible changes in the organ that makes us who we are. The educational systems of the world make such changes at scale, across large swathes of society.

Potions for the Mind

In Plato's *Phaedrus*, the character Socrates argues against the long-term cognitive detriments of the written word. It may sound quaint to us today; and it is all too tempting to dismiss such arguments as silly. Yet taking the argument seriously allows us to look at our modern issues in a clearer light. So, let us engage in the exact paradox that Plato poses for us – to read writings about the drawbacks of writings.

Socrates says (Cooper 1997):

> Among the ancient gods of Naucratis in Egypt there was ... Theuth, and it was he who first discovered number and calculation, geometry and astronomy, as well as the games of checkers and dice, and, above all else, writing.
>
> Now the king of all Egypt at that time was Thamus, who lived in the great city in the upper region that the Greeks call Egyptian Thebes . . . . Theuth came to exhibit his arts to him and urged him to disseminate them to all the Egyptians. Thamus asked him about the usefulness of each art, and while Theuth was explaining it, Thamus praised him for whatever he thought was right in his explanations and criticized him for whatever he thought was wrong.

The god Theuth then tried to convince the king that the gift of writing, "once learned, will make the Egyptians wiser and will improve their memory." He called it "a potion for memory and for wisdom."

Yet, what Plato said (that Socrates said (that Thamus said)) almost 2,500 years ago turns out to identify the exact skull/skin barrier problem that is the subject of this section:

> [Writing] will introduce forgetfulness into the soul of those who learn it: they will not practice using their memory because they will put their trust in writing, which is external and depends on signs that belong to others, instead of trying to remember from the inside, completely on their own. You have not discovered a potion for remembering, but for reminding; you provide your students with the appearance of wisdom, not with its reality. Your invention will enable them to hear many things without being properly taught, and they will imagine that they have come to know much while for the most part they will know nothing. And they will be difficult to get along with, since they will merely appear to be wise instead of really being so.

A root concern here is that having access to writing will encourage people to write things down rather than memorize them. We know, from our historical vantage point, that such arguments did nothing to slow the tidal wave of the written word. Still, it is interesting to consider that today's elite memory athletes are capable of staggering feats of memory using techniques that were created and taught in ancient Greece – suggesting that perhaps Plato was not entirely wrong in his prediction about the degeneration of human memory.

These techniques are not taught in today's schools (note-taking is). The method of loci or the "mind palace" technique is trained by almost all memory athletes, enabling them to perfectly memorize many randomly shuffled decks of cards, lines of abstruse poetry, and giant strings of random numbers. If there was ever a Golden Age of Human Memory, it probably is not our present day – where entire books (e.g., *The Shallows: What the Internet Is Doing to Our Brains*, Pulitzer finalist in 2011) are published about the not-always-positive effects that immediate access to information has upon faculties such as memory.

We strive to remember less when we have effortless access to more. Most do not need to train their memory in a world full of potions for reminding.

A grandmaster of memory can memorize 1,000 random digits in an hour, memorize the order of 10 decks of cards in an hour, and memorize the order of one deck of cards in under two minutes. But such skills require dedicated training over many years. Such training gives the brain a new ability – like an upgrade – but at the cost of training time. We must weigh wetware upgrades against others that can be acquired in a similar amount of time: for example, fluency in Spanish, fluency in Java, mastery over a domain of mathematics, sharper writing skills, and so on.

The twin challenges facing an education system are 1) Which upgrades should a society systematically install in the brains of *all* citizens? and 2) What processes will cause students to acquire said wetware upgrades?

Science and Schools

The learning sciences are concerned with how wetware upgrades of various kinds, across various fields, can be most efficiently accomplished. Obviously, this is critical. Although there may be disagreement from society to society, or from year to year, about what students ought to learn (Spanish or Java? Dactylonomy or paper-based arithmetic? Combinations of both?) – there is rarely disagreement about whether learning should or shouldn't be efficient. Obviously, if time is to be invested in learning, all things being equal, we would like to invest less and get more.

On the one hand, we have a growing body of science about how to make learning significantly more efficient – yet we have an education system that is often slow to adopt such insights.

To name one example: It was discovered in the late 1800s that "spaced repetition" of content helped learners remember it. That is, reminders after 5 minutes, after 10, a day later, a week later, and so on, promoted significantly more learning than cramming the same number of exposures into a smaller amount of time.

In the 1970s, the Leitner system of using flashcards was intended to help people wield this scientific result to learn more effectively. In the 1980s, the system was encoded into software packages like SuperMemo. Educational content such as the Pimsleur language learning system makes significant use of spaced repetition.

Such insights have yet to find themselves deeply embedded in pedagogy, curriculum, teacher training, textbooks, and student assessments. Just to rephrase that: We've known for more than a century that learning can be enhanced by something as simple as paying attention to the precise frequency at which you remind students about things. This is such a simple principle that anyone can do it with a deck of flashcards and a few shoeboxes. It's simple enough that entire textbooks and coursework *could* be redesigned with spaced repetition in mind – significantly increasing the amount that students learn. And yet – no successful systemic attempt to incorporate this finding has arisen in the last 100 years.

The grandfather of one of this book's authors opened his Ph.D. thesis in 1977 with the following depressing analysis of the education system of the day (Foster 1977):

> The national government of the United States, in particular, has sought continuously to challenge the communities to accept new and improved ideas in education, and through federal support has encouraged the trial of innovations and the expansion of educational opportunities. In fact, in the intervening years since Lyndon B. Johnson signed into law the Elementary and Secondary Education act in 1965, the Federal government has granted over fifty billion dollars to educational agencies for specific and general improvement of education. Unfortunately, there seems to be a distinct negative discrepancy between the expenditure to secure adoption of innovations and the actual adoption of them.
>
> [Jerrold] Zacharias was confident in 1960 that with one hundred million dollars per year for curriculum development he could transform the quality of United States' education. By 1966, he dejectedly confessed, "It's easier to put a man on the moon than to reform the public schools." Zacharias learned that the development of new curricula, materials, and techniques cannot secure educational quality without changing the ways in which schools operate and teachers teach.

He laments, as do we, that this is not a new problem, and no solution seems to be forthcoming:

> We seem, therefore, to still be facing the same dilemma Comenius wrote about in 1632:
>
>> For more than a hundred years much complaint has been made of the unmethodical way in which schools are conducted, but it is only within the last thirty years that any serious attempt has been made to find a remedy for this state of things. And with what result? Schools remain exactly as they were.

We seem, therefore, to still be facing the same dilemma one of our grandfathers wrote about in 1977. Science discovers. Schools remain as they were.

Since then, the backlog of unimplemented, ignored discoveries has only grown.

Mindset

Luckily, the relevant science isn't that complicated, and it has been the subject of enough bestselling books and NPR podcasts in the last decade that much of it may be quite familiar.

Let us begin with "mindset" – a word that comes to us from psychology, but which exploded into the public consciousness with Dr. Carol Dweck's bestselling book *Mindset: The New Psychology of Success*. Through her decades of scientific research, she discovered two distinct mindsets, ways of thinking about oneself, that profoundly affect how students learn, grow, respond to failure, and generally achieve success in life.

Her first contribution? She expanded our vocabulary by defining and naming these mindsets. To the belief that one's abilities are given, unchangeable, and fixed – she gave the name "fixed mindset." To the belief that one's abilities can be changed and are growable – she gave the name "growth mindset."

In her own words (Dweck 2007):

> In a fixed mindset students believe their basic abilities, their intelligence, their talents, are just fixed traits. They have a certain amount and that's that, and then their goal becomes to look smart all the time and never look dumb. In a growth mindset students understand that their talents and abilities can be developed through effort, good teaching, and persistence. They don't necessarily think everyone's the same or anyone can be Einstein, but they believe everyone can get smarter if they work at it.

With the benefit of these (now named) concepts in hand, she proceeded to do three more world-changing things: She discovered a way of determining which mindset an individual possesses; she showed that the mindset an individual possesses has profound short- and long-term effects on the individual; and she showed that an individual's mindset can be changed.

In a beautiful meta-move: She showed scientists that mindsets themselves can grow; mindsets themselves do not have to be fixed. An individual's fixed mindset can become a growth mindset. And we as a society can have a growth mindset about mindsets themselves – systematically converting fixed mindsets into growth mindsets through our teaching practices.

> In one study, we taught them that every time they push out of their comfort zone to learn something new and difficult, the neurons in their brain can form new, stronger connections, and over time they can get smarter.... Students who were not taught this growth mindset continued to show declining grades over this difficult school transition, but those who were taught this lesson showed a sharp rebound in their grades. We have shown this now, this kind of improvement, with thousands and thousands of kids, especially struggling students.

It's the kind of result that every scientist dreams of – something that can help thousands upon thousands, yet is conceptually very simple. All you have to do is teach students what neuroscientists already know to be true about human brains. Scientists know that brains can change. We know they are neuroplastic. We know that people can gain cognitive abilities they did not always have. Now, thanks to Dweck, we know that helping students understand these things can profoundly affect their grades and their lives. The dark corollary is that we now know something else: *not* teaching students these things can also profoundly affect the same things, but in the bad way. When we know a better way, is it ethical to maintain the status quo?

The question is moot. Scientists discover. Yet schools remain as they are.

True, teachers can now buy growth mindset posters to put up in their classrooms. But would Plato have had faith in the power of words painted upon posters hanging on walls? And only on *some* walls – at that. The static written word is powerful, but not *that* powerful.

And where is the widespread adoption at the systemic level? Where is the structural implementation of this simple idea across a broad section of our education system? The benefits to thousands upon thousands could be expanded to millions upon millions with the use of neuroscientific language throughout textbooks, curriculum materials, teacher training, and parent involvement programs.

But large-scale change is difficult. The education system wasn't built for flexible change – much as the stone automata of ancient Greece were not. Those animated figures would have to be torn down and rebuilt to make them behave differently. Tearing down an education system is not so feasible.

Perhaps the scientists of today are powerless save to lament, as Comenius did in the 1600s, that schools are hard to change.

Comenius was the "Father of Modern Education," earliest champion of universal education, leader of many schools, and advisor to many governments across the Holy Roman Empire. He saw these flaws in the earliest of education systems.

The problems we face today are not new.

Metacognition

Dweck's mindset work intersects with a more general topic of well-known scientific interest: Metacognition.

As the word "meta" implies, this is "cognition about your own cognition" or "thinking about thinking." It's an idea that dates back (at least) to Aristotle, but which has received enormous support from empirical learning studies.

As the book *How People Learn* puts it (Bransford and Practice 2000):

> A "metacognitive" approach to instruction can help students learn to take control of their own learning by defining learning goals and monitoring their progress in achieving them.

Put so simply, it almost feels trivial. Of course, students should take control of their learning and internally monitor their own progress. The nontrivial part of the problem is that metacognition isn't an inborn skill.

Indeed, students often fail to assess their own level of knowledge correctly and often fail to employ the right problem-solving strategy for the right task. To make matters worse, because all metacognitive processes are hidden from view, teachers often fail to realize that students struggle with metacognitive activities and also fail to realize that they must explicitly teach these skills (Bransford and Practice 2000):

> Because metacognition often takes the form of an internal conversation, it can easily be assumed that individuals will develop the internal dialogue on their own. Yet many of the strategies we use for thinking reflect cultural norms and methods of inquiry (Hutchins, 1995; Brice-Heath, 1981, 1983; Suina and Smolkin, 1994).

Research has demonstrated that children can be taught these [metacognitive] strategies, including the ability to predict outcomes, explain to oneself in order to improve understanding, note failures to comprehend, activate background knowledge, plan ahead, and apportion time and memory.

Unfortunately, these skills often aren't explicitly taught. Formal metacognitive assessments are largely absent from classrooms, as well as from state and national standards. To their credit, the prose of some textbooks does attempt to draw attention to metacognitive things. But then again – can we entrust the training of a mental activity this important and dynamic to the static written word?

Plato's Socrates's Thamus's critique of the Egyptian god rears its head, forcing us to ask if metacognition (or anything, for that matter!) is something that can be taught to children solely via the written word.

Recall that the speaker in Plato's dialogue is, in fact, the father of the Socratic method – the use of skillful questioning by another human being. The dynamic back-and-forth (what the Greeks called "dialectic") was considered the proper way to train the mind. It was the static written word's inability to cause this dynamic back-and-forth that was the root of the critique. As Plato describes it:

> . . . [W]riting shares a strange feature with painting. . . . [They] stand there as if they are alive, but if anyone asks them anything, they remain most solemnly silent. The same is true of written words. You'd think they were speaking as if they had some understanding, but if you question anything that has been said because you want to learn more, it continues to signify just that very same thing forever. When it has once been written down . . . it doesn't know to whom it should speak and to whom it should not. And when it is faulted and attacked unfairly, it always needs its father's support; alone, it can neither defend itself nor come to its own support.

Brains are more complicated than any machine we human beings have ever constructed. Yet, unlike these simpler machines, brains never come with instruction manuals. Quite the paradox! Modern school systems do not recognize "metacognition" as a literacy worthy of study in its own right (like math or science), relegating it to the status of – "it's up to the teacher to teach it, if they happen to know about it, and if they decide to do it." That often equates to "never," which is probably the reason for the incredible popularity of online courses for adults like Coursera's "Learning How To Learn," (associated with McMaster University and the University of California San Diego). For the more than 40,000 adult learners who have rated the course, this may have been the first time metacognitive techniques were explicitly taught to them. For the time being, it will be up to online courses and a few enlightened teachers – in spite of widespread agreement among scientists and the educated public that explicit metacognitive training matters.

Deliberate Practice

Deliberate practice is another idea that has received considerable public attention, in part due to the best-selling book *Outliers* by Malcolm Gladwell. The idea is better attributed to scientist and "meta-expert" K. Anders Ericsson.

As *How People Learn* sums up Ericsson's ideas:

> It is clear that different ways of using one's time have different effects on learning and transfer. A considerable amount is known about variables that affect learning. For example, learning is most effective when people engage in "deliberate practice" that includes active monitoring of one's learning experiences (Ericsson et al., 1993)

Note the implied metacognitive aspect of deliberate practice in that last sentence. An hour of mindless practice is not the same as practice that includes active monitoring. Ten thousand hours of mindless practice is not equal to ten thousand hours of the other kind. Ericsson has been publishing books on deliberate practice since 1991 – applying the idea to expert performance across a broad range of fields: arts, sciences, and sports. He provides compelling evidence for the importance of *how* students practice. And yet . . .

Scientists discover; schools remain the same. Homework assignments go out and come back. Ideally, we would target the majority of our efforts at changing *how* students think, rather than simply ensuring *that* students think. Yet – teachers cannot be there beside all students at all times. Nor can we read students' minds. Is the discovery, then, for naught?

Second Language Acquisition

fMRI studies place code comprehension into that same region of the brain capable of processing speech, signed languages, written languages, shadow puppets, music, artificial grammars, and essentially anything that is linguistic in nature.

Linguist, scientist, and political activist Stephen Krashen is a world-class expert on language acquisition. In 1998, this scientist found himself defending bilingual education in California when it came under attack with Proposition 227 – which required that students with limited English proficiency be taught almost entirely in English. The bill passed, severely reducing the number of bilingual classes in California. Although it was finally repealed in 2016, the number of credentialed bilingual teachers had fallen dramatically. An upcoming shortage of bilingual teachers has been predicted by the California Department of Education (Darling-Hammond et al. 2018). As Krashen prophetically put it in the early 2000s (Krashen 2002):

> Without a serious, dedicated and organized campaign to explain and defend bilingual education at the national level, in a very short time we will have nothing left to defend.

How odd that just a few decades later, the idea of computer language instruction throughout K-12 education would be fueling the crisis that Krashen was fighting – becoming crystal clear in Florida's attempt to replace Spanish with Java. This crystallization demonstrates that the attack against bilingual education has morphed. It is no longer monolingual education versus bilingual education – but rather has become a battle between two forms of bilingual education. It's as if we have a battle for which kind of language (formal or natural) shall be systemically installed in the Broca's regions of millions.

The stronger economic pressure is, of course, for formal languages. These are the languages with which we control the automata of the world – the hardware and software all around us. Minds fluent in these languages get paid more. Demand is higher. Such economic pressures will only increase as our world becomes more and more reliant on software. Is this then what the world has come to – a utopia/dystopia crossroads?

Dystopia. Will the findings of second language acquisition scientists like Krashen be used to more effectively teach the very subject that most endangers second language education as we know it? Students learning Java can be taught Krashen's theories, just as easily as those learning Spanish. That the theories didn't originally come from studying Java students will not be relevant in the dystopia that simply doesn't care about foreign language education.

Utopia. Or will we find that teaching computer languages with pedagogies inspired by foreign language instruction makes the value of foreign language instruction all the more obvious? Perhaps we'll find that the idea of dropping Spanish in favor of Java makes as much sense to people as dropping math in favor of science, or reading in favor of math.

It is in the spirit of this latter utopian idea that we now cover some of Krashen's ideas and apply them to coding education. Our hope is that coding can be a unifying force: a subject that helps weave together the other things we teach (math, reading, science, history, languages, etc.), along with things we don't but should (e.g., metacognition, mindset, deliberate practice, and coding itself).

Krash Course

Krashen's most critical contribution is to give a more precise definition to two English words, "acquisition" and "learning." Language acquisition and language learning are not the same, and one is significantly more important than the other (Schütz 2002).

Ask yourself, which of the two seems to be the important one? The answer is not intuitive to everyone – including foreign language instructors themselves.

Acquisition is a subconscious process, whereas learning is not. Learning, as defined by Krashen, is what happens when teachers explicitly teach – whereas acquisition requires no such explicit instruction. Acquisition, according to Krashen, requires only one thing: meaningful interaction in the target language.

Krashen's message: Interact, and you shall acquire. As Aristotle said:

> For the things we have to learn before we can do them, we learn by doing them.

This all seems agreeable enough, but we haven't gotten to the controversial corollary: that certain things that might seem important to teachers and students are actually not important and should be deemphasized to make room for more meaningful interactions in the language. For example, Krashen argues that teachers should *not* explicitly teach grammatical rules.

For many, this idea is both intuitive and not. On the one hand, we all know that this must be what happens when children are learning their first languages – like "sponges" they "soak up" language without needing to learn metalinguistic words like "noun," "verb," "gerund," or "past participle." Although children do receive grammatical corrections from parents, it's obvious that the vast majority of the input they receive is packaged as meaningful interaction, not explicit instruction.

As Chomsky puts it (Chomsky et al. 1995):

> We are designed to walk.... That we are taught to walk is impossible. And pretty much the same is true of language. Nobody is taught language. In fact you can't prevent the child from learning it.

On the other hand, until Krashen's contributions to scientific literature, it was not necessarily clear that it would be true when learning one's second language. And indeed, before Krashen, the history of second language acquisition was littered with pedagogies that prioritized explicit instruction: learning, instead of acquisition.

To make matters worse, these other pedagogies occasionally worked – especially when explicit grammatical instruction was given *in* the language being learned – "immersive instruction." Yet, as Krashen argues, this is an illusion we need to see past:

> . . . both teachers and students are deceiving themselves. They believe that it is the subject matter itself, the study of grammar, that is responsible for the students' progress, but in reality their progress is coming from the medium and not the message. Any subject matter that held their interest would do just as well.

Scientists discover; yet schools remain the same. Or do they? To his credit, publishing hundreds of articles and books, and delivering hundreds of lectures – Krashen is one scientist who has been slowly bringing about large-scale change. This is a more hopeful version of the story: A scientist discovers; a scientist lectures to thousands over the course of a couple decades; schools slowly change . . . Immersive second language education is becoming more mainstream – though de-emphasizing explicit grammatical instruction has not yet become something that we all accept without question. Twenty years of science advocacy, and the ideas are still not used by *all* language teachers. Many still cling to older teaching methods, with considerably less scientific justification.

It's not nothing. But it is a far cry from systematic adoption. There is nothing structurally in place to ensure that foreign language students are first taught the English metalanguage pertaining to "acquisition" and "learning." A student who is truly fluent in the metalanguage should be able to differentiate instantaneously between pedagogical activities that promote acquisition and ones that promote learning. They should know that their educational "diet" ought to be highly skewed toward acquisition. If they don't, they may spend their time on suboptimal learning activities at the expense of more useful acquisition activities. They may even erroneously accuse teachers of "not teaching" if they aren't lecturing about grammar.

In a parallel universe, students would be comfortable raising their hands and asking pointed metacognitive questions: "Why are we spending these valuable minutes learning when we could be acquiring?"

In which of these universes the coding classrooms of our world will reside is a decision we as a society have not yet made. Given that we are building our coding educational infrastructures and practices as we speak – a story *in medias res* – perhaps there is cause for optimism.

Fluency and Expertise

Advanced, native-level fluency is characterized by extremely high levels of speed and accuracy in the target language. The language has been "installed" in the wetware. Productions of utterances in the language seem to flow from the mouth, the hands, or the pen without effort. Comprehension of other people's utterances is equally flawless. You can speak with someone while you drive a car, play mini-golf, eat ice cream, and focus your attention and working memory on higher-level social objectives – like, say, secretly pondering how you will ask your conversational partner on a second date.

In this stage, your working memory and attention have been freed from the shackles. It is as if everything that was once so difficult is being handled by another "system" in the brain – an unconscious one. As it turns out, this unconscious system and its conscious counterpart were given names by Nobel laureate Daniel Kahneman.

As he puts it himself (Kahneman 2011):

> System 1 operates automatically and quickly, with little or no effort and no sense of voluntary control.
>
> System 2 allocates attention to the effortful mental activities that demand it, including complex computations.

They are both "you." One example of system 1 thinking might be detecting that an object is an apple, and that it is on a table within arm's reach. System 1 can be trained. You can produce the answer to $2 + 2 = \_$ without effort or computation, due to training that happened long ago. With the same speed and the same level of effort, a chess master can come up with a correct chess move simply by looking at the board.

These are powerful ideas that have been given other names by other scholars. Hubert Dreyfus described the road from novice to expert as one of increasing "intuition." Novices may learn rules for things, like "Don't move your queen out too early" and make decisions accordingly – whereas experts simply "feel" the right move. They weren't born with these intuitions. They gained them over many years.

Teaching these ideas to students has the power to give them a metacognitive language that can apply to any field – from chess, to mathematics, to writing, to history, to coding. Indeed, high performance in any field requires help from system 1, from our trained intuitions. Dreyfus has been discussing expertise in terms of fast intuition since the 1980s (Dreyfus and Dreyfus 1980). Kahneman's dual-system model with a fast system 1 has been discussed since

2003 (Louisville 2002), giving us today a crystal clear vocabulary for talking about our multiple systems and their relative merits.

Still: Scientists discover; schools remain the same. Where are the standardized tests that assess how much working memory a student is using while they solve problems? Where are the summative and formative assessments that detect a student's levels of acquired intuition in their subjects?

You don't have to be a teacher to know that there is a big difference between a mind that struggles to add $2 + 2$ (perhaps using rudimentary dactylonomy) and one to whom the answer immediately springs to mind. The same is true for the student who must struggle to remember how to write a program and one who can do it while carrying on a conversation about something else.

Give yourself a fluency test. Here's a program from earlier in this chapter (note the spaced repetition). Now close the book and try to write it.

```
#lang dtc/frames/animations

(animation
  `(cat              ,(cat)
    edison-cat       ,(edison-cat)
    first-viral-cat ,(first-viral-cat)))
```

When finished, don't bother to assess yourself on whether you "got it right." That's old school. People fluent in the learning sciences use more precise language for talking about their performance.

There's more than "right" and "wrong." It doesn't matter if you adopt Krashen's definition of fluency, Kahneman's definition of system 1, or Dreyfus's idea of expertise – any of these would suggest that the *speed* at which you get it right is a much more accurate indicator of your level of expertise. Fluency is hard to fake. If you are struggling, you probably aren't fluent. If you look like you're struggling, you probably *are* struggling.

We humans have a knack for detecting such struggles. The signs of bearing cognitive loads show on our faces and in our voices. Yet, it is difficult to observe every child while they work on every problem – and so the signs of struggle evaporate long before being observed by teachers. After we have produced the correct output, signs of cognitive struggle evaporate.

In schools that struggle to get students to achieve average scores on standardized tests, it might seem Herculean to raise the bar even further and demand fluency from students. Then again, it may well be the lack of fluency in basic skills that prevents advancement. We know this to be true in sports, as *How People Learn* explains (Bransford and Practice 2000):

> The problem ... is that attention is a limited resource. Therefore, this step-by-step process of controlling task performance occupies attentional capacity which in turn reduces the performer's ability to focus on other aspects of the performance, such as decision making, fine motor-skills, self-monitoring of energy level and "seeing the field or ice or court." However, with practice, procedural knowledge develops, which operates largely outside of working memory, and thus allows for skills to be executed more automatically. This, of course, has a very positive effect on overall performance by freeing the mind of the need to closely monitor and attend to the more basic, mechanical skills, so that attention can be paid to other processes.

We also know this to be true in language learning. If you understand that "no va" means "doesn't go," but it takes you a full second (1,000 precious milliseconds of attention and working memory!) to realize what it means, then you have already missed the next few words. Your understanding "doesn't go" – not fast enough, anyway.

We can make our brains fast. But we must accept that getting fast is slow.

What It Feels Like to Upgrade Your Own Wetware

Gaining fluency in a second language at an age where you are actually self-aware can be a truly incredible experience. Unlike a baby, you'll have the privilege of observing the process from the inside out.

You'll begin to experience the strange feeling of understanding what's being said or signed without quite understanding *how* you understand. You'll no longer need to focus on any of the individual words or signs. It may almost feel like a kind of vertigo – like, "How am I doing this?"

So it feels to have a well-trained system 1. So it feels to have expertise and "intuitions." So it feels to have fluency.

You'll also notice that you see things differently, correctly – and you'll have *no choice* but to see things this way.

In the 1960s, a scientist and chess master named Adriaan de Groot studied the fact that grandmaster chess players were capable of memorizing extraordinarily large numbers of chess positions – tens of thousands of them. They could memorize new ones at a glance. What de Groot found, however, is that chess players could easily memorize positions like this one:

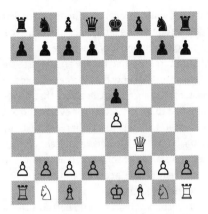

But they could not memorize random positions, like this one:

Memorizable positions needed to be ones that could arise in chess games – ones that contained the kinds of patterns that chess players were accustomed to seeing. With randomized positions, the grandmasters could memorize no better than novices.

Furthermore, it became clear to de Groot that grandmasters were able to memorize the state of those 64 squares by "chunking" what they saw. They saw the board, *not* as a collection of 32 pieces on 64 squares, but as a collection of a much smaller number of chunks.

As *How People Learn* puts it (our emphasis added):

[Due to] limits on the amount of information that people can hold in short-term memory, short-term memory is enhanced when people are able to chunk information into familiar patterns (Miller, 1956). Chess masters perceive chunks of meaningful information, which affects their memory for what they see. Chess masters are able to chunk together several chess pieces in a configuration that is governed by some strategic component of the game.

... The meaningful patterns seemed readily apparent to the masters, leading deGroot (1965:33-34) to note: We know that increasing experience and knowledge in a specific field (chess, for instance) has the effect that things (properties, etc.) which, at earlier stages, had to be abstracted, or even inferred are apt to be immediately perceived at later stages. To a rather large extent, **abstraction is replaced by perception**, but we do not know much about how this works, nor where the borderline lies. As an effect of this replacement, a so-called "given" problem situation is not really given since it is seen differently by an expert than it is perceived by an inexperienced person...

The idea that experts recognize features and patterns that are not noticed by novices is potentially important for improving instruction. When viewing instructional texts, slides, and videotapes, for example, the information noticed by novices can be quite different from what is noticed by experts (e.g., Sabers et al., 1991; Bransford et al., 1988). One dimension of acquiring greater competence appears to be the increased ability to segment the perceptual field (learning how to see).

What a beautiful way to describe what the road to expertise feels like:

Abstraction is replaced by perception.

Abstraction deletes distraction. When perception does abstraction at speeds faster than our conscious mind can follow, we simply see what matters, and only that. Distractions become invisible – deleted by a system deep within our wetware.

When our fast systems have been well trained, we see differently. Indeed, we become unable *not* to see differently. A chess master can never go back and see the board the way a beginner does. A fluent coder can never go back and see programs the way a novice does.

After sustained, long-term wetware growth, we are no more in control of the programmed machinery of our wetware than we are of some of the programmed machines that run our world. Even less so. The external machines can be rebooted, reprogrammed, and redesigned. It is not so easy with substructures of the brain.

Meta-teaching

If we abstract over all of the findings discussed thus far, the single biggest finding from learning science would appear to be a meta-finding: *learning scientists have discovered that the learning sciences should be taught to learners.*

Maybe it's obvious, after all: If we discover how changes can be made within the skull/skin barrier, we should teach that to anyone born with a skull and skin who might desire to change themselves. Let's give this meta-finding a name.

The Fundamental Theorem of the Learning Sciences.
If learning scientists discover that X helps people learn, then students should know about X.

It makes intuitive sense. The wetware of our brain holds many mysteries that have eluded the human race since the birth of our species. Scientists are slowly uncovering these secrets. Children should not be expected to intuitively know this stuff about themselves *a priori*. Adults shouldn't, either.

Some interesting corollaries:

- Teachers should teach the learning sciences to their students.
- Teachers should be lifelong students of the learning sciences themselves.
- Learning scientists should study how people learn the learning sciences.
- Learning scientists should study how to teach the learning sciences.

The same scientific insights that can make a teacher into a better teacher can make students into better students. Why, therefore, silo that information in the minds of scientists? Why silo it in the minds of teachers? Rather, it can be shared among scientists, teachers, and students.

What is called for is a common language among teachers, students, and learning scientists. There's nothing stopping this language from permeating all aspects of education – a "Universal Educational Language," so to speak.

A Universal Educational Language

We have an uphill battle if we wish to change the language of education. Many of our old words (like "learning") carry old meanings – imprecise and ambiguous ones. Perhaps these can be redefined, though: sharpened.

Those fluent in such an educational language would hear "learning" and understand that the word implies training a brain system that is unconscious and automatic. They would understand that their external actions, choices, and environments have the power to change the structure of their brains, causing the growth of new neural connections. They would never speak (or perhaps even think) empty phrases like "I have learned X" or "I have not learned Y" – as if "learned" and "not-learned" were binary terms, the outcomes in a zero-sum game.

Learners fluent in the Universal Educational Language would know that cell growth is no more binary than the growth of a tree. Yes, it is "a tree." True.

But phrases like "That is a tree" are too trivial to have value in the grander scheme of things – like whether it is a sapling or a redwood. Once you possess vocabulary that goes beyond "tree" – the sentence "that is a tree" is hardly worth uttering. Such trivialities would rarely be uttered by those fluent in a language that provides a richer, more expressive vocabulary.

A Universal Educational Language would also have the concept of linguistic extension built into it. Students would speak phrases like "I'm learning X; I wonder if scientists have discovered specific vocabulary about the learning of X. If so, I should extend my own language so that I can fluently discuss those concepts with my X teacher." This would involve learners seeking out the relevant science for whatever they are learning and adding those domain-specific ideas and vocabulary to their educational language.

For coding, this would mean taking very seriously the recent fMRI findings – that code comprehension and general language comprehension are intertwined operations in the wetware of fluent coders. This, in turn, would mean taking very seriously the findings of scientists like Krashen, who have spent their lives discovering and advocating for how fluency should (and shouldn't) be acquired. It would mean understanding and reflecting upon what these findings mean for you (the student) or you (the teacher). It would mean discussing such matters together, at length – to make sure everyone is using the correct educational language, devoid of dangerous misconceptions (which would be recognizable as misspeakings or odd turns of phrase).

But simply clarifying old terms and bringing in new, scientific ones may not be enough. Missing thus far are ways of writing down "educational algorithms" – a key tool of thought for any teacher and learner. The writing of educational algorithms is the written component of the proposed Universal Educational Language.

Yes, algorithms are crucial even when not learning to code. No matter what domain, our procedures have causal effects on wetware growth or lack thereof. Learning scientists use this kind of educational algorithmic language to design experiments – for example:

```
Both groups will take the pre-test.
Group A will play the educational video game.
Group B will listen to classical music.
Both groups will take the post-test.

That is the procedure.
```

Students and teachers should begin to think of themselves as learning scientists, too – equally empowered to design their own experiments – even if only for themselves.

To be concrete, here's an educational algorithm:

```
If today is Monday:
   Open your Monday deck of cards
   Study them for 5 minutes
   Put the hard ones into the Wednesday deck


That is the procedure.
```

This is a portion of the Leitner system mentioned earlier, written down as an algorithm that anyone who understands English can run. Will a student faithfully follow such a procedure? Perhaps not today. But the students of the future? Yes, if they are fluent in the Universal Educational Language. They will have been trained to write, run, analyze, evaluate, gather data, and revise their educational algorithms – a generic skill that they may apply to all learning domains. These are techniques borrowed from coding but applied to wetware instead of to software – suggesting that the study of coding has deep human value even when we aren't coding computers at all.

Here's another algorithm, one that can be used to great effect when learning ASL.

```
Go to an ASL social event
   Awkwardly try to communicate with people


Go home.
   Make flashcards for all the words you learned
   Put them in your Monday deck


That is the procedure
```

A few things here. First, note that this algorithm interweaves with the algorithm for the Leitner system (by putting cards in your Monday deck). This is a key feature of algorithms: They may refer to and interact with each other as part of a larger system – a more complex algorithm with sub-algorithms nested inside of it.

Some algorithms may apply to the time span of a week (such as what to study on which days); other algorithms may apply to the time span of just minutes (such as how to study a deck of flashcards, or how many times to practice a guitar riff before taking a break).

Let us compare the above to a worse ASL educational algorithm:

```
Go to an ASL social event
    Sit there and watch people


Go home


That is the procedure
```

The great thing about algorithms is they can be written down and textually compared with other people's algorithms. Teachers can read, tweak, and comment upon them. And such high-level algorithms require relatively little coding fluency: The language is simply structured English.

The Universal Educational Language must include this written component. It is too powerful not to use. Indeed, it can even be applied at a meta-level – algorithms about writing and refining algorithms:

```
On Mondays:
    I will review my performance data

    If I'm not happy with my growth,
        I will review my algorithms
    Else
        I will eat a cookie
```

Furthermore, expert students would be trained to revisit their algorithms frequently, even to co-construct them with other students and with their teachers – discovering bugs and sub-optimalities in the process. We've seen students whose lives changed when they switched from this algorithm...

```
Go to lecture
Read textbook
Do homework
```

... to this algorithm...

```
Read textbook
Go to lecture
Do homework
```

The fact that they discovered this in college is the real tragedy. But it isn't their fault. It is easier to reflect upon learning and growth when one has a powerful, abstract language for reflecting on such things. The corollary: It can be hard to even *think* certain thoughts without specialized written and spoken languages for thinking them.

Without being trained to write down and think critically about one's learning algorithms, why would students be expected to do so? Luckily, coding education is precisely the field of writing down and thinking critically about such things. So there is all the more hope that our current global endeavors to integrate coding with the rest of education can transform education in the process.

The Loop of Being Human

Automation without; automation within. Distributed cognition; enhanced cognition. Software/hardware; wetware. We have choices when it comes to how we work around the limitations of being human.

The hard part is that the internal and external are never entirely separate. Creating a long-term, structural change *inside* the skull/skin barrier requires creating structures *outside* of it. And vice versa.

If it sounds like this implies a loop: It does.

Crafting an effective learning environment around our skulls and skin is a skill that resides within the skull and skin; but that skill can also be nurtured to greater and greater fluency by the learning environment that surrounds it. We pick up the subject of loops, including this one, in the final chapter.

To be continued . . .

Chapter 4
Ends

"If anything is meant by man-machine symbiosis, it is the existence of such abilities on the man side of the 'membrane', for there is no partnership here between man and machine, merely the existence of a growing, but never perfectly organized, inventory of tools that the competent can pick among, adapt and use to multiply [their] effective use of the computer."

"The most important computer is the one that rages in our skulls and ever seeks that satisfactory external emulator."

"In man-machine symbiosis, it is man who must adjust: The machines can't."

"You think you know when you learn, are more sure when you can write, even more when you can teach, but certain when you can program."

Alan J. Perlis

A WIZARD'S TALE

Learn to Teach; Teach to Learn

The ancient wizard cleared her throat as she led them through a door into a windowless room – about the size of their old simulated sleeping quarters. "These are your new dorms," she announced. "As you can see, there are beds in the corner. And of course . . ." she pointed at three desks along one wall, " . . . computers."

Three computer terminals sat, one on each desk – a command prompt blinking on each.

"This is the second and final stage of education in the House with No Name. You can run a command to unlock the door at any time," said the ancient wizard, "but your final grade will be calculated the moment you do. It will be an average of the grades of every student in the original simulation at that moment, from first-year students to graduating seniors."

"What!?" the three young wizards exclaimed at once.

The ancient wizard continued, "Food will be delivered three times daily. Bed and laundry service, every three days. There's a bathroom and shower through that door. If you need fresh sheets or soap or food, there's a command you can run." She gestured at the computers.

"So, we're trapped here?" said Harmony.

"You were trapped before," the ancient wizard pointed out. "That's how school works. You're just trapped in a different classroom."

"But it's not fair," said Rob. "How can our grades be averages of the other students' grades? That's not going to teach us anything! That's not school!"

The ancient wizard ignored Rob and looked at Henry, adjusting her bifocals. "Those computers have access to everything – the source code for the whole simulation. The beds have direct cranial links, so you can test any new code you create before you push to production. And . . ."

She walked to one of the terminals and typed:

```
(spectate cafeteria)
```

On screen a window opened, showing a live feed of the kids milling about in the cafeteria, mashed potatoes on the floor. Everyone was moving in slow motion. The Python kids were in the middle of a ring of other students. Everyone seemed to be in a state of confusion about where the House of No Name students had disappeared to.

"You're in control now," she said. "You get to decide what they do in their classes, what they study, what tests they take."

"Th-that's too much responsibility!" said Henry.

"No!" cried Harmony. "We don't know how to code! You can't ask us to write code that teaches other people how to code! That's too meta!"

"Besides," added Rob, trying to sound reasonable, "each of the Great Houses uses a different language – and we don't know *any* of them."

On the prompt, the wizard typed:

```
(spectate python-classroom-1)
```

Suddenly, they were looking through a virtual window into a classroom where several upperclassmen from House Python were listening to a lecture where a teacher wearing Python robes was writing on the blackboard in the front of the room. The blackboard had a drawing of something that looked familiar to Henry:

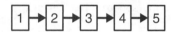

It was labeled "The Linked List," though, not "Story."

"Linked lists," said the ancient wizard. "The fact that they are learning about linked lists on this particular day at this particular time at that particular level – it's all coded in. The curriculum, the homework, the tests. It's all simulated. It's all software."

Henry cut in: "Okay, so if we can reprogram the whole system, what's to stop us from just giving everyone an A?"

"The council of wizards will review your pushes to the Git repo," said the ancient wizard. "Your code won't get into the master branch unless it gets past our automated tests, and our review process."

"Fine," said Henry, trying a different tactic, "what's to stop us from just sitting here and not making changes then? We'll just get the average of what everyone would have gotten in the first place."

The ancient wizard chuckled. "You'd be surprised how many students fail and flunk out of wizard school. It's the year 2117, and we still haven't figured out how people learn coding. Every semester, the average is a C on our fluency assessments. We haven't figured out how to raise the average since 2090. But the kids enjoy the Warner Brothers *Harry Potter* avatars, so at least there's that."

"And we're supposed to raise the average?" said Henry, sitting on one of the beds, knees weak.

"You must learn to teach," she said. "So you can teach to learn."

"But we're here to learn how to code!" said Henry. He was starting to have trouble breathing – much like that moment in the Great Hall, so long ago now.

"Indeed," said the ancient wizard. "You will have to teach yourself a great deal about coding, and about learning, and about teaching. Effectively, you will have to teach yourself to write code that teaches others how to write code. Do you have any doubts that when you have mastered these arts, you will be a wizard? Indeed, you will be a meta-wizard."

The three fell silent, exchanging glances with each other.

"But how can we teach them?" said Rob. "Even if we learn everything there is to know about coding and how to teach it, we're not *in* there. How can we really have any effect on what they learn?"

"No teacher is ever 'in there,'" said the ancient wizard, tapping her skull. "Teachers *can't* get in the wetware. We can only build structures around it. We control environments, not minds. But . . . " the wizard went on, "if you *do* need to enter the simulation to impersonate a teacher or a student, you are welcome to do so."

The ancient wizard turned to leave, taking a set of keys from her pocket and inserting them in the door to lock it from the outside. Then she paused, a different look in her eyes.

"For what it's worth," she said, "when I entered this room, in 2090, I wasn't half the wizards you are today."

She shut the door. The lock clicked, leaving them in silence, save the low hum of the air-conditioning vents in the ceiling.

Montage

With nothing but time on their hands, learn they did.

For the first year (only a semester in the actual simulation), they did little but read the documentation, distributing their cognitions across every inch of their walls (pure whiteboards). They covered it with notes and diagrams. Whenever they needed new markers, of any color, they merely had to order through their terminals. So it was with anything they needed – always arriving with the next day's meal, slipped with the food tray through a slot under the door to their "classroom." Rob became fond of calling it "the jail cell."

Trapped inside whatever it was, they devoured documentation about the education system they had once been trapped inside. They learned how to launch the simulation in development mode, so they could enter into it with the cranial links in their beds, able to experience the running code and any changes they made to it. There were no other students in developer mode, of course. Exploring the vacant classrooms and eerily silent hallways of the school was a bit creepy – but the software supported a `simulate-students` flag, which, when set to `true` would populate the school with NPCs who would walk around, laugh, talk, and simulate going to classes.

In a way, that was creepier – all of these automatons walking the hallways, speaking lines of dialog that were scraped from the real simulation's students, but weirdly mixed up. Listening in on their conversations was like listening to some bizarre form of English where, as conversations went on, it became clearer and clearer that words had no meaning.

"I've got a *ton* of homework," one might say.

"The game jam is coming up. Are you going?" one might reply.

"Chad and Emily are together. Everyone's talking about it."

"And then we *destroyed* their rooks with that code that Tanya wrote!"

They were perfect abstractions of human minds – something much simpler, easier to reason about, a collection of stats and pre-coded behaviors. These abstractions were things the three wizards could tweak to study the emergent behavior of the system.

Henry, Rob, and Harmony learned the language for configuring the behavior of the bots – that is, tweaking their class schedules, their extra-curricular probabilities, their study probabilities, their propensity to bully others, and so on. The system could run thousands of side-simulations, aggregating data and reporting back metrics: from hallway congestion to expected performance on upcoming exams.

And of course, always in reach was the real simulation – the one with real students, the one the documentation referred to as "production." For the first semester, they neither entered production nor pushed new code to the production branch. They merely studied the system.

And they got a C, which surprised none of them. The outcome had been predicted by the production system's statistical models weeks before. Too many students were struggling in the production simulation – their grades on the final exams grew more and more predictable as the days approached, as they continued to fall behind in lectures, as they began to skip homework assignments to go watch the evening's wizard duels in the cafeteria. That the average would be a C became inevitable.

But for the three wizards, the C felt somewhat satisfying – inspiring, even. And it wasn't just because they had watched the cool kids fail in slow motion, having to repeat their classes that semester. It was because they had learned more about coding by watching that C average manifest itself within the student body than they would have doing anything else. They watched people go to class, watched them study, watched them take exams – across all the Houses, across all the years. They learned by watching.

By the time first-year exams came around, the three young wizards could have aced them. They could have aced the second-year exams, too. But they didn't care. There was something about the meta-problem, the problem of the C average itself that had captured them. It was the simple: Why?

Why did some students struggle? Why did some succeed? How exactly did some minds craft good educational environments for themselves and others not?

Such questions began to dominate their conversations and, inevitably, their whiteboards. The system documentation contained thousands of pages about the science of learning – which they devoured. But the ultimate problem appeared to have no solution – which made them eager to push code to production, patching problems the school's own architects could not.

At first, Rob was of the opinion that the assessments themselves were flawed. He argued that if the average on an exam was a C, then it was too hard.

Yet Harmony noted that the people making As were not, according to the data, geniuses. Indeed, many of them were normal people. And of those who failed, the same was true. Normal people.

If they simply changed the exams, she argued, it would merely hide the problem, allowing it to lurk under the surface.

And so they turned their attention to what the documentation called "interventions" – changes to the code in production to improve student outcomes.

Henry would never forget that first push to production. Although there would be many more – that first deployment was truly special. It was like writing their first line of code all over again – only this time, they weren't just saying "hello" to the world. They were causing it to change.

Their first intervention was a simple one – merely an extension of the gesture recognition system that would detect when students "accidentally" shoved into each other from behind in the cafeteria – that, and other signs of bullying. The reasoning was that the cool kids would have more time for studying if they weren't busy picking on other students. It wasn't a bad push. It made it past code review and into production.

The thing was, the impact on grades was small. Yes, people were happier, overall. It was an improvement. But the cool kids found other ways to waste time – fighting duels and playing computer games. They failed another semester of coding. It was not the last time Henry would feel what he came to call "intervention disappointment" – realizing that the one thing his experiments proved was that the real world was more complex than his models of it.

There was the semester when they tried to institute mandatory evening study sessions, which helped. But the students who needed it most tended to spend it doing the wrong sorts of things – like watching the night's wizard duels. It had no statistically significant effect.

There was the semester where they instituted mandatory classes about how to study. But the students who tended to do poorly in their other classes failed to study for this meta-class, too. So, once again, the intervention seemed to help the students who were already doing well do even better.

Their interventions helped, but never as much as they expected. Again and again, what they thought were silver bullets turned out to be puffs of smoke.

On the bright side, each success gained them more and more credibility with the council of wizards that oversaw their pushes to production. This gave them the ability to make larger, more structural changes.

Harmony instituted a program that would detect struggling students early, identifying them for specialized interventions. This worked well, and for the first time, raised the average grade to a B. Their pride swelled – perhaps too much.

Galvanized by this success, the three began to pursue even deeper restructurings of the education system – leading to what the three would later refer to as "the Dark Times." They began to legislate the first language that students had to take. There were many different Houses, yes, but all students would have to begin with a drag-and-drop language, like Scratch.

Things seemed fine at first – but then the parent complaints began. Many of these students were children of developers who used "real" languages like Python and Java in the "real" world. When they learned that their children were "being forced to learn Scratch," they called the system a "dystopia" and threatened to pull their kids out of "this Orwellian system."

The intervention had to be dropped. This was the first time, in fact, that one of their pushes to production had to be rolled back. It was the first time that they had to reckon with the fact that the system they were studying was not entirely self-contained – not the airtight petri dish they'd thought.

So, the next semester, they tried the same thing again, but with Python. This was a different kind of disaster. Students who would have taken Scratch or a gentler introduction to programming were completely unprepared for the tedious and error prone act of typing code directly into a text editor with one's own fingers and seeing the unfiltered error messages shouting at them in red text. The grades by the second week were lower than ever, causing the system to predict a D-average by the end of the semester. The changes had to be rolled back, and damage-control protocols had to be applied.

When they presented their next idea to the council of wizards, it was met with more resistance than usual. The idea was to make everyone go through the first semester of the House with No Name's curriculum – to learn about the history and structure of language itself. The way cooler way.

The council said they would allow a single month of such curriculum, not a full semester. During the first week, though, the student body staged several protests in which they gathered in the Great Hall and chanted, "Teach us coding! Teach us coding! Teach us coding!"

The changes had to be rolled back. For the third time, an experiment was abandoned.

Sobered by the Dark Times, the three began to pursue subtler ideas.

Some semesters, they entered the production simulation as teachers and actually taught in classrooms – teaching all languages, from Python to Racket – hoping that working directly with students would give them some insight, some secret magic, that would teach them how to teach coding. They became skilled teachers, fluent users of the Socratic method, and fluent employers of Krashen's input hypothesis: structuring their classrooms to maximize hands-on use of the languages and to minimize lectures on grammatical concepts.

With this, the Dark Times lifted, and the average climbed to a B+ when their next push wove their insights into the software itself.

In their naivety, though, they thought they were almost done. A B+ was almost an A!

Years went by, though, and they could not manage to tip the needle all the way.

By this time, Rob had already been awarded a Ph.D. for his groundbreaking work on the use of transcranial direct current stimulation of Broca's region while students were working on homework assignments.

Harmony had been given hers years before for her training of neural nets to detect struggling students.

Henry, always the slow one, was currently working on a multiyear project to figure out how to gamify all of coding education. Everyone loved wizard chess, he reasoned. So, if students could just channel that energy into learning to code, then . . . success! Right?

He tried banning the use of pre-written scripts during wizard duels – requiring all contestants to write their own. But many simply stopped playing wizard chess and gravitated toward other games. Others stopped watching duels when the gameplay became lukewarm. The very energy that Henry was trying to harness was starting to dissipate.

He tried instituting classes whose entire curriculum was based around learning to code for wizard chess. It was a popular class, and certain students enjoyed it.

But Henry found it hard to figure out how to teach the less flashy aspects of coding, like linked lists, to people who were hooked on writing scripts that could launch exploding pawns into the defensive rooks of one's enemies. A nontrivial population of such students grew more and more dissatisfied with the less well-crafted dopamine cycles of non-gamified classes. They wanted everything to be "fun" and "not boring" – but they provided no particular insight into how that was supposed to be accomplished on their behalf.

Feeling that his wizard chess curriculum might be causing a kind of brain damage, he attempted to roll back the change. But this caused the student body to stage another protest. There were too many addicts already. The council of wizards made Henry push it to production again.

They even ended up giving him a Ph.D. for it. But all Henry cared about was that B+ average. It was a constant reminder that their years of work had failed to do the thing they set out to do.

Loop Back

"Maybe we shouldn't be surprised," said Henry. "It's not like other fields have solved this problem. Reading and mathematics are critical literacies, too – and not everyone achieves the expected degree of fluency in those."

"We can't just give up," said Harmony. "Not after this long.'"

"I'm not saying we should give up," said Henry. "I'm saying we should go back."

Rob laughed – then coughed. "Oh, wait . . . you're serious?"

"The more I learn about learning," said Henry, "the more I think I've forgotten what it's like to be a novice."

"But back?" said Rob.

"What if we lose our memory?" joked Harmony.

"If?" said Henry, no smile. "To truly be novices again, we *must* lose our memories – at least temporarily."

When it finally dawned on Rob and Harmony what he was saying, Harmony said, "And how do you propose we do that?"

"I've been reading the docs about simulation-induced amnesia. I think I know how . . ." He picked up a dry-erase marker. "I'll draw a diagram."

Rob scratched his beard. Harmony adjusted her bifocals.

The Beginning

Henry arrived at coding wizard school along with hundreds of other students and was ushered into the Great Hall, where they all stood, milling about until a respectable, ancient-looking wizard took the stage. A hush fell over everyone.

"A sorting shall now commence!" he announced. "We must assign all of you into your various Houses. Each House at this prestigious school champions a slightly different way of learning how to become a coding wizard. I will now explain precisely how that works . . ."

Henry, who could not pay attention to lectures for very long, leaned over and asked his new friends, "How does it work? How many Houses are there?"

His better-informed friend Harmony replied, "There are over a thousand, with more begin added every day."

"Over a thousand!" hissed Henry. There was no *way* he was going to end up in the same House as his new friends.

"But," his goofy but loyal friend Rob said, "I've heard that the sorting algorithm takes your preferences into account. So, you can basically choose which House you start in."

Henry sighed with relief. "Good, which one are you both picking?"

"Definitely Py–" Harmony started. "Um, actually . . . I'm not sure."

Rob looked thoughtfully at the hat. "Yeah, my dad said I should pick Scratch, but . . . I don't know . . ."

"I'm not sure why," said Henry, "but I wish I could pick all of them."

At that moment, someone shoved into Henry from behind. He turned around to find three cool kids, all using variations on the classic Draco avatar.

"You know . . ." said Henry with a thoughtful grin. "I think I'll join Python."

"You should," said the Draco with blue eyes.

"It's the best one," said the one with red eyes.

"Python is power," said the one with green eyes.

Henry chuckled as he joined the queue to be sorted. Although this was the beginning, he had a feeling he had been here before – and that he would be again.

The End

A LANGUAGE WITHOUT
Our Road Thus Far

We have come to the part where we must finally make a true programming language out of the fledgling Story Language. A brief montage is appropriate.

Once upon a time, our language was merely a way to write abstractions of stories:

```
#lang dtc/story/images

beginning -> middle -> end
```

And then it began to grow and change form, smaller in a way, but prepared for a growth spurt:

```
#lang dtc/story+/images

(beginning middle end)
```

Single Stories began to include Stories within.

```
#lang dtc/frames/animations

(animate
  `(beginning middle end))
```

To an arbitrary depth, Stories (within Stories (within Stories)).

```
#lang dtc/frames/animations
 (animate
  `(beginning ,(cat) end))
```

And now, the language faces its true coming of age – we will now permit the power of naming. Let us not dally, like parents crying when their children go off to kindergarten. Let us simply allow it to happen.

Definitions

```
#lang dtc/complete

(define the-story
  `(beginning middle end))
```

It's that easy. Now anytime you say the-story, you get back `(beginning middle end). This allows us to package up arbitrarily long Stories into what appear to be very short Stories. Extending a language ("teaching" a computer what something means) is as easy as using define.

After making the above linguistic extension, you can now say:

```
(image the-story)
```

And it will produce the expected image:

But there are actually two kinds of definitions. Here's one of the second type.

```
#lang dtc/complete
```

```
(define (the-story ____)
  `(beginning ,____ end))
```

This is truly powerful. Unlike defining just another vocabulary *word*, this definition defines another *grammatical structure*.

This may seem like an innocent thing, but that's the thing: It isn't just one thing. Defining one thing opens the floodgates for an *infinite number* of new things.

Let's explore this simple infinity via examples.

```
(the-story `middle)
```

This gives us:

```
`(beginning middle end)
```

Whoever uses your extended language now, however, can supply anything they want as the second Moment in a Story that begins with the-story. For example: another word.

```
(the-story `MIDDLE)
```

This gives us:

```
`(beginning MIDDLE end)
```

Or an image:

```
(the-story (cat))
```

This gives us:

```
`(beginning         end)
```

Or, we could even nest another story:

```
(the-story `(start-middle middle-middle end-middle))
```

The output:

```
`(beginning
  (start-middle middle-middle end-middle)
  end)
```

Even this seemingly odd construction is perfectly okay, too:

```
(the-story (the-story (the-story `MIDDLE)))
```

The output:

```
`(beginning
  (beginning
   (beginning MIDDLE end)
   end)
  end)
```

In theory, this could continue indefinitely. Before defining the-story, you couldn't say anything related to (the-story ...) without getting an error. Now, you can say an infinite number of things you couldn't have said before.

What treasures might be hidden within that infinity?

Becoming the Machine

As Alan Perlis put it (Perlis 1982):

> To understand a program you must become both the machine and the program.

Let us become the machine (or in this case, the language) and ask how it handles programs like the ones above. We'll go slowly through a story that only really lasts an instant.

In the beginning, there was the triple-nested Story:

```
(the-story (the-story (the-story `MIDDLE)))
```

In mathematics, the innermost set of parenthesis is what gets handled first. So it is with most programming languages. You can think of the computer handling those expressions simply by replacing them with their definition – with the code you would have written yourself if you hadn't used the defined word there – automating a tiny cognitive task on your behalf.

To make that idea concrete, the innermost parentheses would be converted (on your behalf) to `(beginning MIDDLE end), which is what (the-story `MIDDLE) is defined to be. This would yield:

```
(the-story (the-story `(beginning MIDDLE end)))
```

But the computer isn't finished! Now the automation proceeds. The next innermost interpretable Story will be evaluated, giving:

```
(the-story `(beginning (beginning MIDDLE end) end))
```

And finally:

```
`(beginning (beginning (beginning MIDDLE end) end) end)
```

Now that the entire result is an uninterpretable Story, there is nothing left to do. Such stories mean what they mean. So the program is complete.

You could animate the Story of the computer's interpretation steps like so:

```
#lang dtc/complete

(animate
  `((the-story (the-story (the-story `MIDDLE)))
    (the-story (the-story `(beginning MIDDLE end)))
    (the-story `(beginning (beginning MIDDLE end) end))
    `(beginning (beginning (beginning MIDDLE end) end) end)))
```

Sometimes animations are clearer than anything we can print in books.

Loops

Additionally, our language now has the ability to perform the magic of infinite loops. We didn't need anything named "loops" in our language to get it to work; with the ability to name things, such infinities come free.

Here's a short, finite description of a program that will loop infinitely.

```
#lang dtc/complete
```

```
(define (forever-print ___)
  (print ___)
  (forever-print ___))
```

Note the self-reference. The definition of forever-print contains itself.

You can run this program – and there will be no infinite loop. It is simply a definition. It "teaches" the computer a new word. The infinity is hidden within that word – a kind of linguistic potential energy.

To summon the infinity, one can simply write:

```
(forever-print "HELO")
```

The language, at runtime, will replace this with the definition of forever-print:

```
(print "HELO")
(forever-print "HELO")
```

The first line will print "HELO", and then the second line will get replaced with its definition, which gives:

```
(print "HELO")
(forever-print "HELO")
```

The first line will print "HELO", and then the second line will get replaced with its definition, which gives:

```
(print "HELO")
(forever-print "HELO")
```

The first line will print "HELO", and then the second line will get replaced with its definition, which gives:

```
(print "HELO")
(forever-print "HELO")
```

And. So. On.

The meta-word define grants the power to write self-referential programs with ease. It gives anyone who uses the language the ability to connect two wires – tapping into CPU resources at will, effortlessly commanding the electrons of the computer in front of them or in the cloud, to do their bidding forever. Even beyond death. You just use a word in its own definition: The thing that English teachers say you must never do – it becomes a tool for immortal power.

Mad Libs

Let's say a few words about those blank lines (___) in definitions. You can actually have as many of those as you want. You just have to differentiate them.

```
#lang dtc/complete
```

```
(define (mad-lib ___1 ___2 ___3 ___4)
  (~a "Once upon a time, a man named Charles "
      ___1
      " invented a machine called the Analytical "
      ___2 "."
      " One day, " ___1 " met someone named Ada "
      ___3 "."
      " They wrote the first computer programs for the"
      " Analytical" ___2 ","
      " which is why they are known as the first computer "
      ___4 ".")))
```

(Are you wondering what the ~a means? This might be a good time to check out the documentation for this language at **dont-teach.com/coding/docs**. But you already knew that, of course.)

Naturally, we can now write Stories that produce various versions of the text.

```
(mad-lib "Leibniz" "Stepped Reckoner" "Jacquard" "Luddites")
```

This provides the dubious historical account:

Once upon a time, a man named Charles Leibniz invented a machine called the Analytical Stepped Reckoner. One day, Leibniz met someone named Ada Jacquard. They wrote the first computer programs for the Analytical Stepped Reckoner, which is why they are known as the first computer Luddites.

Anything that matches the pattern (mad-lib __1 __2 __3 __4) is grammatically valid.

You get as many "slots" as you want. In fact, you can name them whatever you want; they need not be blank lines. Think of them like vocabulary words that are only relevant within the confines of the definition.

Here is another version of the same story generator, but which communicates more clearly the kinds of things that the writer intended to be placed into each slot:

```
#lang dtc/complete

(define (mad-lib2 last-name-1
                  machine-name
                  last-name-2
                  kind-of-person)
  (~a "Once upon a time, a man named Charles "
      last-name-1
      "invented a machine called the Analytical "
      machine-name "."
      "One day, " last-name-1 " met someone named Ada "
      last-name-2 "."
      "They wrote the first computer programs for the"
      "Analytical" machine-name ","
      "which is why they are known as the first computer "
      kind-of-person "."))
```

Which style you choose in your definitions is up to you. The language doesn't care. However, the golden rule always applies: Programs are for people to read. So ask yourself who your audience is, and which is easier for them to understand.

Turing Completeness

In this chapter, we have infinity in the palm of our hand. In the last, we could build arbitrarily tall towers of cats.

Two miracles in a row is enough to make anyone ask: Will the powers of languages always continue to surprise us? Might they even now have powers that we know nothing of yet – undiscovered magic? What will our children discover? And our children's children?

In some sense: yes. There will always be programs that have not yet been written that, once complete, solve problems in surprising ways or that change the world unexpectedly. There will always be S/stories to be written.

However, in another sense: no. And this goes for both stories and Stories.

For stories, there are limits – quite simply, those of the mind. We think of stories as "out there" – but they exist to be taken in. As such, they have a certain form, a form that helps them fit "into" the mind, a form that does not overly tax it, a form that is not overly long, a form that unfolds smoothly, a form that has rhythmic ups and downs, a form that has thematic cycles, a form that has throughlines and arcs. Knowing what we know about human minds, we could probably come up with "story laws" that could specify a few sorts of things that simply are not stories – excluded on the basis of form alone. A file full of binary code does not tell a story – whereas a README file telling us it is the hacker's encrypted launch codes does. A 2-hour movie might; a 200,399,923-hour movie does not; a 1-paragraph summary of it might. And so on.

Analogously, there are certain things a Story (or any computer program) can definitely *not* be – no matter what, due to the fundamental nature of what it means to "compute" something. Programming languages must abide by certain laws, meaning that at least to a small degree, they will not surprise us. These laws are a bit like the Law of Gravity, but stronger, because they are mathematical laws. They are more like the law that says $2 + 2 = 4$ than the law that says an apple will fall to the ground.

What follows in this section is a lighthearted explanation of the concept of "Turing completeness." Note that mathematicians like Turing himself would have used much more formal languages and metalanguage to explain the same concept. We will do our best with natural language.

Alan Turing is famous both for being played by Benedict Cumberbatch in the *Imitation Game* and, building upon the work of Polish codebreakers, for mechanizing the breaking of Nazi codes during World War II. One of his greatest works of mathematical and philosophical magic was to show, before Java and Python existed, something like:

If $2 + 2$ is 4, then anything Java can do, Python can do, too.

That's pretty cool. No doubt you'll agree with the $2 + 2$ part, but the second part might come as a surprise. It might even irritate some Java programmers to know that Python has this property.

But there's no need for irritation. Turing also showed essentially that:

If $2 + 2$ is 4, then anything Python can do, Java can do, too.

So at least it's fair.

And to make matters even more interesting, he showed these things more than half a century before either language would be invented. So, of course, he couldn't have used the words "Java" or "Python" in his original paper in 1936 (Turing 1936).

In reality, Turing's proposal is all the more profound because it *doesn't* mention languages by name. It abstracts across all languages. A better translation of the logical extension of Turing's idea might be something more like:

If 2 + 2 is 4, then anything #lang X can do, #lang Y can do, too.

...as long as X and Y are both "Turing-complete languages."

What then is a Turing-complete language? To be deserving of this title a language must be capable of calculating whatever a Turing Machine could. Let us imagine such a metaphorical "machine," a collection of four things:

- **The tape** – An infinitely long strip filled with small "cells" on which symbols can be written – including the "blank" symbol. This is an abstraction of the human memory, extended with as much paper as we might wish.

- **The head** – The head of a Cyclops with a single giant nearsighted eyeball that can peer very closely at one tape cell at a time. With its pudgy hands, the Cyclops can move the tape left or right, giving its eye a closer look at the next cell over. Taking its job seriously, the Cyclops only moves the tape one cell at a time.

- **The state** – A single small tablet of eternally wet clay on which a single symbol can be written at a time.

- **The code** – A logbook full of entries that all start with, "If you are looking at symbol T on the tape and have symbol C on the clay..." and end with any combination of the following:
  - a new symbol to be written on the tape,
  - a next cell to look at (the one to the left, the one to the right, or the current one)
  - a new symbol to write on the clay tablet,
  - whether to stop computing.

The Cyclops is trained to be placed in a room with the state tablet and the instruction book. It can be given the starting cell on an infinite tape. Then, it will dutifully, and with the utmost accuracy, carry out the procedure implied by the logbook. At each step it will look at the tape symbol (T), look at the clay symbol (C), and look up what to do in the instruction book.

It will do so. Unless finished, it will repeat from the top. And. So. On. It may continue forever.

Such a Cyclops is analogous to a Turing Machine – no more powerful, no less. It is easy to prove, and we leave it as an exercise to the reader.

Exercise

Look up the real definition of a Turing Machine. Compare its parts to the ones above. We have kept the names (tape, head, state, and code) the same as most descriptions. We have only changed the language of their definitions.

Compare our language to the more traditional, mathematical language. Write your own metaphors for each part of a Turing Machine, and for the process of "computing."

With this picture in mind, we are ready to confess that the 2 + 2 is 4 thing was just a small magic trick on our part – a bit of educational scaffolding to remind you that this is no scientific theory. It is a mathematical one, requiring only arguments if you wish to be convinced – not labs, not experiments.

Let's begin to give a more formal formulation:

Anything #lang X can do #lang Y can do, and vice versa – as long as X and Y are Turing-complete.

Okay, how then does a language prove itself to be as powerful as a laser-focused Cyclops whose mind is extended by mystical artifacts? We leave this as a (more challenging) exercise to the reader.

Exercise

This one is not for novices. We give it as a reason to come back to this book one day.

For a programming language of your choice, create a game that simulates the Cyclops. Players of your game should be able to write instructions in the logbook (according to the format above), set the initial clay tablet symbol, and set the initial contents of the tape.

They should then be able to press "Run" and watch the Cyclops do its job – exactly as described above.

Congratulations, by simulating a Turing Machine within another language, you have just proven that language to be as powerful as a Turing Machine. Anything a Turing Machine could do, your language can do – via your game, which has one inside.

Although not all coders can do it, the above exercise can be completed in most modern programming languages you've heard of – with a few exceptions (e.g., HTML). Doing so is not always easy – but that's never the point. If it can be done, it is Turing-complete.

The true historic work of magic is officially known as the Church-Turing thesis. It is actually worded a bit more like this:

> Any procedure that is "effectively calculable" can be computed by either Alonzo Church's "lambda calculus" or Alan Turing's "Turing machines," and vice versa.

Anything that is Turing-complete gets to join the club of being able to compute anything "effectively calculable" – along with Turing Machines and the lambda calculus. Python, Java, Racket, and `#lang dtc/complete` programs are in the club.

The lambda calculus is a formal language that is a bit like `#lang dtc/complete`, in that it involves the same kind of substitution operation that we meditated upon in the **Loops** and **Mad Libs** sections above. But Alonzo Church was quite the wizard and managed to show that this language doesn't actually *need* the power of naming things to do all the same magic as languages that do have the `define` meta-word. At least in theory. The cognitive load of having no names for things makes this language (like Turing Machines) impossible to use for practical purposes.

The fact that Turing Machines and the lambda calculus – seemingly very different ways of describing computation – are actually equivalent is deep and fascinating in itself. The fact that either one can compute any "effectively calculable" procedure is the real point, though.

What then does "effectively calculable" mean? It's an adjective that describes a procedure that can be written down as a sequence of instructions that can be followed by a hypothetical person with infinite time, pencils, and paper. Although the instructions may contain loops, causing the person to work for thousands or billions of years, at the expense of perhaps all the pencils and paper in the universe, the work must eventually be complete in order for the task to be called "effectively calculable." Also, to deserve the name "effectively calculable," the task may not require of the person anything *but* pencils, paper, and time. They may not use special machines, for example.

Lastly, each step of the written instructions should be easy for the person to follow – requiring no ingenuity.

In other words, it is whatever a mind extended by infinite storage space can compute with very little thought. It's a definition of a kind of "thinking" that abstracts away as much human thought as possible, so that what remains is something simple enough to be encoded in the machines of the world.

There are limits to the kind of "thinking" known as computation. For example, Turing showed that one cannot write a program that can, in general, tell if other programs will crash on some input. A program might be able to detect *some* crashy programs, but not all of them. This is a limitation inherent to Turing Machines, which means it is a limitation inherent to all Turing-complete languages – Java, Python, and `#lang dtc/complete`. A full inventory of the limits of computation are well beyond the scope of this book – but interested readers can Google the "Halting Problem."

In spite of their limitations, though, Turing-complete machines and languages run our world. Yes, all they are doing is mindlessly crunching symbols, reading and writing from that digital paper known as "computer memory." But that very mindlessness is enough to automate countless manual and mental tasks for the human race – with no end to automation in sight.

With a tower of languages between us and the binary numbers stored as electron configurations in hardware, we are empowered to think at a semantic level much closer to our human languages, ignoring the mathematics and physics underneath. We can write a program equivalent to "Make an animation of cats" or "Serve a webapp backed by a MySQL database," and we need not think about what calculations the CPU must inevitably do in order to make our stories come true.

We owe our ability *not to think* about certain things to the great abstractors that came before us – the wizards who built the languages we use. We stand upon the tower of their construction. The deletions beneath our feet are what elevate us.

What seems like magic is, underneath the surface, simply matter doing math on the mind's behalf. Actually, that still sounds like magic, doesn't it? Welcome to the digital world. Welcome to coding.

Ifs

Caesar might have commanded his generals:

```
Attack the barbarians.

If you are winning, press on.
If you start to lose, retreat.

That is the procedure.
```

Or a teacher might instruct a student:

```
Begin studying the flashcards.

If you get them all correct, eat a cookie.
If you get something wrong, eat a cookie and start again.

That is the procedure.
```

Or an enlightened student might instruct themselves:

```
Begin studying the flashcards.

If I get them all correct,
    I should teach someone to make sure I understand.

If I get something wrong,
    I should teach someone so I learn better next time.

That is the procedure.
```

That Stories and stories must branch is a necessary evil stemming from the fact that we mere mortals do not have perfect information about the future.

As we write programs for computers, there are many unknowns. Having something built into the language to handle ambiguity is a critical tool for minds that must write programs that run in spite of unknowns.

So, in addition to define, we now add the final critical keyword to our language: if.

This gives us a tool for dealing with Stories like (current-day) whose output is different depending on what day it is:

```
(current-day)
```

On a Monday, this gives:

```
`monday
```

But 24 hours later, that same program gives:

```
`tuesday
```

Using `if` along with the above behavior lets us write our own Stories that differ depending on when they are run. Thus, we need not know ahead of time what day the machine will execute the program.

```
#lang dtc/complete

(define (schedule-today)
  (if (eq? (current-day) `tuesday)
      `(wake-up get-tacos go-to-sleep)
      `(wake-up study-flashcards go-to-sleep)))
```

That means tacos on Tuesday and flashcards otherwise. Such conditionally branching stories can be nested in other branching stories, creating more than two branches:

```
#lang dtc/complete

(define (schedule-today)
  (if (eq? (current-day) `tuesday)
      `(wake-up get-tacos go-to-sleep)
      (if (eq? (current-day) `wednesday)
          `(wake-up wash-clothes go-to-sleep)
          `(wake-up study-flashcards go-to-sleep))))
```

But deep nestings like this can be hard on the eyes, and a load on the mind, so languages often provide a convenient way of flattening a branching structure out. In our case, such a magic word is cond, allowing us to express the plan for seven days of the week without seven levels of nesting.

```
#lang dtc/complete

(define (schedule-today)
  (cond
    [(eq? (current-day) `monday)
     `(wake-up make-programs go-to-sleep)]
    [(eq? (current-day) `tuesday)
     `(wake-up get-tacos go-to-sleep)]
    [(eq? (current-day) `wednesday)
     `(wake-up wash-clothes go-to-sleep)]
    [(eq? (current-day) `thursday)
     `(wake-up think-about-languages go-to-sleep)]
```

```
[(eq? (current-day) `friday)
 `(wake-up go-fishing go-to-sleep)]
[(eq? (current-day) `saturday)
 `(wake-up do-nothing go-to-sleep)]
[(eq? (current-day) `sunday)
 `(wake-up do-nothing go-to-sleep)]]))
```

In the interest of spaced repetition, we shall note that the above can also be written as follows, with a splice:

```
#lang dtc/complete

(define (schedule-today)
  `(wake-up
    ,(cond
       [(eq? (current-day) `monday)    `make-programs]
       [(eq? (current-day) `tuesday)   `get-tacos]
       [(eq? (current-day) `wednesday) `wash-clothes]
       [(eq? (current-day) `thursday)  `think-about-languages]
       [(eq? (current-day) `friday)    `go-fishing]
       [(eq? (current-day) `saturday)  `do-nothing]
       [(eq? (current-day) `sunday)    `do-nothing])
    go-to-sleep))
```

You can think of both if and cond as tiny micro-languages embedded in the larger dtc/story-complete language. Both if and cond let you say the same thing you could with the other.

Although you could get away with knowing just one, you run the risk of having other wizards make fun of you if you use one where the other would have been clearer. We have our cultural norms. We build them into our languages: #lang dtc/complete merely follows in the footsteps of every other modern language. They all provide many forms of conditional branching.

Extending Language

Perlis strikes at the heart of language extension and language creation (Perlis 1982):

> There will always be things we wish to say in our programs that in all known languages can only be said poorly.

Sometimes rectifying this problem is as simple as adding a single `define`. Perhaps this single new word or grammatical construct is the thing we always wished to say but could only say badly before.

Sometimes we must resort to using `define` many times, adding a variety of new words and constructs that, when combined, say the thing we always wished to say but could only say badly before. Sometimes this can amount to thousands of lines, sometimes millions.

Inevitably, when creating large amounts of code we must also name new concepts and ideas in English – extending both our programming languages and the natural language we use in and around that software artifact. This, however, is not as easy as using a `define` – for other people do not permit new ideas to be so easily planted into their wetware.

This is why the answer to the analogy is most certainly *not* computers.

```
teacher : students :: programmer : _____
```

We teachers cannot program our students' minds the way programmers program computers. Correct is:

```
teacher : students :: programmer : junior programmers
```

We are inventors not just of code, but of ideas, of words, of systems of thought, of language itself. By choosing to become a coder, you are choosing to become a lifelong teacher of your own linguistic creations. By choosing to become a coder, you are also choosing to become a lifelong student of other people's linguistic creations.

A LANGUAGE WITHIN

So lernt man lernen: Der Weg zum Erfolg

It was in 1885 that German scientist Hermann Ebbinghaus found that spacing out learning over time is superior to learning the same amount in one session. It can be reduced down to a single sound bite that goes unheeded by students everywhere: "Don't cram." Or a single sound bite that goes unheeded by textbooks everywhere: "Do repeat."

With more than a century of scientific study behind it, the spacing effect has been measured many times over in labs throughout the 1900s and into the 2000s, and is still actively being studied today. Without a doubt, inserting spaces between bouts of learning leads to longer retention and more effective use of student learning time. Why this scientific research hasn't been wholeheartedly embraced by the educational institutions of the world is a question that has been asked since the 1980s (Dempster 1988). Scientists are still asking it today (Kang 2016).

In the 1970s, a German science journalist named Sebastian Leitner developed a system for studying flashcards based on spaced repetition. This system has since been algorithmified many times over in software like Anki and SuperMemo, allowing users to create digital flashcards that the computer will show to them at key intervals. We will create our own implementation in this chapter – a fitting way to close the loop. We will leave you with the ability to use your coding skills to create software to practice coding (or any other subject).

Leitner's book *So lernt man lernen* translates to "How to learn to learn" – a title that beautifully captures the meta nature of his ideas. Learning his system doesn't teach you a language, or a science, or a field of mathematics. It teaches you something more powerful than these because it *isn't* specific; it's a system that has abstracted away the details of *what* you are learning, so that it can focus on the *how*.

To learn the system is to learn a way to learn.

Making the flashcards is really the hardest part, so we'll spend the most time here. Just to pick a completely random example topic, let's make flashcards out of some of the concepts from this very book.

As you work through the examples, either on a computer or in your mind, we invite you to ponder how cool and meta you are for being able to write code that helps people learn to write code. Via the computer, you can now program brains. It's advanced magic, but you are truly dabbling in it even now. You may even choose to turn the magic upon yourself if you wish, a reinvestment that will compound your learning over time.

A card must have a front and a back.

```
#lang dtc/complete

(image
  `(to-name powerful-act))
```

We'll display things differently later, but for now, this produces our familiar Story image.

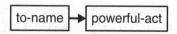

Or, if we want to embed English into a Moment (complete with spaces and punctuation), we can write the Moment with quotes:

```
#lang dtc/complete

(image
  `("Naming things"
    "Powerful linguistic act"))
```

Invoking that power of naming:

```
#lang dtc/complete

(define naming-is-powerful-card
  `("Naming things"
    "Powerful linguistic act"))

(image naming-is-powerful-card)
```

Exercise

It's probably more useful to display a flashcard as an `animation`. Change the above code to an animation. And add a few more named cards.

Here's another:

```
#lang dtc/complete

(define cuneiform-year-card
  `("Cuneiform writing system dates back to _____"
    "3500 BC.  Fertile Crescent.  Ancient Mesopotamia."))

(image cuneiform-year-card)
```

Note that if you want to add line breaks to the text, you can use the \n character anywhere inside the quotes. It's like a character that is equivalent to pressing enter. The name of this character is the "newline" character.

Exercise

Add newlines between the sentence fragments on the back of the previous card.

While you're at it, add a few more named cards with facts worth remembering.

Suppose you don't want to forget the name of that thing you just learned. Let's make a flashcard out of it.

```
#lang dtc/complete

(define adding-newlines-card
  `("How do you make a \"newline\" character?"
    "Put a \\n between the \" characters."))


(image adding-newlines-card)
```

Hmmmm. What's with all of the backslashes there? This often happen in language design: We decide to make something with a special meaning – like \n, but sometimes we want to talk *about* that thing without triggering its special meaning.

For example, the quote symbols must surround the English we are embedding in our code (e.g., "HELO"), but sometimes English itself *contains* quotes. So we need to be able to syntactically differentiate between a quote that signals "This is English; don't interpret it like code" from one that is simply meant to be an uninterpreted quote embedded in the English. To allow you to do this, you use a backslash. A backslash before a quote gives you a literal quote – not one that has a special meaning.

Exercise

Make a flashcard to remind you about how to display a literal quote character:

```
#lang dtc/complete

(image
  `("How do you display\na literal quote\ncharacter?"
    "____"))
```

Note that this is a bit tricky. You want the result to be something like:

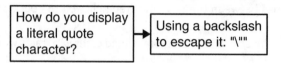

Notice that it contains a literal quote and a literal backslash. **Hint:** To create a literal backslash, put another backslash before it. Think of the backslash as a special escape symbol for other symbols, including backslashes.

If you found that last exercise annoying and you're hoping that you don't have to remember it (i.e., maybe it's just a weird quirky thing that only applies to the languages in this book)... sorry. These particular rules for dealing with human-readable text are used in almost every modern programming language: Java, Ruby, Python, Racket, and so on. No matter the language, when you start embedding English text in code, you'll inevitably have to also embed literal quotes and literal backslashes within that text. That punctuation is part of English, too.

Exercise

Make a flashcard that reminds you how to produce a literal backslash.

The output should have two backslashes in it – because that's how you do a literal backslash. But the code that produces the output may need to have more than two backslashes in it.

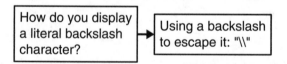

We haven't yet given a name to Moments that look like English – ones that start and end with a quote. These are called "strings" – because they are metaphorically a bunch of letters, numbers, or punctuation "strung" together. All modern languages provide some way of dealing with strings. It's what lets your computer say, "Helo" to the world, without having the slightest clue what the word "Helo" means or that it's misspelled. Strings are another kind of data: It means what it means.

Exercise

Make a flashcard to remind you what a string is.

Strings and escape characters can be tricky, so don't worry if you don't get them at first. Much more important is the basic idea of the flashcards, which you could make a flashcard about, like so:

```
#lang dtc/complete

(image
  `("What's the basic Story that describes a flashcard?"
    `(front back)))
```

Yes, that was a flashcard about a flashcard. More generally, since we're coding flashcards that are about coding, it may help to have a way of displaying code as a picture. It would be weird to have a deck of coding flashcards with no code on them:

```
#lang dtc/complete

(image
  `("How do you turn a flashcard Story into a picture?"
    ,(image-code
       `(image
          `(front back)))))
```

The sub Story above that begins with `image-code` takes a Story and makes a pretty picture out of it, as if it were code you'd written, with nice colors and everything.

Exercise

Make a flashcard to remind you how to turn a Story into an animation. Define a flashcard to remind you how to `define` a new flashcard.

Heavily nested code can increase cognitive load.

```
#lang dtc/complete

(image
  `("How do you escape an uninterpreted Story to\n
```

```
make one of its Moments an image?\n
Example: Animate a flashcard with a picture\n
of a cat on the back."
(image-code
  `(animate
     `(cat ,(cat))))))
```

Definitions can be used to decrease the level of nesting. Here's a rewriting of the above. It does the same thing, but now, it uses a flow of definitions, each one allowing the next to be shorter and more succinct – closer to our natural language. Each line, taken alone, is then easier to comprehend, the cognitive burden diminished by the power of naming (the power of "chunking" things within a name of your choice).

```
#lang dtc/complete

(define question
    "How do you escape an uninterpreted Story to\n
    make one of its Moments an image?\n
    Example: Animate a flashcard with a picture\n
    of a cat on the back.")

(define answer
  (image-code
    `(animate
       `(cat ,(cat)))))

(define animation-card
  `(,question ,answer))

(image animation-card)
```

Exercise

Take the above program and type it in. Run it. In the interactions window, type question, then code-for-answer, and so on. Anything you define, you can look at.

Definitions break your code into smaller pieces, each with a name that allows you to inspect it.

Use this "flow of definitions" writing style shown above to define your own flashcard with a coding question on the front and the correct code on the back.

Try to become fluent in this style. Fluency implies that you are effortlessly able to come up with logical English names for the bits of code you are writing. This might not sound like much – but consider: Wetware with this ability must, in some way, be better at translating between English and code.

That can't be a bad wetware upgrade for a coder, whose job is to do such translations. Plus, it's a style that helps your reader.

You just learned how to write code to make digital flashcards about coding – a technique that can be used by either teachers or students of coding. Plus the same technique works for non-coding cards, too.

This is the power that abstract tools give us. The more abstract they are, the more likely they can be applied by many people, to many things, including themselves.

Designing Your Deck

Now that we know how to make cards – `( front back ) – and display them – either ( image `(front back)) or (animate `(front back)) – we are ready to make a deck of cards.

If a Story with two Moments describes a single flashcard, what is the Story that describes a *deck* of flashcards? One very natural one is to simply make each individual flashcard Story be a sub-Story (or Moment) in a frame Story for the deck:

```
#lang dtc/complete

`(( front back )
   ( front-2 back-2))
```

That's really it. If you want to study a deck of cards, we made the convenient animate-deck for you, which is like animate, but it pauses and lets you think about the card until you press any key to continue.

```
#lang dtc/complete

(animate-deck
 `(( front back )
    ( front-2 back-2)))
```

Exercise

Be a scientist and run the following experiment. Set a timer. Copy the following code (which has 15 flashcards). You can type it in for extra practice, or you can copy/paste it from the end of the documentation page at **dontteach.com/coding/docs**.

Begin studying. Be serious about it; don't cheat. How many minutes before you can go through all flashcards without mistakes? How many times did you run the program?

```
#lang dtc/complete

(define dtc-trivia-deck
  `(("Year of first program comprehension fMRI study?"
     "2014")

    ("American Sign Language shares what \"modality\" or
      \"channel\" with computer languages?"
     "The visual-spatial modality, or channel")

    ("The oldest known story-within-a-story dates back to?"
     "Ancient Egypt (18th to 16th century BC).
     King Cheops' 5 sons tell 5 stories about magic and
     miracles.")

    ("Both the backslash and the backtick serve a similar
      abstract purpose.  What is it?"
     "To \"escape\" the thing that comes after it.  The
     backslash precedes a literal quote or a literal
     backslash.  The backtick precedes a literal
     (uninterpreted) story.")

    ("Programming comprehension, understanding American Sign
      Language, and reading English have all been
      shown to activate which part of the brain?"
     "Broca's area.")
```

```
("In a Story that describes a flashcard, how many
  Moments are there?"
 2)

("In a Story that describes a tic-tac-toe board, how
  many Moments are there?"
 9)

("In a Story that describes a deck of cards, how many
  Moments are there?"
 "It depends.  As many as there are cards in the deck.")

("In a Story that describes a game of chess, how many
  Moments are there?"
 "It depends.  As many as there are moves in the game.")

("In a Story that describes a game of tic-tac-toe, how
  many Moments are there?"
 "It depends.  As many as there are moves in the game.
  But no more than 9 and no less than 3.")

("Write a simple program that animates through a deck
  with two cards, both of which have pictures of cats
  on the back."
 (image-code
   `(animate-deck
      `("What does an early Youtube cat look like?"
        ,(first-viral-cat))
      `("What does an old photo of a cat look like?"
        ,(cat)))))

("Write a simple program that animates through the
  numbers 1 to 10."
 (image-code
   `(animate
      `(1 2 3 4 5  6 7 8 9 10)))))
```

```
("Write a simple program that shows a picture of a Story
  whose three Moments are three images of cats."
 (image-code
   `(image
     `(,(cat) ,(edison-cat) ,(first-viral-cat))))))

("Write a program that shows a picture of a Story
  whose first Moment is a string and whose second is
  a chessboard."
 (image-code
   `(image
     `("What does the starting state of a chessboard
       look like?"
       ,(napoleon/turk 1)))))))))


(animate-deck dtc-trivia-deck)
```

The System

The final step of the Leitner system is the part that actually makes it "the Leitner system." Instead of organizing your cards into a single deck, you must organize your cards into decks that you study with different frequencies. This part can be customized for your life and changed over time, but one way to start might be as follows:

Split your cards into three decks – an "every day" deck, a "Tuesdays and Thursdays" deck, and a "Fridays only" deck. Start by putting all your cards in the "every day" deck. The basic rules for when cards move from deck to deck are simple: When you get a card right, move it one deck up (e.g., from "every day" to "Tuesdays and Thursdays"); when you get one wrong, move it one deck down (e.g., from "Fridays only" to "Tuesdays and Thursdays," or if it's already in the "every day" deck, keep it there).

While performing the above, you are changing the Story of what you will be studying *while* you are studying. When you get a card right, the Story of what will happen on Tuesday changes; when you get a card wrong on Tuesday, the Story of what you will do the next day changes. In other words, the Story of your own studying becomes something that you are constantly rewriting according to the rules of the Leitner system. But the frame story (the Leitner study system itself) does not change.

Could you change those rules? Yes: The final exercise in this chapter asks you to do exactly that. When you do find a version of the Leitner system that works for you, though, you can keep that part fixed and unchanging. The day-to-day study stories may change – but the system you have built *around* those stories will remain constant.

Here's one way to set up a file for studying in this way.

```
#lang dtc/complete

(define everyday
  `(("Python first released" 1989)
    ("Ruby first released" 1995)
    ("Racket first released" 1995)))

(define tuesday
  `(("C++ first released" 1979)
    ("C first released" 1969)
    ("Java first released" 1996)))

(define friday
  `(("Lisp first released" 1958)))
```

Whenever you want to study a deck, simply wrap that Story in one that begins with animate-deck. If today is Monday, you might run the following in your interactions window.

```
(animate-deck everyday)
```

If today is Friday, then you'll study the every day deck and the Friday deck:

```
(animate-deck everyday)
(animate-deck friday)
```

If you wanted randomize the order of a deck, you can use shuffle, which shuffles the order of Moments in a Story randomly.

```
(animate-deck (shuffle everyday))
```

Note that shuffle is a symbol void of card-related sense – it doesn't just work for Stories that represent decks of cards. You can shuffle the elements of any Story. It could be an abstract Story whose moments are largely meaningless:

```
(shuffle `(a b c d e f g h i j k l))
```

```
`(a l e h k f g d b c i j)
```

Or you could shuffle the pieces on a chess board:

```
(shuffle (napoleon/turk-raw 1))
```

```
`(B p p _ p P P _
 _ _ _ _ N _ Q b
 _ p n _ _ _ _ N
 _ p _ P r _ _ _
 R _ K p P _ _ r
 q P _ k P _ R _
 b P _ n _ p P _
 B _ _ _ _ p _)
```

What you get back is yet another Story, which can often be used grammatically wherever the unshuffled Story was used. For example, we can scramble and display the pieces that were on the board during any move of Napoleon's famous game.

```
(image-chess
  (shuffle (napoleon/turk-raw 1)))
```

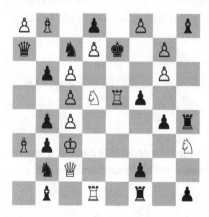

Interesting. This simple line of code generates precisely the kind of chess position that Adriaan de Groot used in his experiments.

Whether you shuffle your cards or not, the important thing to remember is that whenever you finish studying, your job is to reorganize your cards according to the Leitner system rules – either moving cards up or down if you get them right or wrong. As you inevitably learn more and more, the cards will begin to migrate from the every day deck to the Friday deck, where they will stay.

If you one day learn a deck of cards so well that even studying them on Fridays is excessive, you could make a once-a-month deck or even a once-a-year deck.

Unburdening Yourself

If you're happy with your Leitner system as is, great! It's already, in many ways, an improvement over Leitner's original system – which used physical cards and physical shoeboxes or folders. The computer flips the cards for you, so you need not burden your fingers. It shuffles things for you, so you need not trouble yourself there, either. But there are a few things that could, perhaps, be automated.

For example, if today is Tuesday, you have to subject yourself to the arduous task of thinking, "Is today Tuesday?", and then remembering that you need to run (animate-deck tuesday). How inconvenient!

Maybe we could define a Story that unburdens the mind further.

```
(define (dont-make-me-think)
  (cond
    [(eq? (current-day) `tuesday)
     (animate-deck (shuffle tuesday))]
    [(eq? (current-day) `friday)
     (animate-deck (shuffle friday))])

  (animate-deck (shuffle everyday))))
```

The Story (dont-make-me-think) will play out differently on Tuesday and Friday than it does on any other day. It does so by using a conditional branch. It asks the computer what day it is. And it decides what to do accordingly.

It might seem small. But such unburdenings add up.

Advanced programmers could even automate the process of moving cards between decks. But we cannot teach you everything about programming in one book.

Parting Exercises

With the Leitner system, you get to take full advantage of the spacing effect in whatever way is most optimal for your own brain.

We'll end this thread with three exercises that are fairly difficult. You may want to read through them now but come back to them later.

Exercise

This exercise is a chance for you to make a real contribution to the world at large, using the basic coding skills you've learned so far in this book. Yes, it's true. You don't even need to be a fluent coder before writing Stories that have a positive impact.

Make a deck of 50 or more flashcards on a topic of your choice. It doesn't have to be about coding or even about computers. History, math, science, arts, philosophy – anything goes.

If you upload that deck to the forums at **dont-teach.com/coding/forum**, it'll become part of a larger corpus of flashcards contributed by other readers of this book. Each contribution expands the study options available for everyone in the world.

It's a community-driven educational technology that we will organize on the forums.

Use the following template.

```
#lang dtc/complete

(define my-deck
`(
  ;Change these cards to whatever you want.
  (front back)
  (front-2 back-2)
  ;Put in as many additional cards as you want.
  ))
```

Exercise

The version of the Leitner system described here uses three boxes. However, there are many other variations. Come up with one that you think would work just as well or better for you or someone you know.

Describe that system as precisely as possible, and post it for discussion at **dont-teach.com/coding/forum**.

LANGUAGES WITHOUT

The Flood and the Tower

Babbage sketched out the first thing we consider today to be a Turing-complete machine. He and Lovelace sketched out programs that would run on that sketch of a machine. If we count those sketches as the world's first software, they were the first drops of rain in the flood to come.

Today, the world's software consists of 2 billion lines of code. Just kidding: that's just at Google alone (McCandless et al. 2015). One source estimates that a flood of 111 billion lines of code pours out of the minds of developers worldwide each year (Ventures 2017). This flood of stories rewrites our world.

These lines of code have overturned entire industries.

The movie rental industry was born, grew to adulthood, and was on its deathbed in 2010 when Blockbuster filed for bankruptcy — customers having been swept up by newborn software giants like Netflix. At their peak, Blockbuster employed 60,000 minds (Graslie 2013), serving 25 million customers per month in America (News 2010); Netflix employed just over 7,000 in 2018 (Watson 2019), serving 62 million subscribers in America and 148 million globally (Pallotta 2019). That's the leverage that comes from the software that Netflix wove.

Software gives seemingly magic power to the people, teams, organizations, and businesses that know how to leverage it. As it turns out, Blockbuster was aware of this. As they steadily lost customers throughout the 2000s, they did start automating things with software. They signed on 2 million subscribers to their online platform in 2007 (Reuters 2007). They even attempted to deploy an automated kiosk system in 2009, to compete with Redbox. But ultimately, it was too little too late. Blockbuster folded in 2010; today Netflix accounts for almost 1/3 of the traffic on the internet (Luckerson 2015).

Car manufacturers weren't always software companies. They are now. That wheel you turn and those brake pedals you press are just your way of communicating with software produced by the car manufacturer. Pilots of airplanes are likewise pulling levers and pressing buttons that talk to the plane's software. Software is very literally flying through the air all around us.

Oil and gas companies must leverage software and data analytics to compete with each other. So too must farmers crunch the numbers on weather projections and satellite data. So too must financial companies buy and sell stocks with algorithms. So too must hospitals, health care, and insurance companies increasingly resort to managing their operations with the help of intricate software systems.

The keyword here is "must." Organizations must change to succeed, or they must change to survive. Either way, that means resorting to software to streamline operations, improve communication, and innovate faster. The software arms race has driven the global economy to become so fundamentally software-driven that it is hard to think of a single industry or major sector of civilization as we know it that can afford to do without it. Companies, governments, and individuals all embrace software.

There are Luddites today who resist, to be sure. But the loom has grown too large to smash. It weaves itself bigger and stronger by the day. It was an unstoppable singularity long ago.

It used to be the case that we could look around and see things that coders had no part in producing. Today, that is impossible. Pick any nearby object, hard or soft, electronic or not, and ask yourself, "How did this get here?" or "How was this made?". Odds are, the story of that object was shaped by multiple software systems – those involved in its design, manufacturing, and distribution.

This is the economy that coders have built, not brick by brick – but line by line. The code of the world, a multilingual tower of Babel, is the edifice for which Babbage and Lovelace laid the first stone.

They are two sides of the same thing – the tower of code and the flood of software, the textual edifice and its stories in motion.

Soft Is the New Hard, and the Old Hard

Babbage is often credited with inventing the computer – yet he never did build his Analytical Engine – that device to weave algebra like flowers and trees. He managed to build small parts of it before his death in 1871. His son continued for twenty years to build it, but also failed. Parts of the Analytical Engine have been constructed, as Babbage intended it, but the entirety has not – even to this day.

Babbage's most profound contributions were not the machines he built, but rather his writings *about* his unborn machines. Babbage's hardware design processes exactly mirror the design of all complex "hard" things today – that is, he built it "in the soft" first. No computer chip, no city bridge, no car engine, no rocket ship, nothing of importance is built "in the hard" first. We build them first with our soft technologies, our languages: the spoken word, the written word, diagrams... and software. Because Babbage had no software on hand to create a working simulation, he used the soft technologies he did have: the written word, mathematical notations, and diagrams. And with these, he wove a simulation of his machine in the wetware of those with whom he collaborated, and those who came after him.

Lovelace's understanding of that machine allowed her to weave with it in her mind. Before it had even been built, she was capable of seeing, in the distance, that machine's ability to do numbers, algebra, music, and more. She and Babbage were some of the first minds (extended with paper and pens) that could run such simulations.

Today, our simulations of unborn hard technologies run the same way, in minds – but we also have an additional option: to write a software simulator, freeing the mind of the need to imagine the complex processes of invisible machines. We can render its inner workings to the screen before they ever work in the hard. Aided by software, our imagination can leap beyond its cognitive limitations.

Babbage and Lovelace didn't just write a machine and program into life, they wrote a new kind of writing into life. They wrote a new way of thinking into life. Today, that kind of writing allows us to describe, simulate, visualize, share, combine, and iterate upon hard things long before they become hard. From the soft, hard things crystallize.

But the power of the soft works the other way, too.

The cloud computing revolution was a softening of the hard – or the software-ification of hardware. Programmers now have, at their fingertips, vast and inexpensive cloud computing resources. We can "spin up" virtual (software) machines with arbitrary amounts of RAM, memory, and computing power. Underneath the software machines are hardware machines – but not necessarily in a one-to-one ratio; indeed, one hardware machine may host several software machines, or one software machine may sprawl across multiple pieces of hardware. Yet to the programmer deploying their software in the cloud, these details are abstracted away. You *feel* like your software is running on whatever hardware you requested from the software that runs the cloud. In reality, your software may be running on software (which is running on software (which is running on software (which is running on software))).

What of the hardware at the bottom, then? Where is it heading? For a time in history, it seemed that the hardware industry was driving the whole world – with computing speeds doubling every two years. But Moore's "Law" turned out to be what everyone (including Gordon Moore) knew it to be all along: not much of a law at all. The doubling of hardware speed began to slow down dramatically as it ran up against *actual* laws: physical laws like the fact that putting too many transistors too close together makes the computer faster, but also hotter.

This led to the inevitable: chips that cannot get faster without becoming uncoolable and hazardous.

Yes, hardware can still get cheaper, smaller, easier to access, more ubiquitous. The analogies are the clay tablets of Babylon. These tablets were large and difficult to produce, giving way to papyrus, then to paper. Today, paper and ink would appear to represent the end of that road – the cheapest, most ubiquitous substances that enable the infinitude of human written expression. You can buy paper in loose leaf, in many colors, in notebooks, with holes, with lines, with grids, and so on – but at the end of the day, it's all just paper. What you write on it is what matters. In other words, writing surfaces have become as soft as possible, while still being exactly hard enough for today's uses. Years of abstraction have deleted anything hard or heavy.

Computing hardware is also racing to the bottom in terms of cost, weight, thinness, and its ability to be virtually sliced into whatever size you need. Hardware is softening and perhaps, one day, will become as abstract as paper. Today, we effortlessly copy software from old machines to newer ones – as if to underscore that the hardware was only ever just a vessel for the software in the first place. We pour the software out into the next vessel and the next and the next – no vessel any more important than the previous one. It's as easy as copying cuneiform from one clay tablet to another. Actually it's easier, because the work of the scribes can be performed by software as well.

Nothing escapes the impact of software: not the economy, not the government, not science, not education, not hardware, and . . . not even software. It's true, we leverage software to transform software. Languages like Racket or Java or Python are pieces of software; but they act more like looms that transform our programs into apps, webpages, data visualizations, and so on. You know: more software. The levels of meta-weaving don't stop at just one, though. Consider the Racket language – which weaves the programs written in this book. With that language, we wove `#lang dtc/story/cats` and `#lang dtc/frames/animations`, which in turn weave your programs into whatever they happen to describe. And Racket itself was woven, in part, with code written in the C programming language, which itself was woven, in part, by code written in assembly language.

Abstraction's Arrow

As Alan Perlis put it:

> We will never run out of things to program as long as there is a single program around.

It seems we will never stop creating languages as long as there is a single language around, either. As our throughput of 111 billion lines of code per year steadily and unpredictably transmogrifies everything in its path, the world inevitably changes. As the world changes, the kinds of changes we wish to make to the world change, too, causing the programs we wish to write to change. We then create new languages that are specially designed for *those* sorts of changes.

In our experience, students assume this means that computer languages are on a trajectory to collide with human languages, at which time we will all simply code in English (or Spanish, or Chinese). For some reason, this "utopia" always sounds both plausible and desirable to novice programmers – though in fact it is neither plausible nor desirable. But for those who are not yet fluent in a programming language, it is an understandable lament. Similarly, a native English speaker living in a Deaf community might lament that, "Things would be so much easier if only everyone could just understand me." Becoming as fluent as everyone in *their* language is a long road fraught with frustration and embarrassment. Furthermore, it is all too easy for non-speakers and non-signers to underestimate the value of languages they do not know, and thus to view the road ahead as *only* containing frustration and embarrassment, when in fact it *can* be viewed as a road filled with joy and enlightenment.

To wish that all computers would just "know English" is a similar kind of lament. At first glance, it might seem that making the computers understand English would save us time – plus it would be cool.

We can't argue with that.

It's harder than it sounds, though, and (worse) it would be a step in a dubious direction for most software.

To see that it's hard, consider how easy it is to make a computer understand `#lang dtc/story/cats`. This language is vastly simpler than English; its documentation fits on one not-too-long webpage. It is *because* it is small and simple that every word and grammatical structure in the language has been given a precise definition (using `define`); for all cases of ambiguity, an `if` has already been used to unambiguously handle the ambiguity.

As an example, consider this fictitious English-y computer language:

```
#lang dtc/English

Turn the cat red, then rotate it, please.
```

Is this really better than the following?

```
#lang dtc/story/cats

(rotate (redify cat))
```

They both express the same idea. But the phrase "turn the cat red" is shortened to `(redify cat)`; the "then rotate it" is expressed with `(rotate _)`; the punctuation has been deleted; and the unnecessary "please" has been deleted. If you wanted to implement `#lang dtc/English`, one way might be to write a program capable of reading in English phrases like "Turn the cat red, then rotate it, please" and performing all of the above deletions (removing punctuation and unnecessary words) – ending up with something abstract and simple, like `(rotate (redify cat))`, which could perhaps be run similarly.

We've come back to the old skull/skin barrier question again: Should people take the time to train their brains to write in computer languages; or should we make computers capable of understanding the breadth and depth of human language? Only this time, the question has taken on a different tone. It's no longer as simple as – should we do arithmetic on our fingers or on a calculator? Now, we are asking a lot more than addition and subtraction from those machines on the far side of our collective skin/skull barriers. We are coming very close to asking them to do what we ask other human minds to do – namely: to make sense out of our ideas no matter how they are written.

Would our fictitious English-y language be able to make sense of this?

```
#lang dtc/English

pls make the cat red and then
rotate it after you make it red!
```

You might argue this doesn't count because it's not grammatically correct and contains a misspelling. Fine. Maybe this, then?

```
#lang dtc/English

Computer, please make the cat red.
Upon making it red, I would like you to
    rotate it.
```

Or:

```
#lang dtc/English
```

```
Rotate the cat,
    but only after
        you first make it red.
```

Or:

```
#lang dtc/English
```

```
Rotate the cat after coloring it red.
```

All of these are valid. Will #lang dtc/English accept all of them or only some? If it must accept all of them, we must face the fact that there may be a lot of ways to express the same concept, and we must handle them all somehow. If it only accepts some such ways – then the language isn't really English, is it? Rather, it's a more specialized version of English that users of #lang dtc/English will now have to learn. They will have to learn what the language *doesn't* accept – what your abstractions have deleted.

The designer of #lang dtc/English must face a choice then: Handle many ways of saying the same thing; or force users to learn the canonical way of saying the thing. The former is hard for you, the designer; the latter requires people to learn your language.

It's not really a hard choice. Just the task of getting the computer to understand the myriad of ways that an unrestricted human writer might express the concepts of color shifting and rotating an image of a cat is subject to an immediate explosion in complexity. Something that was an easy task in #lang dtc/story/cats becomes seemingly impossible to do for all cases in #lang dtc/English. It's enough to make any sensible person ask, is it *really* that hard to learn vocabulary words like rotate, red, and cat? Is it really that hard for someone to write basic constructions like (rotate (redify cat))? It takes time and thought on the part of the learner, yes. But many have achieved fluency in one or more programming language; no one to date has created a computer that can be programmed in English.

Even if someone *did* create such a miraculous programming language, where any English sentence is "understandable" by the computer – we would then be forced to ask the tough question: What does "understandable" mean? Sometimes English is ambiguous; sometimes even human beings have trouble understanding each other's precise meanings. Does the magical language just randomly pick between available interpretations? Does it ask you for clarification? We could call these two strategies, respectively: `#lang makes-a-best-guess` and `#lang asks-for-help`. If an airplane were programmed in either of these, we would drive instead. Airplanes shouldn't have to second-guess their programming; and pilots shouldn't have to clarify a coder's intentions on the fly.

The code that runs our cars, our airplanes, our stock markets, our voting systems, our scientific experiments – these are programs with value because, once written, we no longer have to think about them. On the other hand, if such programs were running within some kind of magical `#lang` that is "under-standing" thousands of lines of ambiguous source code per millisecond – we would think about our programs quite often, as they do unpredictable things or suddenly stop to ask what the programmer originally meant. And even if users *knew* what the programmers were thinking, how would they clarify things? The best tool we have for clarification is, of course, programming languages themselves. Circular.

Thus the whole quest to build `#lang dtc/English` would be difficult, and even if it worked, it's the kind of language that would be quite the burden on working memory and attention. In one way or another, users would end up back where they started – programming in more precise languages. So it's safe to say we won't stop programming in precise languages anytime soon.

This very idea – to create a program that could understand English – was left as an exercise to the reader in 1950 by none other than Alan Turing himself. Actually, Turing's exercise was a bit harder – because it requires creating a program that can both understand written English *and* generate responses that fool people into thinking it's a human mind talking to them. No language designer to date has passed Turing's test.

Coders prefer to take on challenges that our linguistic tools are better suited for. As Perlis puts it:

Within a computer natural language is unnatural.

Every one of those 111 billion lines of code we write yearly is written in a formal language because those languages have a kind of power that natural lan-guages do not. They say only what they need to say, and they say these things in a formal, unambiguous way. They are either correct or not correct – nothing murky and unclear, nothing "both right and wrong," as we often find in everyday human utterances.

So yes, the languages we code in will continue to change over time – but not in the direction of becoming more ambiguous or more "human." Rather, they will become increasingly streamlined and tailored to the problems that matter to human minds. Furthermore, as software inevitably floods every nook and cranny of human experience, as more and more people find themselves swept up in the wave, we will find that the number of languages multiply – applied to more and more problems by more and more coders. The diversity of language is on a divergent trajectory, a linguistic nova.

Coding allows you to control the matter of the world, the electrons, the pixels on screens, the communication lines of the internet. Your fluencies in computer languages won't arrive spontaneously, like magic – no more than Spanish or Chinese fluencies would. But once you have them, you'll begin to seem like you have magical powers to others, able to weave together larger and larger systems, capable of more and more impact on the world around you.

Just remember: Languages aren't power; fluency is power.

Within a computer, natural language may be unnatural; however, within a human mind, computer languages can *become* quite natural indeed. Many who embark on the road to becoming a coder do fail – misunderstanding the nature of the road they are on. People who think fluency can be achieved simply by being exposed to facts and ideas in a classroom will fail just as surely as someone who thinks they can learn Spanish just by attending class and memorizing verb conjugations. Knowledge, coverage, exposure, awareness – none of these are equivalent to fluency.

The surest way to fluency is to use the language outside of class – a lot. In our experience as teachers, the students who learn the fastest are the ones who figure out how to make programming into play.

Then, they play in their free time.

Languages are power – but languages are not easy to learn. So in truth: Learning is power. Then again . . . learning is not easy, and all too many students don't know how to do it effectively. So in truth: *Knowing* how to learn is power.

The impacts of software are now apparent worldwide, as is the growing need to learn how to write it. What is not yet apparent is whether our education systems can be altered to teach the writing of software effectively, at a grand scale. If we can, then we can finally bridge the gap between the importance of software to the human race and the number of human beings who know how to write it.

But if we can't, then our world's stories will continue to be written by a few, highly fluent individuals.

The rest will never know what stories they cannot write.

LANGUAGES WITHIN

The Education Bottleneck

When a developer joins a new team, there is an immediate educational bottleneck. They must "ramp up" (as it is often called — a term borrowed from economics and business (Terwiesch and Bohn 2001)). This means learning about the codebase of their new team — its story to date. Perhaps the software is brand new — and the story is only just beginning. Or maybe years have gone by, and the story is being joined *in medias res*. If so, there may already be a giant artifact of millions of lines, an invisible machine, an edifice of thought — all manifested as lines of text. Bit by bit, a new developer must learn the linguistic edifice's nooks, crannies, and magic staircases.

Code that ostensibly is "written in Python" will still take a fluent Python programmer time to learn — to develop the even-more-specialized fluency related to this *particular* Python code, the ideas that *this* Python code expresses, the metalanguage used in and around *this* business ecosystem within which the Python code resides. Code is always embedded in and shaped by context and history.

Yes, even expert developers experience returns to being novices — learning on the job, but learning nonetheless. The office becomes the classroom. We developers loop back to this beginning with surprising frequency, finding ourselves not yet fluent in the peculiarities of some new land (whether it be a software system, language, library, framework, or tool).

Yet, we are not without techniques for such loop backs — we know how to learn from each other. Sometimes we learn through writings called "documentation" or etchings called "diagrams"; sometimes we learn through oral traditions called "meetings," "code reviews," or "scrums"; sometimes we learn by reading the ancient texts — studying long into the night. Sometimes we even learn by *editing* the ancient texts themselves.

As the flood of software grows, so does this educational undercurrent. Software companies are all education companies — at least internally, for their own programmers. Whether it was consciously designed or not, there exists an "education system" in and around any software project. The larger the project, the more complex the education system. Brand new programmers at a software company are highly paid students, often taught by highly paid teachers.

So if coding education is critical in the software industry and critical in K-12 education worldwide, it would seem that coding education unites us all. It's not something we grow out of or graduate from. It's part of the definition of the field: We wield programming languages – tools that allow users to extend them with new definitions that weren't there before and that no one knows about except the writers. These things no one knows about often have to be learned by others when they join, *in medias res*, the stories we are writing.

The kind of coding educational environment we collectively build at the K-12 level will shape the backstories of every coder who joins those stories. Getting the K-12 environment right matters. To help shed light on how to get it right: a flashback – to the world's first environment for learning coding.

History's First Coding Students

In some sense or another, Ada Lovelace had a model of Babbage's Analytical Engine in her mind. She was able to conceive of its parts and their motion clearly enough that she was able to program it on paper without ever seeing the program run. How did she learn to do this in an age before coding education was a thing, before there was the Hour of Code, before the national CS Education Week, before Ada Lovelace Day? In part, she had a superb general education: because her father was a philandering poet, her mother was determined to teach her mathematics and logic to ensure that she didn't dabble in poetry and end up like her father. She was an avid reader and writer, tutored by some of the greatest minds of the time, a mathematical prodigy, and fluent in several languages. Babbage dubbed her "Enchantress of numbers." She wrote a program for calculating the Bernoulli numbers in her notes as she was translating a French article about Babbage's machine.

She and Babbage were some of the few people in the world capable of writing programs for the Analytical Engine. All of the programs they wrote solved mathematical problems – and were essentially translations from the mathematical ideas and notations, in which they were already fluent, into a notation that Babbage was designing – the "Notation" in his notes (Babbage 1826). Ada's program was published as follows:

Diagram for the computation by the Engine of the Numbers of Bernoulli. See Note G. (page 722 et seq.)

But that is not how it would have been entered into the Analytical Engine – which would not have had a keyboard for input and a screen for output. Rather it was to have punch cards for input and – elegantly – a punch card puncher for output (Collier 1970). One might wonder: Could a resulting punch card be fed back into the engine as a new program, which would then produce a new punch card, and so on?

Exercise

Can you write a program in one of this book's languages whose output is a valid program in another of this book's languages?

In any event, the "Notation" carried sufficient information to allow someone who understood the machine to hand-compile it into a punch card representation. Had the machine existed, Babbage and Lovelace would have been able to feed these punch cards into it by hand. Such a stack of compiled code would have looked like this, the technology borrowed from the automated looms of the day:

How did Ada Lovelace learn to program? How did she build Babbage's machine in her mind? At the earliest gleaming of software's dawn there were already multiple languages at play in the minds of the earliest programmers, who were superb masters of their own native languages, too. They used the languages they knew to design new languages – the written Notation and the language of punched holes in cards. And they ran these programs, in various forms, in their extended minds – on wetware interacting with paper, an act of distributed cognition that allowed them to simulate the workings of hardware that had never been built.

They did, in the 1830s and 1840s, what coding students today must do – install in their wetware the ability to write programs in multiple Turing-complete languages. They could not, interestingly enough, achieve fluency by today's standards in the languages they designed. Without the benefit of a real computer, they could not test their programs; not surprisingly, both of them made mistakes. Ada is famous for catching what Babbage called a "grave mistake" (Babbage 1864), and Lovelace's program printed above contains one error that seems never to have been caught by either of them. The small error, almost impossible to see, is occasionally caught by modern programmers who take on the recreational task of translating her program into a modern computer language (Target 2018).

Programmers in a world before programmable machines, they wrote only a small number of programs, wielding only a small number of languages. Although they could not achieve the levels of fluency that people today can, they did quite well for being the first coding students (and coding teachers) of all time.

Abstractly speaking, this environment consisted of writing letters to each other. Before the end of this book, we will call upon teachers of coding to do something similar – reaching out and connecting with each other through the power of natural language and storytelling.

(environment (mind (fluency)))

It might seem today, with the benefit of educational software, scientific findings, and our historical vantage point, we should have an easy time building coding educational environments. Still, what should an ideal environment for training fluent coders look like? And how does that ideal compare to what the world is actually building today?

For one thing, we know an ideal environment must be capable of nurturing people over a long period of time. We know that the road to fluency is paved with more programs than what Babbage and Lovelace wrote. Exactly how many more, though, is hard to say.

The fact that we don't know the answer to this question is an indicator of the larger issue: A brain's journey to become a coder is largely uncharted territory – even though many have walked it since Babbage and Lovelace made those first unsteady steps. Most people who have learned to code can tell you the story of how *they* recollect learning it, but no one is in agreement about exactly how to teach it to others – let alone build systems that do so at scale. To make matters worse, the moment we are fluent, we – by definition – cannot quite see things the way novices do anymore. The more fluent we become, the more we must rely on science to understand the novice brain.

Turning to science: One of the most consistent findings throughout the decades is that a disturbing fraction of students have not succeeded in introductory programming courses (McCracken et al. 2001). So at least we know one thing: Coding is either 1) hard to learn, 2) hard to teach, or 3) both. To make matters worse, such findings have been repeated time and again in classrooms at the world's top research institutions – where the professors were fluent in the languages of the time, where the university students had top-of-the-line hardware and software, and the students were already well educated before beginning their first coding classes. Students frequently failed anyway. If a subject is hard to learn or hard to teach under these optimistic circumstances, it probably won't be easier in, say, a 3rd grade class of underperforming students in a school with no IT department. It might not be easy for anyone. Learning and teaching languages rarely is.

Furthermore, with the preponderance of scientific research having been done at the university level, K-12 education is left comparatively without the light of science, at least for now. Thus, K-12 education systems must fumble in the dark to assemble the first public infrastructures for producing a population not just fluent in the computer languages of today, but capable of becoming fluent in the computer languages of tomorrow. It's a tricky problem.

To make matters worse, a pesky quirk of the economy: The average salary for teachers in America is a far cry from the $105,000 that is the current average for software developers (Bureau of Labor Statistics 2019). Individuals who enjoy teaching and coding are immediately placed in a dilemma with a strong economic bias toward going to work for Google rather than the local school district. A corollary is that the more fluent a K-12 educator becomes, the more the same dilemma sneaks up on them.

Some might argue that K-12 educators do not need to be as fluent as professional software engineers – using, by analogy, mathematics: We do not require, say, 3rd grade math teachers to have the same proficiencies as working mathematicians. True. But on the other hand, we do require 3rd grade Spanish teachers to have near-native fluency in adult Spanish, not just fluency in 3rd grade Spanish. We certainly require 3rd grade English teachers to be fluent speakers of adult English, not just 3rd grade English. In fact, this is true at all levels of instruction, for all teachers of language.

The moment we recognize a subject as a language is the moment we know in our hearts that we must raise the bar – both for teachers and for students. Fluency becomes necessary for teachers and the end goal for students.

The recent fMRI studies localizing program comprehension in the same regions that process Spanish and English is an inconvenient truth for those who might have argued that fluency was unnecessary for teachers. As of 2017, scientists observed what coding fluency looks like in the brain: The same regions light up when you see code or English. Fluency is not a unicorn or abstract idea; it's a real, physical thing – observable in the gray matter located in and around Broca's region. Now that we know this, it seems quite natural to ask educators to have the very wetware upgrades they are supposed to be instilling in others. It seems strange to ask a teacher to help a student travel a neurocognitive road that they themselves have not traveled.

Still, this *is* an admittedly high bar. Perhaps there's an argument that waiting for teachers to become fluent before teaching is simply too slow. Perhaps software has become so ubiquitous, and the general public so extravagantly left behind by the explosion of our world's software infrastructure, that having *any* kind of coding instruction at the K-12 level is better than nothing. After all, if teachers become fluent eventually (via teaching), then things can only get better in the long run, while still being "better than nothing" in the short term.

But that's a big "if" – or, a big "conditional branch." One side of the branch may lead to a utopia of fluency, but the other may lead elsewhere. Which story will come true? Whether teachers become more and more fluent as they teach depends very much on *how* and *what* they are teaching. For better or worse, the how and what are being decided by forces external to education systems themselves. A non-trivial amount of Silicon Valley venture capital money is currently being spent to create products and "out-of-the-box curricula" that enable teachers to teach coding without knowing how to code. It sounds like a contradiction in terms – but that's the marketing.

One company, Tynker, has received over 10 million dollars of venture funding to create online software to teach coding to K-12 students. Their pitch to educators as of this writing? "No experience required!"

A clip from their website, with our emphasis added:

Built for Educators

No experience required! Plus, free training for schools.

It's not an entirely empty promise, either. The lessons are interactive: You simply put your students in front of the software. Hard parts of being a coding teacher are supposedly done for you now. Taken to the extreme, that's one kind of utopia perhaps – the Silicon Valley kind: where curriculum and instruction are dominated by software produced at tech companies; the role of a "teacher" is merely standing in the same room as the students and making sure they are focusing attention and working memory on the software. It's an abstraction of what "teacher" once meant.

In 2013, Microsoft purchased the indie game Minecraft for $2.5 billion (Peckham 2014). Within months, they had announced their new product: Minecraft Education Edition, with Minecraft-based educational experiences and out-of-the-box lesson plans in language arts, science, history, math, arts, and, of course, coding. By 2017, they were providing Minecraft-based coding instruction through their online coding education platform MakeCode, complete with interactive lessons, tutorials, and entire 14-week "introduction to computer science" courses. Perhaps the utopia has truly arrived: Teachers without fluency can now enroll their students in online courses that cover everything from function definitions to conditional branching to loops to the assigning of variables. It's worth noting that none of these courses claim to create "fluency," but rather to "cover" the concepts. Either way, their pitch to educators as of this writing? "No experience required!"

Our emphasis added:

About this Course

This is a semester-long course targeted at middle school grades 6–8, as an introduction to Computer Science. The course is written for teachers who may have never taught computer science before. During this course, students will explore concepts in computer science through Microsoft MakeCode and Minecraft.

Google has launched Google for Education, which seeks to be an entire out-of-the-box infrastructure for education: Get Chromebooks for all your students, link them to Google's cloud, get curriculum for every subject – and, of course, coding EdTech software. Their CS First curriculum is free and covers all the usual basics – variables, functions, ifs, loops, and so on. Their pitch to educators as of this writing? "No experience required!"

No CS experience required

CS First empowers every teacher to
teach computer science with free
tools and resources.

Everyone from venture funded startups to big tech has a potion that seeks to make it effortless to teach coding. In order to use these, you simply need to redefine "teach coding." Instead of defining it as something that requires fluency from the teacher, you now can define it as the activity of placing students in front of the software, and simply allowing them to learn through video tutorials and software interactions.

On the one hand, it seems that Plato might approve of EdTech and our increasing reliance upon it. These writings of today are neither silent nor still – but dynamic and alive. Our writings can answer the questions of students. They can administer tests and gather metrics. They can build data models of student progress. They can adapt and reorganize as necessary. They are potions for remembering *and* reminding.

It's almost like they have a teacher inside. The common term "automated tutoring system" certainly implies this.

Luckily, the degree to which coders will be able to delete human coding teachers from the equation may itself be thwarted by as-yet-undiscovered laws of language learning. It can be hypothesised that fluency, as a generalized Broca's region process, must to some un-abstractable degree be transmitted between minds interacting in real-time – thus securing a kind of job security for language teachers, which would extend to coding teachers. Language education apps of today like Duolinguo, while of obvious value, don't seem quite sufficient enough to yield real fluency. They don't claim to. Even EdTech enthusiasts know in their heart that nothing can quite match the power of interacting with a human teacher, someone speaking our native tongues, a storyteller, someone who can connect what we are learning to what matters to us.

What is most likely to happen (and indeed is already happening in the coding classrooms of the world) is a kind of hybrid – where educational software tools are used increasingly by teachers worldwide. What this teacher/software hybrid will evolve into and how it will affect students depends very much on what that software looks like and how teachers employ it.

Today's "no experience necessary" potions aren't necessarily bad things in the grand scheme of things. In fact, many of them can be truly life-changing classroom tools if used well. Many are built to be fun, and many have high educational value. The only advice we offer is this: Look at them like any technology that unburdens the mind. We should think critically about how they should be leveraged in classrooms.

Calculators unburden the mind, but we still view their use with some suspicion – apparent from our continued teaching of arithmetic concepts in early education. A student mind that can *only* do arithmetic with a calculator is lacking a degree of fluency that it ought to have; a teacher mind that can *only* teach coding with an out-of-the-box EdTech software can be regarded analogously.

Will the reliance upon certain kinds of EdTech software have adverse effects? It depends on what we allow the software to delete. Externalizations are always double-edged: They free the mind of a task, but at the expense of any long-term cognitive benefits that performing such a task might have had.

In asking about the optimal educational environment for student minds, we have arrived at the crucial question of how and what to externalize from teacher minds. If we want to get ubiquitous coding education right, we have to get this part right. The evolving definition of "coding teacher" matters – as does the question of which people are empowered to co-author that definition.

Co-Authoring the EdTech Story

If there are not enough fluent coding teachers around, software plus non-fluent teachers will always be better than that. The thing with voids is that when they can be filled with something, they will be.

The power of EdTech in the short term to be better than nothing may allow it to scale very quickly, allowing us to complete our worldwide project of installing coding education at all levels of K-12 education long before fluent coding teachers are the norm in coding classrooms. One early definition of "coding teacher" may very well end up being, at least in the short term, anyone who watches the kids while they sit at the computer. If it really requires "no experience," then any teacher at any school can do it: English teachers, history teachers, math teachers, science teachers, gym teachers.

That's not a bad thing at all. Let us name this diverse first generation of coding teachers, fluent or not, the Babbage and Lovelace generation. And they deserve a name, for some of the greatest power to weave the stories of education's future is actually in their hands – not in the hands of software companies.

If there's any piece of advice we could give to the Babbage and Lovelace generation of teachers, it would be simply this: Be lifelong coding students. It's the least we teachers can do if we are the ones helping to install coding education alongside our other societal literacies: math, reading, science, and history. If coding truly deserves to be among these pillars of society, then it needs to get messaged to students as something with lifelong value – by teachers who actually believe that frame story.

How can teachers, fluent or not, simultaneously 1) teach coding, 2) be lifelong students of coding, and 3) message to students the deep human value of coding?

Teachers can actually do all three by doing just one thing: storytelling. Coding is a form of writing that can turn fictions into facts. One doesn't need to be an expert, or even very fluent, to begin thinking and writing in this way. In fact, to begin making positive impacts, one needs nothing fancier than the languages taught in this book, and no more fluencies than whatever you may have gained simply by reading through the code examples herein.

To assist with helping teachers tell such stories, below is a series of three exercises – three story prompts, so to speak. To make these even more powerful, we'll abstract over their subject matters. They are for coding teachers, English teachers, science teachers, history teachers, art teachers, and so on. Each can be repeated one time, or thousands.

Exercise

Imagine you're at the whiteboard, teaching. You begin to draw a diagram. A voice within you begins to speak.
It says:

> Did you just draw a diagram on the whiteboard? Did you employ a "visual vocabulary" to communicate with your students – maybe a combination of lines, arrows, words, colors, annotations, stick figures, and/or other pictures?

And the voice is right. Of course you did. You're a communicator. Such written communications are powerful teaching tools. You've mastered that vocabulary.

But consider: Could code be written to draw that diagram for you? And are there times when such automation might benefit you? Only you can answer that. And that's what this exercise is about.

Consider the following sample (fictional) responses below. Use them as a template for your own (nonfictional) responses.

I'm a history teacher. As I was standing at the blackboard drawing a timeline of Napoleon's retreat from Moscow, my inner voice said something along the lines of:

This timeline looks vaguely like the Story images I remember seeing in *Don't Teach Coding*. I communicate with timelines *all the time*! If I could write code that produces a timeline image, then maybe I could take all of that code and `define` it as a simple vocabulary word – like `timeline-image`, so people could write something like:

```
(timeline-image
  `(["24 June 1812"
      "Napoleon leaves with 685,000"]

     ["14 December 1812"
      "Napoleon returns with 27,000"]) )
```

Then, maybe I could ask my students to generate similar diagrams to embed in their essays.

Maybe I could even release my language online and see if other history teachers and students worldwide might want to use it.

So I went home and posted this on **dont-teach.com/coding/forum** because that was the exercise. (I didn't wait until after I had coded something – because that wasn't the exercise.)

Here's another perfectly fine sample response:

I'm an organic chemistry teacher. I was drawing diagrams for chemical reactions. My inner voice stopped me in my tracks.

I got some help from some other coders online and made a sweet language for generating molecular reaction diagrams with code like:

```
C2H4(g) + H2O(g) --> C2H5OH(g)
```

My language automates the process of generating nice, fancy images from the boring alphanumeric text.

I thought that was going to be all, but to my pleasant surprise, I found that I could compose the language I had written with one someone else had written . . . for making slideshows! Now I can code my own organic chemistry PowerPoint slides without using PowerPoint, and I'm even working on automatically generating quizzes and tests now.

I posted about my `#lang o-chem` on the forums so that organic chemistry teachers can find it.

That last one was an overachiever. Don't let people more fluent than you intimidate you into not starting. Let them inspire you. As we tell our students: Have a growth mindset.

Above all, note that the last assignment and the ones that follow aren't about writing code – but about storytelling, which is much bigger than coding. In part, they're about building habits of perceiving, whenever it is there, the *value* that writing code might bring. They're also about articulating that value to others in written natural language. A single lament in one's native tongue is a fine way to start a software story – whether you're going to code the software parts or someone else is. Powerful stories are written both in code *and* in natural language. Sharpening your ability to write such linguistically diverse stories comes from the act of attempting to write such stories – not from already knowing how to write such stories before you start. What we must know before we can do, we learn by doing.

Exercise

This is similar to the exercise above, but for a more complex communication tool than static images. These are known as: Images in motion.

Or, as others call them: Animations.

Here's a sample response.

I was teaching my class a song to remember the countries of the world. Each time we said a country name, I pointed at the country on the map.

My arm started to get tired, and I remembered that in *Don't Teach Coding* it said something about automation being the point of coding.

That gave me the idea to code up an animation, where the countries would light up in the appropriate order. First, I looked at **dont-teach.com** to see if someone had already done something like this.

I found a language for generating static images of world maps with highlighted countries. It wasn't an animation, but I realized I could just use the `animate` magic word from this very book to animate all the frames in the order I wanted. Or any order, really.

Now my arm isn't tired, and I can even adjust the speed to increase the challenge. Sometimes I have the animation randomly show one of my students' faces on top of a random country.

The kids think it's hilarious. It taps into the same facial-recognition dopamine cycle that makes Facebook so addictive. Science! It's like I'm coding their brains.

Exercise

For our final exercise, we repeat the above for an even more complex communication tool than moving images.

The next level up? Not just animated, but *interactive* images. Some call them games. Others call them simulations, or systems. They go by many names.

These are one of the most powerful kinds of experiences code can produce. It allows the coder to design a back-and-forth, dynamic, real-time experience between mind and machine – a kind of automated dialog that would no doubt have interested Plato, writer of dialogues. The automated dialogue's potential for education is untapped and within easy reach of today's Babbage and Lovelace generation.

Here's a sample response to this exercise.

I was grading my students' essays and realized that 40% of them had not read the assigned readings. Within this population, 100% of them seemed to be under the impression that I wouldn't notice.

The voice inside my mind said:

Maybe they would read if I made a simple game out of the reading assignment. Like, at the end of each paragraph, the computer would pose an ethical question:

```
Do you think Tom Sawyer did the right thing?

A) He never does.
B) Only if we redefine "right."
C) Yes.
D) All of the above. E) None of the below.
```

And then, regardless of what they answered, the computer would respond with a meme containing a photo of a random student in the class. Then it could play one of several available fart noises and give them a random number of points.

With the help of the internet, I made one such silly assignment, and it was a hit. So now I do it with all of my assignments, and I'm supposed to show other teachers how to do it at next month's professional development brown bag lunch meeting. Some of the students are asking to be able to write their own. All in all, it turned out to be faster and more rewarding than waiting for a Silicon Valley startup to raise millions in venture funding to create it for me.

These three exercises will make you more fluent while you simultaneously start stories that matter for yourself and others. It's okay to start more stories than you finish. Keep starting stories until one of them catches your mind in such a way that you can't stop thinking about how awesome it would be to write more, if only you could write the part that has to be written in code. Then go out and learn precisely enough coding to help you with what you need to write. This will streamline your learning process and help you navigate the vast linguistic seas out there. There's a lot that *can* be learned. What *should* be learned is best guided by your own stories – the ones you're writing for yourself and those you care about.

That's it, abstractly. Just write stories. Whenever portions of your stories need to be written in code, try to write those parts, too. Repeat until fluent. Then continue repeating. That is the procedure.

Inevitably, some teachers who follow this fluency procedure will grow so fluent that they leave to work at Google, Microsoft, Amazon, Facebook, or Netflix. It cannot be avoided. It's just economics.

Many teachers will stay, though. They're the members of the Babbage and Lovelace generation that matter most, uniquely positioned to write the stories of education's future.

Babbages and Lovelaces of Education

Optimistically speaking, we hope the historical record of the future will read something like this:

The earliest K-12 public infrastructures for teaching coding alongside reading, writing, mathematics, science, and history began in dozens of countries in the early decades of the 2000s. It became the global standard by the year 2030.

Although off-the-shelf EdTech solutions filled the sudden demand for coding instruction, a population of teachers eventually grew fluent enough to write code and share it with each other via cloud-based version control technologies of the time, such as Github.com and Bitbucket.com. That, in retrospect, may have been the tipping point. More software led to more collaborations, which led to increased fluency within what we now call the Babbage and Lovelace generation of coding teachers.

Increasingly fluent teachers began to tell their students stories about their *in media res* open source EdTech projects, stories about how these personal quests had begun and where they were going. The effect on students was profound – some even becoming inspired enough to participate in these projects themselves. Making pushes to software projects before graduating high school became the norm for hundreds of thousands of students in those early years.

To the Babbage and Lovelace generation, we owe the educational culture of today – with its unique blend of oral storytelling traditions coupled with written traditions, such as the `"Hello, World"` ritual, the First Push to Production ceremony, and Design a Language in Honor of Ada Lovelace Day – all of which are still celebrated in most parts of the world today.

Looking back, it's hard to pinpoint the exact moment when the singularity began – the moment the old definition of "education" had been completely rewritten by teachers and students from within. What we do know is that the definition slowly changed into what we now call education today: the act of fluent citizens publicly collaborating on the global project to program our own brains, via our own software, for the good of the world.

So, don't just "teach coding." Let the pursuit of fluency transform you in such a way that you get to participate in the ongoing redefinition of what the term "teach coding" means. Software has that power. Thus, fluency has that power.

With enough software written by enough teachers from within the education system, maybe we can finally adapt our schools in ways that have been impossible since Comenius founded them. Software, after all, can be built for change in ways that no harder technology can, reprogrammable from within, without having to be torn down and rebuilt.

The reprogrammable, software-driven education system – it's not a utopia in and of itself. It's more like a strategy for *finding* a utopia – paving the way by building a system that can be flexibly adapted, coherently discussed, and written by fluent coders who care about making that system into the best version of itself. The more we accomplish this, the more we can entertain levels of optimism that would have impressed even Leibniz. Who knows? Perhaps we'll stumble upon an unexpected blend of various utopian visions, perhaps a blend that leads to the *best* of all possible utopias, with the best of all possible education systems, written by the best of all possible coders: our best possible selves.

This Final Section Has No Name

Channels from mind to matter are not magical fictions. They are called computers, and they are everywhere. Every successful utterance in a programming language changes the world in some small way at runtime. Very literally, the matter in the world changes. Electrons move, transistors flip, pixels light up. A grain of sand is not a heap, but as you add grains of sand, one at a time, eventually you have a heap. That first program you write...

```
#lang dtc/complete

(print "HELO")
```

... may displace less than a grain of sand's worth of electrons on your personal computer – hardly enough matter to matter. But those first steps are the most important. As you gain fluency, you gain power. You can begin to displace electrons in the cloud, electrons on the other side of the world, electrons on other people's computers. Your writings will be able to move motors, send emails, display web pages, store information in databases, respond to user interactions. At some point, the fluencies in your brain will allow you to write software that moves electrons in brains – extending or enhancing cognitive abilities. Are those electrons enough matter to matter? It certainly can be.

Wittgenstein once ended a much more famous book about language with:

Whereof one cannot speak, thereof one must be silent.

It's hard to argue with that. We won't.

Still, we'd like to end this book about programming languages with an opposite tone. Fluent coders are wizards of language; we can weave stories that change the world. Those changes can be profound and far-reaching. Our changes can outlive us. They can span the skull/skin barrier. They can span the globe.

Wizards, wizards in training, and wizards who train other wizards:

Of what we wish to change, we must not remain silent. We must write the stories of the future. We must weave the next world.

That is the procedure.

The End
And, to be continued...

Conclusion

As you might expect, we had to omit much in our attempt to write a short interdisciplinary book across the fields of computer science, linguistics, history, and learning science. For the ideas in this book that we never explicitly named, hopefully this conclusion will serve.

NEXT STEPS: LEARNING SCIENCES

What you choose to do next is up to you. But, in accordance with the Fundamental Theorem, we will first list resources related to learning.

- *How People Learn.* This book should be required reading for anyone with a brain. It's the closest thing we've found to an instruction manual.
- *Learning How to Learn.* This online course will make you a more effective human being, no matter what you are studying.

For a treatise on the use of second language acquisition theory for teaching/learning coding, we recommend the excellent article by Scott R. Portnoff: "The Introductory Computer Programming Course Is First and Foremost a Language Course."

Also recommended: Gain fluency in a brand new natural language – a fluency you didn't acquire "for free" as a child. Language learning as an adult isn't easy. The quest to do so will teach you more about second language acquisition than this book ever could.

On that note, consider American Sign Language. Like our programming languages, it is a visual one. Learning it will expand your very definition of what language means.

NEXT STEPS: LANGUAGES TO LEARN

If you want to take the road less traveled and become a programmer who thinks differently from the average developer, become fluent in these:

- Racket
- Prolog
- Haskell

But beware. After becoming fluent in these, you'll no longer understand why people have trouble understanding Python, Java, or C. It will make it harder for you to empathize with novices.

NEXT STEPS: CODING

If you want to learn about computer science (not just one language, but something deeper), there are many paths. We'll recommend a few of our favorites – ones we've watched beginners walk down many times. They always walk back changed for the better.

- *How to Code: Simple Data* – an online course provided by the University of British Columbia through the edX platform. You can audit the course online for free. We also recommend the second course in the series, *How to Code: Complex Data*.
- *How To Design Programs* – one of the best introductory textbooks in computer science. It's free at **htdp.org**. Don't just read it. Do the exercises as many times as necessary to become fluent. Hint: Make flashcards.
- *Beautiful Racket* – a free online book about creating your own programming languages.
- *The Little Schemer* – a book that teaches programming via Socratic dialogue. Plato would be proud.

NEXT STEPS: SOFTWARE ENGINEERING

Depending on the size of the software artifact, programming feels different: Programming "in the micro" (a few lines) requires a different set of cognitions from programming "in the small" (a few hundred or a thousand lines), which requires a different set of cognitions from programming "in the large" (many thousands of lines or more).

The study of how we programmers must write, behave, and interact at various levels of textual complexity is called "software engineering."

Some resources:

- **The Mythical Man Month** addresses the odd paradox that adding more coders to a project can slow things down. More person-hours leads to less getting accomplished.

- **No Silver Bullet** is an essay that addresses the fact that software projects can become monsters that cannot be slain.

NEXT STEPS: HACKER CULTURE

We should never forget that being a coder is more about you and less about the corporations that you might end up working for. It is a human thing – a kind of free speech, a kind of self-expression, a kind of writing. The authors re-read the following frequently, to be reminded of who we are:

- **Hackers and Painters** – a book by hacker and entrepreneur Paul Graham.

- **In the Beginning There Was the Command Line** – an essay about Linux by sci-fi author Neil Stephenson.

- **The Cathedral and the Bazaar** – a book by Eric Raymond on the magic that is Open Source software.

NEXT STEPS: HISTORY

If you liked the historical lens of this book, we have a few recommendations:

- **"Breaking Smart" Season 1** is a series of online essays about the past and future of software engineering: **breakingsmart.com**. Read them, get inspired, change the world.

- *Computerphile* and *Numberphile* are YouTube Channels with a diverse selection of fascinating historical and technical videos.

- **Extra Credits** is a YouTube channel with tons of cool stuff. Find them at **becausegamesmatter.com**. Their chronologically first video on the history of writing is a logical place to start. Their videos about games and game design will be of interest to coders. Their game lens makes their historical analyses all the more relatable to coders.

NAMING THINGS: COMPUTER SCIENCE

We'll now "pull back the curtain" and try to name some of the ideas that we may have only touched upon implicitly in this book. We'll name them explicitly here, so you can find them in the world beyond.

- **Language Oriented Programming (LOP)**. First introduced in the 90s, this is a powerful and growing idea that has the power to transform how people learn programming and how programmers interact with each other professionally. It's a worldview worth adopting. The Racket language leads the way in this endeavor.

- **Theory of Computation**. This branch of computer science involves asking questions like: What is computation? Those interested in Turing-completeness should look there for similar gems. *Godel, Escher, Bach: An Eternal Golden Braid* is one of the best books ever written on the subject.

- Miscellaneous terms:
  - The idea of a function whose definition contains itself is called a "recursive function."
  - The style of programming that involves extending languages via creation of new functions is called "functional programming."
  - Languages with lots of parentheses are often referred to as "Lisps." Scheme is a Lisp. The ideas of escaping out of a Story with a comma (from Chapter 3) come to us from these languages – but the original concept was created by Willard Van Orman Quine. "Quasi-quoting" is the term to look up.
  - Writing programs that read other programs is called "writing an interpreter" or "writing a compiler" or "making a programming language."
  - Writing programs that produce other programs is called "meta-programming." Duh.

- The idea of a language hierarchy that contains languages successively more difficult to parse was formally fleshed out by Chomsky – see "Chomsky hierarchy."
- What we called Stories also goes by the name "expression" – or, in Lisp, "S-expression." The definition is the same: A list of things inside parentheses.

NAMING THINGS: PHILOSOPHY OF MIND

- The idea that minds and computations can be extended into the environment is called "extended mind" or "distributed cognition." The book *Cognition in the Wild* is a beautiful book on the subject – examining naval vessels as complex cognitive/computational systems involving many human minds and their many means of communication.

- The idea that language affects thought is called the "Sapir-Whorf Hypothesis."

- The idea of making a computer that fools other humans into thinking it is intelligent is known as "getting a machine to pass the Turing Test." It is one definition of "intelligent machine."

- The idea that a machine that can fool humans might still *not* qualify as intelligent is argued in a famous response to Turing called "The Chinese Room" argument.

NAMING THINGS: LEARNING SCIENCE

- **Cognitive apprenticeship** is both a practice and a field of research pertaining to the teaching of apprentices by masters – with a particular focus on how masters can model the necessary cognitive behaviors for their apprentices.

- **Communities of practice** is an idea that out-of-school learning happens (and perhaps *ought* to happen) in communities of practice – networks of variously skilled practitioners. Such communities can (and have!) been formed for computer science educators. In one model, a geographically located "master teacher" helps to train other coding teachers in an area.

Teachers who want to weave an environment in which they become more fluent over time would be advised to weave such a social network into existence – either around them geographically, or around them virtually (with the help of the internet).

This book can't change the world alone. We have to build and maintain new social structures that support new behaviors, and that lead to new fluencies. If you need help doing this in your area, we can help.

THANK YOU

Thank you for reading. At any time, for any reason, join us: **dont-teach.com/coding**.

Bibliography

Academic Dictionary of Lithuanian. 2005.

Ravi P. Agarwal and Syamal Sen. *Creators of Mathematical and Computational Sciences*. Springer Publishing Company, 2014.

James E. Aisner. "Global Brands: Connecting With Consumers Across Boundaries." Harvard Business School Working Knowledge, 2000. https://hbswk.hbs.edu/item/global-brands-connecting-with-consumers-across-boundaries (accessed August 15, 2019).

Scott D. Allen. "Benchmarking Microsoft vs Macintosh BASIC." *Mac GUI*, 1984. https://macgui.com/usenet/?group=6&id=453 (accessed September 21, 2019).

David F. Armstrong. "William C. Stokoe, Jr: Founder of Sign Language Linguistics, 1919-2000." 2000. http://gupress.gallaudet.edu/stokoe.html (accessed August 24, 2019).

Charles Babbage. "On a Method of Expressing by Signs the Action of Machinery." *Philosophical Transactions of the Royal Society of London* 116, pp. 250–265, 1826.

Charles Babbage. *Passages from the Life of a Philosopher*. London: Longman, Green, Longman, Roberts, & Green, 1864.

Thomas H. Bak, Jack J. Nissan, Michael M. Allerhand, and Ian J. Deary. "Does Bilingualism Influence Cognitive Aging?" *Annals of Neurology* 75(6), 2014.

Douglas C. Baynton. *Forbidden Signs: American Culture and the Campaign against Sign Language*. Reprint edition. University of Chicago Press, 1998.

Craig M. Bennett, Abigail A. Baird, Michael B. Miller, and George L. Wolford. "Neural Correlates of Interspecies Perspective Taking in the Post-Mortem Atlantic Salmon: An Argument for Proper Multiple Comparisons Correction." *Journal of Serendipitous and Unexpected Results* 1(1), pp. 1–5, 2010.

Jonathan M. Bloom. "Hand Sums: The Ancient Art of Counting with Your Fingers." *Boston College Magazine*, 2002. http://bcm.bc.edu/issues/spring_2002/ll_hand.html (accessed August 24, 2019).

Johan J. Bolhuis, Ian Tattersall, Noam Chomsky, and Robert C. Berwick. "How Could Language Have Evolved?" *PLOS Biology*, 2014.

John Bransford and National Research Council (U.S.). Committee on Developments in the Science of Learning, and National Research Council (U.S.). Committee on Learning Research and Educational Practice. *How People Learn: Brain, Mind, Experience, and School: Expanded Edition*. Washington, D.C.: National Academy Press, 2000.

Quincy Brown and Amy Briggs. "The CS10K Initiative: Progress in K-12 through Exploring Computer Science Part 1." *ACM Inroads* 6(3), pp. 52–53, 2015.

United States Department of Labor, Bureau of Labor Statistics. "Software Developers: Summary." 2019. https://www.bls.gov/ooh/computer-and-information-technology/software-developers.htm (accessed August 24, 2019).

Lord Byron. *The Complete Works of Lord Byron: Including His Suppressed Poems, and Others Never Before Published*. J. Smith, 1832.

Ruth Campbell, Mairéad MacSweeney, and Dafydd Waters. "Sign Language and the Brain: A Review." *Journal of Deaf Studies and Deaf Education* 13(1), pp. 3–20, 2007.

Noam Chomsky, Gene Searchinger, Frederick J. Newmeyer, Lila R. Gleitman, George A. Miller, Lewis Thomas, South Carolina Educational Television Network., Equinox Films, Inc., and Ways of Knowing, Inc. "The Human Language Series." 1995. Educational Television Program.

Andy Clark and David Chalmers. "The Extended Mind." *Analysis* 58(1), pp. 7–19, 1998.

Kristen M. Clark. "NAACP, other groups blast computer-coding proposal as 'misleading and mischievous'." *Tampa Bay Times*, 2016. http://www.tampabay.com/naacp-other-groups-blast-computer-coding-proposal-as-misleading-and/2267336 (accessed August 24, 2019).

Code.org. 2019. https://code.org/ (accessed August 15, 2019).

John Colapinto. "Famous Names: Does It Matter What a Product Is Called?" *The New Yorker*, 2011. https://www.newyorker.com/magazine/2011/10/03/famous-names (accessed August 15, 2019).

Bruce Collier. "The Little Engines That Could've: The Calculating Machines of Charles Babbage." Harvard University, 1970. http://robroy.dyndns.info/collier/ Thesis ... in partial fulfillment of the requirements for the degree of Doctor of Philosophy in the subject of History of Science.

John M. Cooper. *Plato: Complete Works*. Hackett Publishing Co, 1997.

CSforALL. 2019. https://www.csforall.org/ (accessed August 15, 2019).

Peter T. Daniels and William Bright. *The World's Writing Systems*. Oxford University Press, 1996.

Linda Darling-Hammond, Leib Sutcher, and Desiree Carver-Thomas. "Teacher Shortages in California: Status, Sources, and Potential Solutions." Learning Policy Institute, 2018. https://learningpolicyinstitute.org/product/teacher-shortages-ca-solutions-brief (accessed September 2, 2019).

Augustus De Morgan. *Trigonometry and Double Algebra*. Taylor, Walton and Maberly, 1849.

Frank N. Dempster. "The Spacing Effect: A Case Study in the Failure to Apply the Results of Psychological Research." *American Psychologist* 43(8), pp. 627–634, 1988.

dictionary.com. 2019. https://www.dictionary.com/browse/digit (accessed August 21, 2019).

Marloes van Dijk, Evelyn H. Kroesbergen, Elma Blom, and Paul P. M. Leseman. "Bilingualism and Creativity: Towards a Situated Cognition Approach." *The Journal of Creative Behavior* 53(2), 2018.

Edsger W. Dijkstra. *Selected Writings on Computing: A Personal Perspective*. 1st edition. Springer, 1982.

Edsger W. Dijkstra. "Under the Spell of Leibniz's Dream." *Information Processing Letters* 66, pp. 53–61, 2001.

Stuart E. Dreyfus and Hubert L. Dreyfus. "A Five-Stage Model of the Mental Activities Involved in Directed Skill Acquisition." California University Berkeley Operations Research Center, 1980.

Carol S. Dweck. *Mindset: The New Psychology of Success*. Ballantine Books, 2007.

Bradley Ewart. *Chess: Man vs Machine*. 1st edition. Barnes & Noble, 1980.

Luciano Fadiga, Laila Craighero, Maddalena Fabbri-Destro, Livio Finos, Nathalie Cotillon-Williams, Andrew Smith, and Umberto Castiello. "Language in Shadow." *Social Neuroscience* 1(2), pp. 77–89, 2006.

W. Tecumseh Fitch and Angela D. Friederici. "Artificial Grammar Learning Meets Formal Language Theory: An Overview." *Philosophical Transactions of the Royal Society B* 367(159), 2012.

The Florida Senate. "CS/CS/SB 468: Computer Coding Instruction." The Florida Senate, 2016. https://www.flsenate.gov/Session/Bill/2016/0468 (accessed August 15, 2019).

Benjamin Floyd, Tyler Santander, and Westley Weimer. "Decoding the Representation of Code in the Brain: An fMRI Study of Code Review and Expertise." In *Proc. ICSE '17 Proceedings of the 39th International Conference on Software Engineering*, pp. 175–186, 2017.

William Lois Foster. "A Study to Determine the Relationship of Selected Teacher Characteristics to Their Acceptance and Adoption of an Innovative Instructional Program." Northeast Louisiana University, 1977. A Dissertation Presented to the Faculty of the Graduate School of Northeast Louisiana University in Partial Fulfillment of the Requirements for the Degree of Doctor of Education.

Roland M. Friedrich and Angela D. Friederici. "Mathematical Logic in the Human Brain: Semantics." *PLOS ONE*, 2013.

John Fuegi, Jo Francis, Special Broadcasting Service (Australia), and Flare Productions. "Ada Byron Lovelace: To Dream Tomorrow." Flare Productions, 2003. Documentary from Women of Power series.

Gaby Galvin. "Some Say Computer Coding Is a Foreign Language." *U.S. News & World Report*, 2016. https://www.usnews.com/news/stem-solutions/articles/2016-10-13/spanish-french-python-some-say-computer-coding-is-a-foreign-language (accessed August 15, 2019).

Ricardo Gil-da-Costa, Alex Martin, Marco A. Lopes, Monica Muñoz, Jonathan B. Fritz, and Allen R. Braun. "Species-Specific Calls Activate Homologs of Broca's and Wernicke's Areas in the Macaque." *Nature Neuroscience* 9(8), pp. 1064–1070, 2006.

Rev. J. A. Giles. *The Complete Works of the Venerable Bede: In the original Latin, Collated with the Manuscripts, and Various Printed Editions, Accompanied by a New English Translation and Life of the Author*. London: Whittaker and Co., 1843.

Dana Goldstein. "How a State Plans to Turn Coal Country into Coding Country." *New York Times*, 2019. https://www.nytimes.com/2019/08/10/us/wyoming-computer-science.html (accessed August 24, 2019).

James Gosling, Bill Joy, Guy Steele, Gilad Bracha, Alex Buckley, and Daniel Smith. "The Java® Language Specification: Java SE 12 Edition." 2019. https://docs.oracle.com/javase/specs/jls/se12/html/index.html (accessed August 25, 2019).

Serri Graslie. "Blockbuster Fades Out, But Some Zombie Stores Will Live On." NPR's All Things Considered, 2013. https://www.npr.org/sections/thetwo-way/2013/11/08/243967587/blockbuster-fades-out-but-some-zombie-stores-will-live-on (accessed August 24, 2019).

Sarah Grey, Cristina Sanz, Kara Morgan-Short, and Michael T. Ullman. "Bilingual and Monolingual Adults Learning an Additional Language: ERPs Reveal Differences in Syntactic Processing." *Bilingualism: Language and Cognition* 21(5), pp. 970–994, 2018.

Julie Grèzes and Jean Decety. "Functional Anatomy of Execution, Mental Simulation, Observation, and Verb Generation of Actions: A Metaanalysis." *Human Brain Mapping* 12(1), pp. 1–19, 2001.

Jason W. Gullifer, Judith F. Kroll, and Paola E. Dussias. "When Language Switching Has No Apparent Cost: Lexical Access in Sentence Context." *Frontiers in Psychology* 4(278), 2013.

Philip Guo. "Python Is Now the Most Popular Introductory Teaching Language at Top U.S. Universities." BLOG@CACM (Communications of the ACM), 2014. https://cacm.acm.org/blogs/blog-cacm/176450-python-is-now-the-most-popular-introductory-teaching-language-at-top-u-s-universities/fulltext (accessed August 16, 2019).

Mark Guzdial. "Predictions on Future CS1 Languages." 2011. https://computinged.wordpress.com/2011/01/24/predictions-on-future-cs1-languages/ (accessed August 15, 2019).

Frances R. Hammond. "Letter from Frances R. Hammond, Director — Worldwide Economics & Market Analysis Staff." General Motors Corporation, 1993.

Andy Hertzfeld. "MacBasic." 1985. http://www.folklore.org/StoryView.py?project=Macintosh&story=MacBasic.txt (accessed September 21, 2019).

G. Hickok, T. Love-Geffen, and E. S. Klima. "Role of the Left Hemisphere in Sign Language Comprehension." *Brain and Language* 82(2), pp. 167–178, 2002.

History on the Net. "Mesopotamian Education and Schools." *Salem Media*, 2019. https://www.historyonthenet.com/mesopotamian-education-and-schools (accessed August 17, 2019).

Eric Hobsbawm. *Labouring Men: Studies in the History of Labour*. 1st edition. Weidenfeld & Nicolson, 1964.

Stephen D. Houston. *The First Writing: Script Invention as History and Process*. Cambridge University Press, 2004.

Department of Education, Iowa. "Computer Science." 2019. https://educateiowa.gov/pk-12/instruction/computer-science (accessed August 24, 2019).

Walter Isaacson. *Steve Jobs*. Simon & Schuster, 2011.

J. J. O'Connor and E. F. Robertson. "Pythagoras's Theorem in Babylonian Mathematics." MacTutor History of Mathematics (University of St Andrews, Scotland), 2000. http://www-history.mcs.st-and.ac.uk/HistTopics/Babylonian_Pythagoras.html (accessed August 17, 2019).

Peter Jackson. "100 Words of English: How Far Can It Get You?" *BBC News*, 2011. https://www.bbc.com/news/magazine-12894638 (accessed August 24, 2019).

Ministry of Education, Culture, Sports, Science and Technology, Japan. "About the way of programming education in the elementary school stage (summary of discussion) (Translation)." Japan, 2016. http://www.mext.go.jp/b_menu/shingi/chousa/shotou/122/attach/1372525.htm (accessed August 15, 2019).

Tim Jay and Julie Betenson. "Mathematics at Your Fingertips: Testing a Finger Training Intervention to Improve Quantitative Skills." *Frontiers in Education* 2, 2017.

Daniel Kahneman. *Thinking, Fast and Slow*. New York: Farrar, Straus and Giroux, 2011.

Sean H. K. Kang. "Spaced Repetition Promotes Efficient and Effective Learning: Policy Implications for Instruction." *Policy Insights from the Behavioral and Brain Sciences* 3(1), pp. 12–19, 2016.

Yufeng Ke, Ningci Wang, Jiale Du, Linghan Kong, Shuang Liu, Minpeng Xu, Xingwei An, and Dong Ming. "The Effects of Transcranial Direct Current Stimulation (tDCS) on Working Memory Training in Healthy Young Adults." *Frontiers in Human Neuroscience* 13, 2019.

Elaine C. Klein. "Second versus Third Language Acquisition: Is There a Difference?" *Language Learning* 45(3), 1995.

Donald E. Knuth. "Ancient Babylonian Algorithms." *Communications of the ACM* 15(6), pp. 671–677, 1972.

Teun Koetsier. "On the Prehistory of Programmable Machines: Musical Automata, Looms, Calculators." *Mechanism and Machine Theory* 36, pp. 589–603, 2001.

Evelyne Kohler, Christian Keysers, M. Alessandra Umiltà, Leonardo Fogassi, Vittorio Gallese, and G. Rizzolatti. "Hearing Sounds, Understanding Actions: Action Representation in Mirror Neurons." *Science* 297(5582), pp. 846–848, 2002.

Stephen Krashen. "Evidence Suggesting That Public Opinion Is Becoming More Negative: A Discussion of the Reasons, and What We Can Do About It." 2002. http://www.languagepolicy.net/archives/Krash11.htm (accessed September 2, 2019).

Stephen Krashen. "Evidence That Implicit Learning (Subconscious Language Acquisition) Results in L1-like Brain Processing: A Comment on Morgan-Short, Steinhauer, Sanz & Ullman (2012)." 2013. http://skrashen.blogspot.com/2013/11/evidence-that-implicit-learning.html (accessed August 21, 2019).

Richard Kunert, Roel M. Willems, Daniel Casasanto, Aniruddh D. Patel, and Peter Hagoort. "Music and Language Syntax Interact in Broca's Area: An fMRI Study." *PLOS ONE*, 2015.

Sei Kwon and Katri Schroderus. "Coding in School: Comparing Integration of Programming into Basic Education Curricula of Finland and South Korea."

Finnish Society on Media Education, 2017. http://mediakasvatus.fi/wp-content/uploads/2018/06/Coding-in-schools-FINAL-2.pdf (accessed August 15, 2019).

Diana Lambert. "California Adopts First Computer Science Standards for K-12 Students." *EdSource*, 2018. https://edsource.org/2018/californias-first-computer-science-standards-set-for-approval/60198 (accessed August 15, 2019).

Gottfried Leibniz. *Dissertatio de arte combinatoria*. 1666.

Leroy E. Loemker. *Philosophical Papers and Letters (of Gottfried Leibniz)*. 2nd edition. Boston: D. Reidel Pub. Co, 1976.

Dennis Looney and Natalia Lusin. "Enrollments in Languages Other Than English in United States Institutions of Higher Education, Summer 2016 and Fall 2016: Final Report." Modern Language Association, Web Publication, 2019. https://www.mla.org/content/download/110154/2406932/2016-Enrollments-Final-Report.pdf (accessed August 16, 2019).

University of Louisville. "The Grawemeyer Award in Psychology: 2003 – Daniel Kahneman and Amos Tversky." 2002. https://web.archive.org/web/20150723084412/http://grawemeyer.org/psychology/previous-winners/2003-daniel-kahneman-and-amos-tversky.html (accessed August 24, 2019).

Ada Augusta, Countess of Lovelace. *Sketch of the Analytical Engine Invented by Charles Babbage*. Richard and John E. Taylor, 1843. Written in French by Luigi F. Menabrea. Translated by Ada Lovelace, along with her Translator's Notes which are primarily quoted in this text.

Victor Luckerson. "Netflix Accounts for More Than a Third of All Internet Traffic." *Time*, 2015. https://time.com/3901378/netflix-internet-traffic/ (accessed August 24, 2019).

Stephen Manes and Paul Andrews. *Gates: How Microsoft's Mogul Reinvented an Industry – and Made Himself the Richest Man in America*. 1st edition. Touchstone, 1994.

Viorica Marian and Anthony Shook. "The Cognitive Benefits of Being Bilingual." *Cerebrum*, 2012.

Ma. del Carmen Rodríguez Martínez, Ponciano Ortíz Ceballos, Michael D. Coe, Richard A. Diehl, Stephen D. Houston, Karl A. Taube, and Alfredo Delgado Calderón. "Oldest Writing in the New World." *Science* 313(5793), pp. 1610–1614, 2006.

David McCandless, Pearl Doughty-White, and Miriam Quick. "Codebases: Millions of Lines of Code." *Information Is Beautiful*, 2015. https://informationisbeautiful.net/visualizations/million-lines-of-code/ (accessed August 24, 2019).

Harry McCracken. "Apple II Forever: A 35th-Anniversary Tribute to Apple's First Iconic Product." *Time*, 2012. http://techland.time.com/2012/04/16/apple-ii-forever-a-35th-anniversary-tribute-to-apples-first-iconic-product/ (accessed September 21, 2019).

Michael McCracken, Vicki Almstrum, Danny Diaz, Mark Guzdial, Dianne Hagan, Yifat Ben-David Kolikant, Cary Laxer, Lynda Thomas, Ian Utting, and Tadeusz Wilusz. "A multinational, multi-institutional study of assessment of programming skills of first-year CS students: Report by the ITiCSE 2001 Working Group on Assessment of Programming Skills of First-year CS Students." In *Proc. Innovation and Technology in Computer Science Education*, 2001.

George A. Miller, Eugene Galanter, and Karl H. Pribram. *Plans and the Structure of Behavior*. Holt, Rinehart, Winston, Inc., 1960.

Korbinian Moeller, Laura Martignon, Silvia Wessolowski, Joachim Engel, and Hans-Christoph Nuerk. "Effects of Finger Counting on Numerical Development – The Opposing Views of Neurocognition and Mathematics Education." *Frontiers in Psychology* 2, 2011.

National Institute of Korean Language. "Korean Online Dictionary (Translation)." 2019. https://opendict.korean.go.kr/service/dicStat (accessed August 24, 2019).

Otto Neugebauer. *The Exact Sciences in Antiquity*. 2nd edition. Dover Publications, 1969.

Mercury News. "In a Few Years, Blockbuster Goes from Dominant to Besieged." 2010. https://www.mercurynews.com/2010/06/18/in-a-few-years-blockbuster-goes-from-dominant-to-besieged/

D. Nofre, M. Pristley, and G. Alberts. "When Technology Became Language: The Origins of the Linguistic Conception of Computer Programming, 1950–1960." *Technology and Culture* 55(1), pp. 40–75, 2014.

Peter Norvig. "(How to Write a (Lisp) Interpreter (in Python))." 2010. http://norvig.com/lispy.html (accessed August 16, 2019).

Jeffrey A. Oaks. "An Arabic Finger-reckoning Rule Appropriated for Proofs in Algebra – Finger Reckoning." *Convergence*, 2018. https://www.maa.org/press/periodicals/convergence/an-arabic-finger-reckoning-rule-appropriated-for-proofs-in-algebra-finger-reckoning (accessed August 24, 2019).

Bekir Onursal and Surhid Gautam. "Vehicular Air Pollution – Experiences from Seven Latin American Urban Centers." World Bank Technical Paper No. 373, 1997.

Frank Pallotta. "Netflix Added Record Number of Subscribers, but Warns of Tougher Times Ahead." CNN, 2019. https://www.cnn.com/2019/04/16/media/netflix-earnings-2019-first-quarter/index.html (accessed August 24, 2019).

Don Passey. "Computer Science (CS) in the Compulsory Education Curriculum: Implications for Future Research." *Education and Information Technologies* 22(2), pp. 421–443, 2017.

Matt Peckham. "Minecraft Is Now Part of Microsoft, and It Only Cost $2.5 Billion." *Time*, 2014. https://time.com/3377886/microsoft-buys-mojang/ (accessed August 24, 2019).

Alan J. Perlis. "Epigrams in Programming." ACM Special Interest Group on Programming Languages (SIGPLAN), 1982.

Steven Pinker. *The Language Instinct: How the Mind Creates Language.* 1st edition. William Morrow and Company, 1994.

Reuters. "Blockbuster Reaches 2 Million Online Users." Reuters, 2007. https://uk.reuters.com/article/us-blockbuster-online/blockbuster-reaches-2-million-online-users-idUKWEN169220070103 (accessed August 24, 2019).

Giacomo Rizzolatti and Laila Craighero. "Speculations on the Origin of Language." *Friulian Journal of Science* 5, pp. 103–111, 2004.

Ricardo Schütz. "Language Acquisition – Language Learning." 2002. https://www.sk.com.br/sk-laxll.html (accessed August 24, 2019).

United States Security and Exchange Commission. "SEC Form 10-K for Google Inc. (Fiscal Year Ending Dec. 31, 2014)." 2014. https://www.sec.gov/Archives/edgar/data/1288776/000128877615000008/goog2014123110-k.htm (accessed August 24, 2019). Estimate based on number of employees in Research & Development as well as Operations, which are predicted to be primarily software engineers.

Janet Siegmund, Christian Kästner, Sven Apel, Chris Parnin, Anja Bethmann, and Andre Brechmann. "Understanding Programmers' Brains with fMRI." In *Proc. Front. Neuroinform. Conference Abstract: Neuroinformatics*, 2014.

Anne H. Soukhanov. *The American Heritage Dictionary of the English Language.* 3rd edition. Houghton Mifflin Harcourt, 1992.

Firat Soylu, David Raymond, Arianna Gutierrez, and Sharlene D. Newman. "The Differential Relationship Between Finger Gnosis, and Addition and Subtraction: An fMRI Study." *Journal of Numerical Cognition* 3(3), 2017.

Jared P. Tagliatela, Jamie L. Russell, Jennifer A. Schaeffer, and William D. Hopkins. "Communicative Signaling Activates 'Broca's' Homolog in Chimpanzees." *Current Biology* 18(5), pp. 343–348, 2008.

Sinclair Target. "What Did Ada Lovelace's Program Actually Do?" *Two-Bit History*, 2018. https://twobithistory.org/2018/08/18/ada-lovelace-note-g.html (accessed August 24, 2019).

Christian Terwiesch and Roger E. Bohn. "Learning and Process Improvement During Production Ramp-up." *International Journal of Production Economics* 70(1), pp. 1–19, 2001.

C. N. Trueman. "Factories in the Industrial Revolution." The History Learning Site, 2015. https://www.historylearningsite.co.uk/britain-1700-to-1900/industrial-revolution/factories-in-the-industrial-revolution/ (accessed August 24, 2019).

Alan M. Turing. *On Computable Numbers, with an Application to the Entscheidungsproblem*. 1936.

Turkish Language Institute. Büyük Türkçe Sözlük. 2019. http://sozluk.gov.tr/ (accessed August 24, 2019).

Department for Education, United Kingdom. "Statutory Guidance: National Curriculum in England: Computing Programmes of Study." United Kingdom, 2013. https://www.gov.uk/government/publications/national-curriculum-in-england-computing-programmes-of-study/national-curriculum-in-england-computing-programmes-of-study (accessed August 15, 2019).

Natalie Thais Uomini and Georg Friedrich Meyer. "Shared Brain Lateralization Patterns in Language and Acheulean Stone Tool Production: A Functional Transcranial Doppler Ultrasound Study." *PLOS ONE*, 2013. Note: the date of origination of human speech is incredibly speculative.

George William Veditz. *The Preservation of the Sign Language*. National Association of the Deaf Collection (Library of Congress), 1913. Medium: Film.

Cybersecurity Ventures. "Application Security Report 2017." 2017. https://cybersecurityventures.com/application-security-report-2017/ (accessed August 24, 2019).

Andreas Vesalius. *De humani corporis fabrica libri septem*. 1543.

M. H. de Vries, A. C. Barth, S. Maiworm, S. Knecht, P. Zwitserlood, and A. Flöel. "Electrical Stimulation of Broca's Area Enhances Implicit Learning of an Artificial Grammar." *Journal of Cognitive Neuroscience* 22(11), pp. 2427–2436, 2010.

Ernest Alfred Wallis and Leonard William King. *A Guide to the Babylonian and Assyrian Antiquities*. 2nd edition. London: Order of the Trustees, 1908.

Amy Watson. "Number of Netflix Employees from 2015 to 2018, by Type." Statista, 2019. https://www.statista.com/statistics/587671/netflix-employees/ (accessed August 24, 2019).

Rev. C. A. Wheelwright. *Pindar*. Harper & Brothers, 1837.

Alfred North Whitehead and Bertrand Russell. *Principia mathematica*. 6th edition. Cambridge, England: The University Press, 1925.

Wikimedia. "Photo of the Ishango bone." 2007. https://commons.wikimedia.org/wiki/File:Os_d%27Ishango_IRSNB.JPG (accessed October 20, 2019).

Wikimedia. "Photo of the reconstruction of the Turk, a chess-playing automaton designed by Kempelen." 2009. https://commons.wikimedia.org/wiki/File:Kempelen_chess1.jpg (accessed October 20, 2019).

Wikimedia. "A Jacquard loom showing information punchcards, National Museum of Scotland." 2019. https://commons.wikimedia.org/wiki/File:Os_d%27Ishango_IRSNB.JP://commons.wikimedia.org/wiki/File:A_Jacquard_loom_showing_information_punchcards,_National_Museum_of_Scotland.jpg (accessed October 20, 2019).

Richard Winefield. *Never the Twain Shall Meet*. 2nd edition. Gallaudet University Press, 1987.

Nathan Yau. "Recursive Painting in Real Life." 2019. https://flowingdata.com/2019/02/05/recursive-painting-in-real-life/ (accessed August 21, 2019).

Index

Looking for more ways to get involved? In 2020, the authors founded a non-profit called MetaCoders to bring a *new* method of coding education to students everywhere. MetaCoders uses many of the educational elements discussed in this book and has already launched classes in 8 cities as of this publication. We are looking for students, teachers, volunteers, coders, and philanthropists to help us in our mission. Here are just a few ways you can contribute:

Help Us Launch Coding Classes in Your City
We are always looking for advocates to help us launch educational programs in new cities. You can work with MetaCoders as a volunteer or employee to help us find a location for classes, advertise to local parents, and recruit others to our cause. Contact us at **contact@metacoders.org** at any time with information about your city, and we can work together to start teaching kids in your area!

Help Teach Students in Your Area
If you're in any major city, we may very well be looking for teachers in your area already! Visit **https://metacoders.org/join-our-team** to see if we are looking for "Coding Coaches" in your area. Even if we haven't made it to your area yet, and you're interested in teaching with us, send us an email through the email form on our website. We may be able to work with you to get classes setup in your area for you to teach!

Or, if you're looking to teach a small group of children in your area, we also make our curriculum and training materials publicly available to all teachers teaching *free*, no cost classes to kids. This is a great opportunity for educators looking to start coding clubs in rural towns and other areas in need. You can find our curriculum and our training materials on our website at **https://metacoders .org/coaches**.

Help Us Code New Educational Technologies

Do you already identify as a coder? Or are you looking to sharpen your coding skills? We're looking for volunteers to help us build our open source educational technologies. Help us write new programming languages and educational materials for kids from the comfort of your home. Visit **https://metacoders.org/coders** for more information about how to start contributing to the codebase.

Donate to Help Share Coding Education with Kids Everywhere

Our mission is to provide coding education to children nationwide at the most affordable price possible. In order to do that, we need the help of donors! Donations help subsidize the cost of our classes for students everywhere, but also allow us to provide financial assistance strategically to families in need. Visit **https://metacoders.org/donate** to setup a 1-time or recurring donation.

We are also looking for corporate sponsors to our programs. Reach out to us at **contact@metacoders.org** with any questions you have about corporate sponsorship.

ENTHRALLING and
EFFECTIVE LESSON PLANS
FOR GRADES 5–8

STEM
to
STORY

BY 826 NATIONAL

EDITED BY JENNIFER TRAIG

WITH GENEROUS SUPPORT FROM
TIME WARNER CABLE

100% ALIGNED
WITH
COMMON CORE
AND
NEXT GEN SCIENCE
STANDARDS

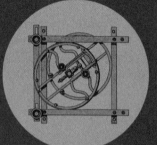

Time Warner Cable

826 NATIONAL

JOSSEY-BASS
A Wiley Brand

Bring STEM to life for students with zombies, rockets, celebrities, and more

STEM to Story: Enthralling and Effective Lesson Plans for Grades 5-8 inspires learning through fun, engaging, and meaningful lesson plans that fuse hands-on discovery in science, technology, engineering, and math (STEM) with creative writing. The workshop activities within the book are the innovative result of a partnership between 826 National's proven creative writing model and Time Warner Cable's Connect a Million Minds, an initiative dedicated to connecting young people to the wonders of STEM through hands-on learning. Authentically aligned with both the Common Core State Standards and the Next Generation Science Standards, this book provides teachers, after-school and out-of-school providers, and parents with field-tested lessons, workshops, and projects designed by professionals in each field. Including reflective observations by arts and science celebrities like Jon Scieszka, Mayim Bialik, and Steve Hockensmith, lessons feature bonus activities, fun facts, and teaching points for instructors at every level. These quirky, exploratory lessons will effectively awaken student imaginations and passions for both STEM and creative writing, encourage identity with scientific endeavors, and make both science and writing fun.

Grades five through eight is the critical period for engaging students in STEM, and this book is designed specifically to appeal to – and engage – this age group. The guided curricula fosters hands-on discovery, deep learning, and rich inquiry skills while feeling more like play than school, and has proven popular and effective with both students and teachers.

- Awaken student imagination and get them excited about STEM
- Fuse creative writing with STEM using hands-on activities
- Make scientific principles relevant to students' lives
- Inspire students to explore STEM topics further

The demand for STEM workers is closely linked to global competitiveness, and a successful future in STEM depends upon an early introduction to the scientific mindset. The challenge for teachers is to break through students' preconceptions of STEM fields as "hard" or "boring," to show them that STEM is everywhere, it's relevant, and it's loads of fun. For proven lesson plans with just a dash of weird, *STEM to Story* is a dynamic resource, adaptable and applicable in school, after school, and at home.

TEACHING AND LEARNING STEM

A PRACTICAL GUIDE

RICHARD M. FELDER

REBECCA BRENT

FOREWORD BY BARBARA OAKLEY

B JOSSEY-BASS

A Wiley Brand

Rethink traditional teaching methods to improve student learning and retention in STEM

Educational research has repeatedly shown that compared to traditional teacher-centered instruction, certain learner-centered methods lead to improved learning outcomes, greater development of critical high-level skills, and increased retention in science, technology, engineering, and mathematics (STEM) disciplines.

Teaching and Learning STEM presents a trove of practical research-based strategies for designing and teaching STEM courses at the university, community college, and high school levels. The book draws on the authors' extensive backgrounds and decades of experience in STEM education and faculty development. Its engaging and well-illustrated descriptions will equip you to implement the strategies in your courses and to deal effectively with problems (including student resistance) that might occur in the implementation. The book will help you:

- Plan and conduct class sessions in which students are actively engaged, no matter how large the class is
- Make good use of technology in face-to-face, online, and hybrid courses and flipped classrooms
- Assess how well students are acquiring the knowledge, skills, and conceptual understanding the course is designed to teach
- Help students develop expert problem-solving skills and skills in communication, creative thinking, critical thinking, high-performance teamwork, and self-directed learning
- Meet the learning needs of STEM students with a broad diversity of attributes and backgrounds

The strategies presented in *Teaching and Learning STEM* don't require revolutionary time-intensive changes in your teaching, but rather a gradual integration of traditional and new methods. The result will be continual improvement in your teaching and your students' learning.

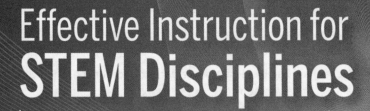

Effective Instruction for
STEM Disciplines

FROM LEARNING THEORY TO COLLEGE TEACHING

EDWARD J. MASTASCUSA
WILLIAM J. SNYDER · BRIAN S. HOYT
FOREWORD BY MARYELLEN WEIMER

Praise for Effective Instruction for STEM Disciplines

"The world of today's learners is a multimode, information-intensive universe of interactive bursts and virtual exchanges, yet our teaching methods retain the outdated characteristics of last generation's study-and-drill approach. New pedagogical methods, detailed and justified in this groundbreaking work, are essential to prepare students to confront the concerns of the future. The book challenges our traditional assumptions and informs the science, technology, engineering, and mathematics (STEM) community of the latest research on how the brain learns and retains information, how enhanced student engagement with subject material and its context is essential to deep learning, and how to use this knowledge to structure STEM education approaches that work."—David V. Kerns, Jr., Franklin and Mary Olin Distinguished Professor of Electrical and Computer Engineering, and founding provost, Olin College

"Every STEM faculty member should have this book. It provides a handy introduction to the 'why and how' of engaging students in the learning process."—David Voltmer, professor emeritus, Rose-Hulman Institute of Technology, and American Society for Engineering Education Fellow

"The poor quality of math and science education and the shortage of well-qualified graduates are acknowledged almost daily in the U.S. press. Here the authors provide much-needed insights for educators seeking to improve the quality of STEM education as well as to better prepare students to solve the problems they will confront in our increasingly technology-driven world."—Keith Buffinton, interim dean of engineering, Bucknell University.